GENTLEMEN'S SONS

In the Spellmount/Nutshell Military list:

The Territorial Battalions - A pictorial history
The Yeomanry Regiments - A pictorial history
Over the Rhine - The Last Days of War in Europe
History of the Cambridge University OTC
The Fighting Troops of the Austro-Hungarian Army
Intelligence Officer in the Peninsula
The Scottish Regiments - A pictorial history
The Royal Marines - A pictorial history
The Royal Tank Regiment - A pictorial history
The Irish Regiments - A pictorial history
British Sieges of the Peninsular War
Victoria's Victories
Heaven and Hell: German Paratroop war diary
Rorke's Drift
Came the Dawn - Fifty years an Army Officer
Kitchener's Army - A pictorial history
On the Word of Command - A pictorial history of the Regimental Sergeant Major
Marlborough as Military Commander
The Art of Warfare in the Age of Marlborough
Epilogue in Burma 1945-48
Scandinavian Misadventure
The Fall of France
The First Victory: O'Connor's Desert Triumph, Dec 1940-Feb 1941
Blitz Over Britain
Deceivers Ever - Memoirs of a Camouflage Officer
Indian Army of the Empress 1861-1903
Heroes for Victoria 1837-1901
The Waters of Oblivion - the British Invasion of the Rio de la Plata, 1806-07.
Soldier's Glory - 'Rough Notes of an Old Soldier'
Craufurd's Light Division
Napoleon's Military Machine
Falklands Military Machine
Wellington's Military Machine
Commando Diary
The French are Coming! The Invasion Scare 1803-05
Military Marching - A pictorial history
Soldier On! - Testament of a Tom
The Glider Soldiers
Sons of John Company - The Indian and Pakistan Armies, 1903-91
A Guards Officer in the Peninsula

In the Nautical List:

Evolution of Engineering in the Royal Navy, Vol 1. 1827-1939
In Perilous Seas
Sea of Memories
Ordinary Naval Airmen
Haul, Taut and Belay - Memoirs of a Flying Sailor

In the Aviation List:

Diary of a Bomb Aimer
Operation 'Bograt' - Memoirs of a Fighter Pilot
A Medal for Life-Capt Leefe Robinson VC
Three Decades a Pilot-The Third Generation
Bob Doe - Fighter Pilot
The Allied Bomber War, 1939-45

GENTLEMEN'S SONS

The Guards in the Peninsula and at
Waterloo, 1808-1815

By
Ian Fletcher and Ron Poulter

SPELLMOUNT LTD
Tunbridge Wells

To Doriam, Debbie and Jack

© Ian Fletcher and Ron Poulter 1992
ISBN 1-873376-00-6

First published in the UK in 1992
SPELLMOUNT LTD
12 Dene Way
Speldhurst
Tunbridge Wells
Kent
TN3 0NX

British Library Cataloguing in Publication
Data:
A catalogue record for this book is available
from the British Library

Printed in Great Britain by
BIDDLES LTD
Woodbridge Park
Guildford
Surrey

GENTLEMEN'S SONS

CONTENTS

SKETCHES AND MAPS

INTRODUCTION

When Major H.L. Aubrey-Fletcher wrote his *A History of the Foot Guards to 1856*, published by Constable & Co of London in 1927, he began by recalling a dinner party at which a lady remarked upon the very fine appearance of the Foot Guards but added that it was a pity they didn't fight. He then went on to say that at the time of writing his book there were still many people who believed that up until the First World War - or Great War as it was called then of course - no Guardsman ever left Britain's shores, a rather ludicrous supposition. He was also rather indignant at an entry in the suggestion book of the Officers' Club which asked when the 'Guardees' were going to do some fighting? He set out to put the record straight by embarking upon a history of the Foot Guards up until 1856, there being no history of the Foot Guards at that time, other than two regimental histories, those of the First or Grenadier Guards, and the Coldstream Guards. There was as yet no history of the Third or Scots Guards.

However, Aubrey-Fletcher's history failed inasmuch as it became a history of the period from the mid-seventeenth century until the Crimean War with references to the Guards included as and when they were involved in actions. There was, perhaps, too much general coverage of events, both military and political, during the period thus leaving the reader somewhat frustrated at the lack of a detailed history of the Foot Guards. *Gentlemen's Sons* is an attempt, not to provide a complete history of the Foot Guards, but rather to give a fairly detailed account of the Foot Guards between the years 1808 to 1815 when they fought with distinction in the Peninsular War and Waterloo campaign.

But *Gentlemen's Sons* is not just another regimental history. The name *Gentlemen's Sons* was given to the 1st Division of Wellington's army in which the regiments of Foot Guards were brigaded, the name deriving from the number of titled officers, the sons of aristocracy and landed gentry and the general 'well to do' gentlemen of society that were to be found amongst their number. By examining their demeanour on campaign, their billets and bivouacs, their often flamboyant camp lifestyle, and their military dress *Gentlemen's Sons* is also intended to give the reader a flavour of what life was like on campaign with the Foot Guards at the beginning of the nineteenth century. It is also hoped that this volume will succeed where Aubrey-Fletcher's failed.

That the Guards were an elite body of men cannot be denied but this was not just because of their socially unrivalled officers corps. They were also a highly trained and disciplined fighting force and it is perhaps fitting that the Guards played a major part in the final act of the final battle of the Napoleonic era, when the First Guards repulsed Napoleon's own Imperial Guard on the slopes of Mont St Jean.

Although both social and military aspects of the Guards are examined in *Gentlemen's Sons* we have also given consideration to the style of dress worn by them on campaign. The uniforms shown in this volume are perhaps not what some would expect to find in a book about British Foot Guards. The extremes of the Iberian weather soon exposed the frailties and deficiencies of the uniforms worn by Wellington's men, driving them to adopt a great deal of non-regulation clothing and other items of equipment. In *Gentlemen's Sons* the Guards are shown as tough, fighting soldiers - Wellington's best - as they appeared on campaign and in the heat of battle, and not as he is often shown, as a chocolate-box soldier on parade at Windsor or St James's. The interpretations of the Guards featured in the colour plates have been taken from primary sources such as the journals of officers and men, contemporary paintings and drawings and the dress regulations of the time. The three Guards regiments gave us access to their regimental archives through which we have been able to show improvised garments, regulation dress, captured items of enemy clothing and equipment, cut down and modified coats and jackets, patched and darned uniforms and improvised footwear and weapons, all worn with pride by the Foot Guards.

Gentlemen's Sons would not have been possible of course without the assistance of the following bodies and individuals. Thanks go in no particular order to Major (Retd) E.C. Weaver MBE, Major (Retd) P.A. Lewis and Lieutenant Colonel T.J. Tedder of RHQ Grenadier Guards for allowing access to the regimental archives and for permission to reproduce the picture of the Honourable Orlando Bridgeman and the cloak given to him; to Lieutenant General The Honourable Sir William Rous KCB OBE for allowing us to use the picture of his great grandfather, J.E.C. Rous and other items in his possession; to Major D.H. Toler and Major (Retd) C.J. Louch, of RHQ Coldstream Guards, for allowing access to the regimental archives and to Lance Sergeant Pearce and Guardsman Dave Milden for their help and assistance there; to Major R.E Whyte, Major C. Brown and Mr K. Coursey of RHQ

Scots Guards for allowing access to the regimental archives and for their assistance; to Captain D.D. Horn MISM of the Guards Museum; to Major General Giles Hallam Mills CB CVO OBE and Major John Mills OBE DL for their help and for the loan of their great grandfather's letters and diary; to Colonel (Retd) Paul Adair: to Dr Peter Boyden and the staff of the National Army Museum, London; to the British Library, London; to Colonel Peter Walton and Major John Tamplin of the Army Museums Ogilby Trust for their help and for allowing reproduction of pictures in the AMOT collections; to David C. Hamilton-Williams for his most interesting views and information relating to the Imperial Guard at Waterloo; and last but not least to Bob Marrion for his time and trouble in supplying items from his own extensive collection.

The illustrations in this book come from the collections of Sotheby's, Christie's, The National Army Museum, The Army Museums Ogilby Trust, RHQ Grenadier Guards, RHQ Scots Guards, The Scottish United Services Museum, the Bob Marrion collection, The Guards Museum, and the authors' collection. The two photographs of the Coldstream Guards Cemetery, Bayonne, were taken by Andy Cook. The maps are based on those in Julian Paget's *Wellington's Peninsular War*, and his *Hougoumont - Key to Victory*, (both published by Leo Cooper, London, 1990 and 1992 respectively), David Chandler's excellent *Waterloo - The Hundred Days* (Osprey, London, 1980), and Major H.L. Aubrey-Fletcher's *A History of the Foot Guards to 1856*, (Constable, London, 1927).

I.F. & R.P. 1992.

THE GUARDS

A few years after the close of the Napoleonic Wars the Duke of Wellington sat down to dine at Hatfield House in Hertfordshire. As the dinner progressed two eminent guests entered into a rather animated discussion as to just who were the better troops - the Guards or the Line regiments. The two men began to argue their respective cases too passionately and at length the great Duke himself was called upon to give his own verdict. "Oh!" he said, "I am all for the Guards - all for the Guards". The triumphant disputant then exclaimed, "I told you so; those fellows in silk stockings have more *blood* about them, and blood will tell."[1] Wellington, however, went to add that he meant the non-commissioned officers of the Guards as he rated these very highly indeed, proof of which can be found in the high number of Guards NCOs that he recommended for commissions in different regiments.[2] That the NCOs of the Guards were extremely efficient cannot be denied but it is the composition of the officer corps, the 'fellows in silk stockings', that gave the 1st Division of the army - in which the Guards were brigaded - its nickname, 'The Gentlemen's Sons.'[3]

Of course, the composition of the 1st Division in the Peninsula was not exclusively confined to the battalions of Foot Guards, for between 1809 and 1814 no fewer than nineteen battalions of Line regiments were attached to the 1st Division, as well as various companies from the rifle regiments, notably the 5/60th, but none of these were ever brigaded with the Guards.[4] In fact, it was not until the Waterloo campaign that the 1st Division, consisting of the 2nd and 3rd Battalions First Guards and the 2nd Battalions of the Coldstream and Third Guards, was exclusively a Guards Division, by which time it could genuinely be given the name, 'The Gentlemen's Sons'. Ironically, this name does not seem to have been applied during the campaign as divisional nicknames had apparently ceased at the close of the Peninsular War when the army was broken up and scattered around the globe leaving Wellington to fight the 1815 campaign with his 'infamous' army of British, Dutch and Belgian troops.

The most often-quoted reference to term, 'The Gentlemen's Sons', relates to an incident towards the end of the Peninsular War when the Guards were positioned near Bayonne in southern France. After five years of hard fighting against the armies of the Emperor Napoleon Wellington's men had fought their way across the Iberian Peninsula and were now across the French border. By December 1813, they had reached Bayonne where the First Guards, under Colonel Tynling, occupied a redoubt by the roadside leading to the town. As the rain fell from a leaden sky Wellington, accompanied by Colonel Freemantle and Lord Hill, happened to pass by on his return to his Headquarters and was somewhat surprised to see so many of the Guards officers holding umbrellas to keep off the rain. Shortly afterwards, Lord Hill galloped over to them and said, "Lord Wellington does not approve of the use of umbrellas during the enemy's firing, and will not allow the 'gentlemen's sons' to make themselves ridiculous in the eyes of the army." A few days later, Tynling received 'a wigging' from Wellington for suffering so many of his officers to carry umbrellas in the face of the enemy and added, "The Guards may in uniform, when on duty at St James's, carry them if they please; but in the field it is not only ridiculous but unmilitary."[5] This little episode quite possibly says much of the Guards' philosophy towards campaigning; to make the best of a bad situation and to pass it off in as comfortable a manner as possible.

When the rest of Wellington's army dubbed the 1st Division 'The Gentlemen's Sons' they were not far from the truth, the name deriving, of course, from the predominance of titled officers and sons of the landed gentry amongst the Guards regiments for when it came to the composition of the officer corps the Guards were unrivalled. They came only from the higher echelons of society, from the landed gentry and from the families of successful merchants and tradesmen[6] Indeed, if one includes those serving on the Staff, this elite body of officers at Waterloo included 7 peers, 25 sons or heirs of peers, 5 knights, 9 sons or heirs of baronets and one son of a knight.[7] Of all the titled officers serving in the British army at the outbreak of the Peninsular War, either in the cavalry and infantry, nearly a third could be found in the three regiments of Foot Guards.[8]

Such were the high purchase prices of commissions that only the well-connected or titled could afford to join this socially exclusive military assembly and even when the young officer had bought his commission he would need a further considerable sum to pay for the not inconsiderable expenses incurred in order to enable him to live in the style and manner expected of the Foot Guards both at home and, wherever possible, on campaign.

Comparisons between the prices of commissions and

rates of pay in 1815 between the Guards and the Line regiments are worthy of note. In the Guards, a lieutenant-colonelcy, for example, cost £6,700, a majority £6,300, a captaincy £3,500 and a lieutenancy £1,500. The equivalent ranks in the Line regiments would cost £3,500, £2,600, £1,500 and £550 respectively. With regard to pay, a major in the Guards received £1 4s 6d per day, a captain 16s 6d, and a lieutenant 7s 10d. Their equivalents in the Line regiments received 16s, 10s 6d, and 6s 6d per day.[9]

The regiments of Foot Guards were, therefore, for the affluent only. An officer of the Guards would expect to pay not only for his service dress but for elaborate state uniforms, worn to the various functions held at Windsor or St James and if the cost of these expensive uniforms was high enough they could expect to pay even higher mess bills during the course of a year, all of which necessitated the need for a considerable private income. Then there were the London clubs, fashionable haunts of the rich, famous and powerful that became meeting places for the Guards. Amongst the most prominent were White's, Boodle's, Brookes's, Arthur's and Graham's. Here, the Guards mixed with politicians and socialites, indulging in various card games such as whist, faro and macao. Fortunes were won and lost at the table and the Duke of Portland's father-in-law, General Scott, won the vast sum of £200,000 at whist. These clubs were concentrated in the west end of London, mainly in the Piccadilly area, and entry into White's in particular was very difficult indeed. Most of the nobility were members and it says much that officers of the Guards were members. They did, of course, have their own club, the Guards' Club. This was run along military lines and the only games played were billiards and low whist. Gronow claimed that the dinner there was cheaper and better than at the other clubs. All in all, it was an expensive business being an officer in the Guards but in spite of this, however, the clamour for commissions in the Guards was often intense and the rate of purchase the highest in the army.[10]

Another anomaly amongst the Guards was the practice of 'double-ranking' whereby the officers of the Guards held both regimental and army ranks. This dated back to 1687 since when a captain in the Guards was ranked as a lieutenant-colonel and to 1691 when lieutenants were ranked as captains. This privilege meant, of course, that a captain in the Guards could exchange into a Line regiment as a lieutenant-colonel, not that many did, however, in spite of the slow speed of promotion in the Guards. For example, in the Third Guards the shortest time in which an ensign of 1809 became a lieutenant was four years seven months and of the 75 ensigns in the Brigade of Guards in 1809 only 18 became lieutenants within five years.[11] Virtually all promotions during the Peninsular campaign were by way of seniority, mainly caused by the deaths of officers in action, rather than by purchase.

As we shall see, the socially elite Guards officers were often scorned and mocked by members of other regiments and it would often come as a great delight to the men of Line regiments to see Guards officers 'getting their hands dirty' as they struggled through the snow during the retreat to Corunna in 1809 or on the hectic, forced march from Brussels to Quatre Bras in 1815. However, the Guards were amongst the best disciplined and highly trained and effective of Wellington's - and Moore's - troops. Witness the arrival of the First Guards at Corunna, for instance, after the terrible and harrowing retreat through the bleak and barren, snow covered mountains of north western Spain in January 1809. Moore's dishevelled army arrived in a sorry state as the pursuing French army closed in on them, but as Moore and his officers watched and waited as the British troops began to arrive they looked on in astonishment as one particular unit came marching over the hill in step as though they were on parade, the sergeants keeping the men in check whilst the drum major twirled his baton around him. Moore turned to Sir Robert Anstruther and said simply, "Look at that body of men in the distance; they are the Guards, by the way they are marching."[12] This is probably the most famous quote of the Peninsular War that refers specifically to the conduct of the Guards but there were many other occasions where they distinguished themselves in action, at Barrosa and Burgos, for example, and on the memorable day of June 18th 1815 when, as Wellington himself later said, the closing of the gates of Hougoumont decided the outcome of the battle of Waterloo.

The officers of the Guards may have been mocked from time to time by the men of the Line regiments but when J.W. Fortescue, the great historian of the British army, wrote that the officers of the Guards were able to command more respect from their men as a result of their upbringing, he was only echoing the thoughts of one of the Peninsular War's most lauded diarists, John Kincaid, of the 95th Rifles, who regretted the fact that more aristocratic families of England did not send their sons into the army as they seemed to be able to command more willing obedience from their men with less effort than others. Fortescue went on to say that, 'no one who knows anything of the subject will dispute the advantage which the habit of command, inherited through many generations and acquired in childhood, may confer upon a man.'[13] This may well be reflected in the extremely low number of Court Martial cases involving the men of the Guards. In the archives of the Coldstream Guards, for instance, Court Martial records show that the vast majority of disciplinary cases involved only trifling offences, misdemeanours such as falling asleep on duty or getting drunk, the universal curse of the whole army. Indeed, on March 4th 1811, Wellington himself issued a General Order stating that since he took command of the army two years previous, there had yet to be a single soldier in the Brigade of Guards to be brought before a general Court Martial and not one of them had even been so much as confined in a public guard.[14] This is praise indeed which says much for the Guards' discipline and the men's respect for their officers.

As with all of Wellington's British troops the Guards were fiercely loyal to their regiments, a loyalty born out of comradeship and of the sharing of the hardships of campaign life. But it was also a loyalty, of course, to king and country for the aristocratic and land-owning Guards had much to lose should the spectre of republicanism materialise at home, in the shape either of Napoleon or of anarchism and revolution. These factors bound the officers of the Guards together in a bond of unrivalled *esprit de corps*. After all, revolution had only recently swept away the aristocracy in France and with the beheading of Louis XVI the rest of Europe trembled lest the winds of change blow over their own lands. The legacies of the Industrial Revolution in England had created an undercurrent of revolutionary fervour in Britain, stirred up by the displaced workers, the poor and the homeless, who looked to France for inspiration. Fortunately for Britain, their was an even stronger loyalty to king and country, for the great majority of Briton's had no desire to see their green, pleasant and happy land trodden underfoot by the armies of the Corsican upstart. Moreover, the broadsheets and satirists of the day did their job well, providing savage-looking cartoons to a genuinely worried British public illustrating the terrible and disturbing consequences of a successful invasion by Napoleon who was quickly transformed into the greatest bogey man this nation has ever known, an ogre whose shadow was cast over the British Isles for nigh on twenty years.[15] It was, therefore, such threats both from without and within that bound the Guards together in a bond of loyalty and allegiance to king, country and regiment at the end of the 18th and beginning of the 19th centuries.

But who were these 'Gentlemen's Sons'? As stated above they were not just peers of the realm, knights, baronets or their sons. They were also the sons of the landed gentry. When they joined the army they joined to see military service, of course, and to fight and defend Britain's shores from the threat of Napoleon. But when they embarked upon service they did so not with a fearsome grimace and warrior-like outlook but with the instincts of a sportsman off in search of his quarry. We find amongst the Guards officers expert shots, keen hunters, trained judges of horses and greyhounds, naturalists, botanists and of course, men with a great sense of style and fun.

John Mills is perhaps a typical example. Commissioned in the Coldstream Guards on December 21sth 1809 at the age of twenty Mills joined the 1st Battalion Coldstream Guards in Portugal in December the following year. He was no son of a titled lord but had sufficient income to live rather well, to entertain and to maintain a 'Stud', consisting of a horse called Docktail, who was taken from the French at Salamonde, as well as two mare mules, Bess and Jenny, and a small mule called Turpin. Mills also supported his private servant, William, a soldier servant named Duckworth who looked after the animals, and Joseph, a Portuguese boy who helped him. He later increased his 'establishment' by employing a batman called Moore.[16] From this one can only shudder to think of the amount of baggage that followed Wellington's army!

John Mills was, of course, first and foremost an officer in the Coldstream Guards but just a cursory glance of his letters and diaries reveals him as a sportsman, never one to pass up the opportunity of going on a hunt, of shooting game or fowl, or of indulging in horse racing, coursing or playing cricket. He held card schools, dinner parties, and dined at monasteries and in the best hotels when in Lisbon. Wherever he went he noted the architecture, the agriculture, he visited vineyards and sampled the local wines and would note and sketch wildlife, birds in particular. In all, one is struck by the level of knowledge and attention to detail displayed in his letters and diaries but he is only typical of the young Guards officer on campaign.[17] After the close of the Napoleonic Wars Mills became a 'man about town' amongst other things, and took up the mantle of Beau Brummel following his demise. A great horse lover, he won many Gold Cups at Goodwood, became a member of the Royal Yacht Club, married 'the pretty heiress in London' and later became MP for Rochester.

The Honourable John Edward Cornwallis Rous was the

son of the 1st Earl of Stradbroke and was a contemporary of Mills. Rous joined the 1st Battalion Coldstream Guards just before the battle of Salamanca in 1812 and like Mills he wrote an account of his experiences during the war.[18] Rous took the war in his stride and his letters show that towards the end of the war, for instance, he was more concerned at missing out on Balls and going to the opera in Bordeaux and Toulouse than he was of staying alive. He bemoaned the fact that he missed the major race meetings back home, such as the Derby, as he was a great horse lover and maintained a sizeable Stud in England. His letters are also full of the trials of maintaining a good table under difficult conditions, of his sporting exploits and his billets and bivouacs. He also displays a remarkable knowledge and assessment of the events, both political and military, elsewhere in Europe. Rous took with him to the Peninsula his younger brother, William, in the hope of getting him an ensigncy in the Coldstream. William travelled with John throughout the campaign of 1812 before obtaining his commission in the regiment in December of that year. Rous later became 2nd Earl of Stradbroke and lived to the ripe age of 91 and would often recount to his grandchildren his adventures in the Peninsula.

Both Mills and Rous are typical of the young Guards ensigns that fought in the Peninsula and at Waterloo. One could go into great detail describing the backgrounds and subsequent careers of dozens of Guards officers but it is hoped that the few following anecdotes will give an insight into the type of officer that gave the 'Gentlemen's Sons' their name and reputation.

Perhaps the most celebrated Guards officer was Daniel Mackinnon, of the Coldstream Guards. Mackinnon was the son of William Mackinnon, Chief of the Clan Mackinnon and was commissioned as an ensign on January 16th 1804. He subsequently served with his regiment at Bremen in 1805, at Copenhagen in 1807 and in between spells at home recruiting he served in the Peninsula with the 1st Battalion Coldstream Guards between 1810 to 1813 and later in Holland in 1814. As we shall also see, Mackinnon was one of the defenders of Hougoumont where he had his horse shot under him, he himself being badly wounded by a musket-ball that struck him in the leg. Mackinnon, however, was more remarkable in the army for his sense of fun and his practical jokes and was a great sportsman and would amuse his comrades by climbing over the furniture of a room like a monkey. He would run and jump against anyone and his comrades would make bets with him that he would not be able to climb up the ceiling of a room or over a roof-top. Even the great clown, Grimaldi, said that Mackinnon only had to don the clown's costume and he would totally eclipse him.[19] He was also a great friend of the poet Byron when the latter was in Lisbon during the Peninsular War.

Mackinnon's most infamous escapade involved him impersonating the Duke of York. Before landing in Portugal after a spell of leave in England, Mackinnon decided to lead the Spaniards into believing that the Duke of York was amongst them. As his ship docked a royal standard was hoisted and as Mackinnon disembarked, accompanied by his comrades who had agreed to play the parts of his aides-de-camp, he wore the star of his shako on his breast. The Spanish authorities were quickly informed of the arrival of 'His Highness' and with much pomp, circumstance and ceremony turned out to receive him whilst a grand banquet was given that night in his honour. At the end of the dinner a huge bowl of punch appeared at which Mackinnon decided the ruse had gone far enough. Getting to his feet, Mackinnon suddenly dived head first into the bowl of punch, throwing his heels into the air, to the great astonishment of the horrified Spaniards and the howls of laughter of his comrades. The indignant Spaniards then reported the hoax to Wellington who subsequently reprimanded Mackinnon.[20]

On another occasion, Mackinnon discovered that Wellington was intent on visiting a convent near Lisbon. This was duly arranged by the lady abbess whereupon Mackinnon decided that he too would visit the convent and when Wellington arrived he appears to have failed to see the handsome features of our Guards officer peering out from beneath a nun's habit, Mackinnon having first shaved his head and whiskers before donning his disguise.[21]

Mackinnon spent a good deal of time with Lord Byron when the latter was in Lisbon and whilst there his time was taken up presenting the local women with, of all things, toothbrushes, having received a supply from England. Living opposite Mackinnon were two pretty Portuguese ladies whom Mackinnon was able to watch from his room nearby as they dressed, undressed, and went through their daily 'ablutions and toilet.' He could not help noticing each day that the two ladies did not brush their teeth and so lost no time in sending across his servant with two toothbrushes, perfumed and neatly packed up. The ladies were delighted with their presents but Mackinnon could only watch in horror as the two ladies, instead of brushing their teeth set to work busily brushing their hair with them![22] Like John Mills, Mackinnon was a dandy of

London society and an associate of Beau Brummel.

It is a well known fact that Wellington loved to surround himself with 'bright young things', officers full of life who seemed to instill the same in him. The Brigades of Guards were usually kept close to his Headquarters in the Peninsula and Wellington could often be found laughing and joking with their officers. They were frequently invited to dine with him also. Being the sons of gentlemen these young officers were equally at home in the dining room, on the dance floor and on the battlefield and whenever Wellington chose to hold a Ball his young officers were, as we shall see, very much in attendance and very much at home. One has only to look at the youthful, boyish faces of some of the Guards officers pictured elsewhere in this book to get an idea of the sort of officer to be found at army Headquarters, many of whom maintained contact with their old commander after the wars. One young officer of the sort with which Wellington would surround himself was Lord James Hay, of the First Guards, who was presented to the Prince Regent at a Ball just prior to leaving for the Waterloo campaign. The Prince was moved to say that he had never seen so handsome a young soldier in the uniform of the Guards. Unfortunately, Hay was later killed at Quatre Bras.

Hay, Mills and Rous are just typical examples of the type of young junior officers in the Guards. At the other end of the scale, however, were the senior officers, men who led from the front and maintained similar ideals and principles as their younger colleagues. Commanding the Guards at Hougoumont on June 18th 1815 during the battle of Waterloo was Lieutenant Colonel James Macdonell, later to be called the bravest man at Waterloo. Macdonell was the third son of Duncan Macdonell of Glengarry and had served with distinction in the Peninsula. When the French gained entry into Hougoumont it was Macdonell who was instrumental in closing the gates and he could be seen walking around the courtyard carrying a huge log in his arms to help barricade the gates. Lord Alexander Saltoun, a lieutenant colonel in the First Guards, was also at Waterloo. The 15th Lord Saltoun, he commanded the light companies of the 1st Brigade of Guards and had four horses shot beneath him. He also played a prominent part in the Guards' defeat of the Imperial Guard at the climax of the battle.

These, then, were typical examples of the officers of the Foot Guards, the 'Gentlemen's Sons', the men who after Waterloo prompted Wellington to say to that interminable gossip Creevey, "that no troops but the British could have held Hougoumont and only the best of them at that."

NOTES

[1] John Stepney Cowell, *Leaves from the Diary of an Officer of the Guards*, (London, 1854), 171-172.

[2] Wellington later said that the non-commissioned officers of the Guards regularly got drunk, usually by eight o'clock each evening, after which they went to bed, but added that they took great care to ensure that their duties were seen to first. Philip Stanhope, 5th Earl, *Notes of Conversations with the Duke of Wellington, 1831-51.* (London, 1888), 18.

[3] The nicknames of the other divisions in the Peninsula were; 2nd Division, 'The Observing Division'; 3rd Division, 'The Fighting Division'; 4th Division, 'The Supporting Division'; 5th Division, 'The Pioneers'; 6th Division, 'The Marching Division'; 7th Division, 'The Mongrels'; the Light Division, 'The Division'. Sir Charles Oman, *Wellington's Army*, (London, 1913), 171-172.

[4] 2/9th, 2/83rd, 1/40th, 2/24th, 2/42nd, 1/61st, 1/79th, 1/50th, 1/71st, 1/92nd, 1/26th, 2/62nd, 76th, 77th, 85th and the 1st, 2nd 5th and 7th KGL were all attached to the 1st Division at some point between 1809 and 1814.

[5] Captain Gronow, *The Last Recollections of Captain Gronow,* (London, 1934), 23.

[6] The term 'tradesmen' should not be confused with the present-day meaning of the word. By definition, a tradesman in the early part of the nineteenth century might be a banker, a lawyer or an accountant.

[7] Philip Haythornthwaite, *Wellington's Military Machine,* (Tunbridge Wells, 1989), 26.

[8] J.W. Fortescue, *A History of the British Army,* (London, 1920), x. 205.

[9] Haythornthwaite, *Wellington's Military Machine,* 26.

[10] Nearly 50% of all commissions in the Foot Guards were bought compared to 17.7% in the Line regiments. Michael Glover, *Wellington's Army in the Peninsula*, (Newton Abbott, 1977). 86.

[11] Ibid. 88.

[12] Lieutenant General Sir F.W. Hamilton, *The Origin and History of the First or Grenadier Guards*, (London, 1874), ii. 379

[13] Fortescue, *British Army*, x. 205-206.

[14] GO March 4th 1811.

[15] For an expert treatment by the British press of Napoleon's threatened invasion the reader should consult Peter Lloyd's *The French Are Coming! The Invasion Scare 1803-05.* (Tunbridge Wells, 1992).

[16] John Mills, June 13th and 21st, 1811. *MSS Journal of the Campaign in Spain and Portugal, 1811-1812.* In possession of his family.

[17] The reader's attention will later be drawn to the journal of Colonel Henry Mackinnon, also of the Coldstream, whose account of the campaigns between 1809-1811 would not be out of place amongst the popular travelogues of this day and age.

[18] See Ian Fletcher, (Ed), *A Guards Officer in the Peninsula: The Peninsular War letters of John Rous, Coldstream Guards, 1812-14.* (Tunbridge Wells, 1992).

[19] John Raymond, (Ed). *The Reminiscences and Recollections of Captain Gronow, Being Anecdotes of the Camp, Court and Society, 1810-1860.* (London, 1964). 63.

[20] Ibid. 63-64.

[21] Ibid. 64. Gronow says that after he heard of the incident Byron was inspired to include a similar episode in his Don Juan. He also said he would say no more about Mackinnon's adventures in the convent but had no wish to be scandalous!

[22] Ibid. 350.

CAMPAIGN LIFE

Life for the Guards in Wellington's army was not all battles and
sieges. Indeed, as we shall see, they might see only one major
action or siege during the course of a year. This changed
towards the end of 1813 as the Allied Army fought its way
across the Pyrenees into France but in the main the army
experienced long periods of inactivity during which, apart
from the odd skirmish or minor action, it passed its time
marching, counter-marching, on routine work, setting up
camp or bivouacs, seeking food and forage, looking to their
horses and their campaigning kit and the many tasks and
chores that made up the daily life of a soldier in Wellington's
army.

This, naturally enough, left the soldiers with a great deal
of free time which they chose to spend in various ways, a
subject that warrants a study itself.[1] These pastimes were many
and diverse enough but the officers of the Guards were able to
indulge themselves to a far greater extent than many other
officers in Wellington's army. One of the main reasons for this
was that the Brigades of Guards were usually kept close to
Headquarters and consequently whenever Wellington gave a
Ball, went hunting or held an investiture with its accompanying
dinner, the officers of the Guards were usually to be found in
attendance.

Hunting was one of the most popular pastimes at
Headquarters and the officers of the Guards could be found
regularly chasing foxes along with Wellington. Indeed, during
the Peninsular campaign the Coldstream Guards even supplied
a huntsman, Tom Crane, who had spent many years with the
Fife Hunt, who appeared at hunts dressed in a long scarlet coat.
When Wellington's Headquarters were established at Freneida
on the Spanish-Portuguese border during 1811 a great deal of
fox hunting took place and many officers took the opportunity
to bring out from England their own packs of hounds.
Unfortunately, on one occasion at Freneida, both Crane and
the pack of hounds were captured by the French when they
chased the fox into enemy territory. Fortunately, the French
returned them safely to their own lines under a flag of truce.[2]

When General Sir Thomas Graham arrived at
Headquarters in 1811 to assume command of the 1st Division
he brought with him an enthusiasm for hunting almost

unmatched by any other officer in the army. He was an outstanding horseman and even at the age of sixty-three could always be seen at the head of the fox-hunters. Wellington himself was another eager rider and would ride hell for leather at fences and ditches, although Captain George Bowles, of the Coldstream Guards, was moved to write, 'Lord Wellington got a tumble two days ago and hurt himself a little. He will certainly break his neck some day.'[3]

Many of the Guards officers were accomplished riders and held a number of race meetings in the Peninsula at which General Graham presided and more than a few maintained good stables at home in England. Ensign John Rous, of the Coldstream Guards, kept a number of horses and greyhounds at the family home at Henham, Suffolk. One of his horses, 'Quiz', won seventeen races including the 1801 St Leger. Rous was also great courser and kept a fine kennel of successful greyhounds.[4] A comrade of his Ensign John Mills, was also a fine horseman and his horses later went on to win many Gold Cups.

As well as hunting foxes many a day was spent shooting hares, partridges, rabbits and woodcocks, as Captain George Bowles, of the Coldstream Guards, wrote:

Beckford and myself, who are living together, have been out shooting two or three times, and had we any dogs might have done tolerably well, it is, however, genuine fagging and such as none but a keen sportsman would go through. It will give you some idea of our hard work when I tell you that I have each day completely worn out a pair of pretty strong shoes. Hares are in abundance about a league from hence. General Graham, whose headquarters are at Segiosa, courses once or twice a week, and generally kills two or three brace a day. In fact hunting, shooting, coursing, and acting plays are the order of the day.[5]

Bowles later wrote home with some delight that he had bagged a good many pintail and wild-fowl and wrote the letter with a pen made from the feather of a bustard which he had shot himself.[6]

Life as a soldier in Wellington's army was hard, the men leading a nomadic, gypsy-like existence as they marched back and forth across the Iberian Peninsula for a distance of what has been estimated at around 6000 miles. But if the hardships on campaign were no less a trial for the Guards than they were the rest the army their tribulations were somewhat cushioned by the knowledge that with private incomes at their disposal they were, however, able to exist in a manner that while not exactly that of the kind they would experience at White's or Crockford's, their London clubs, would, nevertheless, allow them to live in the sort of style that only an officer of His Majesty's Foot Guards could afford. There were, of course, many cavalry officers who had comparable incomes and also a few amongst the other infantry regiments - notably the 43rd Light Infantry - but as a whole there were no other regiments that could possibly live in the style of the Foot Guards. Indeed, when John Rous, of the Coldstream Guards, wrote to his mother on January 11th 1813, it was not just the exuberant boasting of a young officer to his mother:

Nobody dines out without considering that fish in the first course and a roast turkey in the second is what he may reasonably expect, besides which we have plenty of woodcocks. This is merely to give you an idea of the living of the Guards when compared with that of the Line, who live on a pound of tough beef and a pound and a half of bread (per diem) commonly called ration, a thing not known with us when in quarters.[7]

These were, after all, the 'Gentlemen's Sons', and as such were able to procure from home all manner of delicacies and luxuries that were impossible to come by whilst on campaign in the Peninsula.

Ensign Rees Gronow, of the First Guards, recalled the story of the Honourable W. Dawson, a quite remarkable character from his own regiment. Dawson was always to be seen surrounded by muleteers with whom he was negotiating in order to provide transport for his immense personal supply of hampers full of wine, liqueurs, hams, potted meat and other delicacies brought out from England. He also had his own cooks, said to be the best in the army, as well as a host of servants from Spain, Italy, Portugal and even France. Such was the magnificent table kept by Dawson that even Wellington himself dined with him, entering his tent to find, 'a dinner fit for a king, his plate and linen in good keeping, and his wines perfect.' Apparently, Wellington brought Sir Edward Pakenham with him, as well as Colonel du Bergh. Dawson was much loved by his brother officers but they appear to have taken advantage of his good nature for as Gronow relates, his stay in the Peninsula was cut short after about a year. 'He had only a younger brother's fortune; his debts became very considerable, and he was obliged to quit the Guards. He and his friends had literally eaten up his little fortune.'[8]

It was not only food that the Guards brought out from England. Their letters are full of requests for what many today might consider absurd items, such as draw-string purses, barometers, buckled shoes, muffatees, cotton night caps and black neckcloths. Maps were also requested. The most popular maps used by British officers were those printed by William Faden and Don Tomás Lopez. Ensign John Lucie Blackman, of the Coldstream Guards, wrote home on August 7th 1812 requesting a good sized map of Russia in order that he could follow Napoleon's campaign there. He went on to write:

I am in want of a writing desk with a case to it - I should likewise like to have a pair of those short boots that buckle at the side. Tea is very dear. Knives and forks would not go amiss......a large sponge is a great luxury.[9]

Reading matter was also much in demand. John Rous wrote home requesting Hatchard's, the London booksellers, to send him regular copies of the Quarterly Review as well as any other books, 'which it is the fashion for everybody to read.'[10] The eccentric Colonel Edward Sebright, of the First Guards, would read newspapers, but only after he had given them his own brand of treatment. Apparently, when Sebright left for Spain with the Guards he left directions to have the newspapers sent out regularly to him. Upon their arrival his servant would have to dampen them with water after which Sebright would hold them over a fire and exclaim, "Why, my papers smell as if they were only printed last night."[11]
Newspapers were a source not only of information but also amusement according to Ensign John Stepney Cowell, of the Coldstream Guards:

When newspapers reached us they were read with avidity; they contained old news of ourselves, besides endless speculative opinions on the result of the war, each in the plentitude of their simplicity, or, according to their own political views and interests. With one we were all glorious and successful, with another Lord Wellington was an ignoramus and we were all going to a place not to be named in print.[12]

Being always close to Wellington's Headquarters meant that whenever Balls and dinner parties were held the officers of the Guards were usually to be found in large numbers and with such a high proportion of officers coming from the higher echelons on British society the Guards were more than at home at such functions. John Stepney Cowell was often invited to dine at Headquarters and described one such dinner, attended by Wellington and seventeen others, 'among whom were the authorities of the town, some ladies, two commanding officers of the regiments of the Guards, other younger and lively characters belonging to Lord Wellington's personal staff and the corps *en bivouac* in the city's neighbourhood.' The evening was a great success and was rounded off by the two ladies who sang some 'pretty airs'. The two ladies were joined in song by Colonel Fermor, of the Third Guards, who sang several French songs. 'Thus concluded an agreeable evening....and as we returned to our Orson-like life in the fields, we thought with regret of these pleasant hours that had but too speedily passed.'[13]

Of course, the venues for such Balls and parties were not quite up to those held in Grosvenor Square or St James's but they were, nevertheless, always keen to put on a bit of a show. On May 30th the officers of Don Julian Sanchez' corps gave a grand Ball at Fuenteguinaldo to mark their Prince Regent's birthday. The officers of the Guards were naturally invited an in return they themselves decided to return the compliment and give a Ball themselves on King George III's birthday. The Guards constructed a huge hut for the occasion the floor of which was decorated with grass. For supper, the Guards pooled their rations whilst punch was made in camp kettles. Captain George Percival, of the Coldstream Guards, wrote an account of the Ball to his aunt:

I believe I mentioned a Ball that we were to give at Puebla on the 4th of June. It took place and everything went off uncommonly well till after supper when an order arrived for us to march at daybreak the next morning. It was 12 o'clock when the order arrived and having danced from 7 till that time you may suppose we were not a little annoyed at the order, having only two hours bed. Both ladies and gentlemen were much pleased with the Ball. Waltzes were the favourite amusement. I had three different partners, none of which I could fancy beautiful.[14]

When the Guards reached Bordeaux in June 1814 there were Balls a plenty. One such affair was given by the people of Bordeaux in honour of the Duke d'Angouleme which, according to John Rous, exceeded in splendour and taste anything he ever saw in England. The Ball cost 4000 guineas and supper was prepared for 1500 people. Also whilst at Bordeaux some twenty-two Guards officers held a dinner party to mark the end of the campaign.[15] Whilst the Guards were waiting at Bordeaux for the ships destined to take them home to England they took the opportunity of visiting the town's theatre where they saw ballets, comedies and operas. The Guards were apparently very popular in the south of France as they were reputed to carry with them all the gold in the army![16]

The most famous Ball of course was given by the Duke and Duchess of Richmond on June 15th on the eve of the

Waterloo campaign. The venue for this Ball was not the most salubrious - it took place in the workshops of a Brussels coach builder - but was attended by almost every one of Wellington's officers and unlike those held in the Peninsula was graced by the presence of a large number of ladies. The dramatic circumstances in which the Ball was held have caused the event to pass into legend as Wellington's officers tumbled out into the streets to hurry off to rejoin their regiments, many of them fighting and dying the next day at Quatre Bras still wearing their dancing pumps.

Another priority amongst Wellington's men was the procuring of good billets or quarters. In the Peninsula, the French army, with its greater recent experience of war on the Continent, appears to have been most proficient in the art of constructing their camps when compared to Wellington's. The French would erect tents or huts made from branches and leaves and would often form them into streets with squares while ditches were dug in order to drain the ground. Their camps were a hive of activity with everything arranged - from work to amusements - with typical French thoroughness and Gendarmes were even used to keep order. On the other hand, until late in the war, when tents became standard issue, the British soldier seems to have been content to make use of any form of house or building rather than get involved in the construction of sophisticated huts, particularly during the early stages of the war, something which was noted by Ensign Gronow:

An English soldier in camp appeared to be the most uncomfortable of mortals; there was no plan laid down for his recreation, or the employment of his leisure hours, and you might see him either brushing his clothes or cleaning his accoutrements, or else sitting on his knapsack, smoking his pipe to pass the time. We had no large tent wherein the men could congregate to converse, read, or otherwise amuse themselves, and when the weather was wet, they huddled together in small tents, where the atmosphere was worse than the Black Hole of Calcutta.[17]

Of course, as the war progressed and Wellington's men grew more accustomed to the rigours of campaign life they naturally became more adept at creating better living conditions for themselves. As we shall see later, when it came to the subject of provisions the officers of the Guards were able to procure from home, and locally from markets and camp-followers, all manner of consumables, but no amount of money at all could provide them with decent living conditions and they had to take their chances along with the rest of the army. When John Rous arrived in Portugal to join his battalion of the Coldstream Guards in the summer of 1812 he could not help but note the ramshackle condition of the houses:

The houses are all extremely filthy; we find chiefly one chair and a table in our billets which the owners of the house are obliged to give us....the rooms are so small and smell so bad, that I have slept with my shutters (for there are no windows) open every night.[18]

Indeed, he later bemoaned the fact that he neglected to bring from England a mosquito net as he was bitten 'all over by the fleas and bugs.' John Stepney Cowell, also of the Coldstream, was similarly appalled by the condition of their billets in Portugal. In 1811 he found himself billeted at Nave de Haver, close to Fuentes de Oñoro. 'The hovels,' he said, 'formed but a polite excuse for a covering,' and added:

We sat, when indoors (for *in-windows* we could not call it, there being none beyond broken shutters), wrapped in our cloaks, on the family household chests of the poor inhabitants, round a *brazarico*, or pan of hot ashes, to warm the extremities of man; a joke or a cigar in our mouth, to console the stomach or brush up the intellect; our drink, when we could get it, some kind of wine or alcohol, to fill the internal portion of human nature's commissariat depot.[19]

The state of Portugal as a whole left much to be desired and was considered by far the dirtier of the two Iberian nations and many an officer, struck by the far-off beauty even of the capital city of Lisbon upon first arriving, was later horrified to have the illusion dispelled. 'Each step we advanced,' wrote Cowell, 'filth in the greatest quantity and of the most disgusting nature presented itself, accompanied by a corresponding stench.'[20] Ensign John Mills, of the Coldstream, thought the country was 'entirely despoiled' and blamed much of the desolation on the French who laid waste vast stretches of land in their efforts to find provisions, often destroying much that was of little use to them:

You can form no idea of what a ruined country is - the houses in the towns and villages are most of them unroofed - not a vestige of anything that can be called furniture in them; they have burned all the houses that will burn, and the others that have no wood in them they [the French] have entirely gutted.[21]

The general procedure for the allocation of billets involved the quartermasters riding in advance to the next town or village on the line of march whereupon certain districts or streets would be allocated to individual brigades or battalions. Quartermasters would then select the best houses for the commanding officers and mark the doors thus with chalk. The next best houses were allocated to captains and lieutenants, and so on down to the junior officers. Any houses allocated to the rank and file would be marked with the number of men to be housed therein.

In April 1809 Colonel Henry Mackinnon, of the Coldstream, was housed in a room with a library. The house had previously been occupied by a French officer prior to the battle of Vimeiro and in the library he found a copy of *Telemaque*. Mackinnon, in fact, was allotted accommodation in a bewildering array of historic buildings ranging from palaces to monasteries and on one occasion even slept in the house of the Marquis de la Conquesta, a descendant of Pizarro, the conqueror of Peru.[22] However, even he spent nights in houses without furniture or windows. On reading Mackinnon's journal one is struck by the remarkable knowledge he displays of the buildings, history and culture of both Spain and Portugal and his journal would even today make a most interesting guide book.

During the retreat of Wellington's army from Burgos following the disastrous siege there in October and November of 1812, Colonel Freemantle of the Coldstream, although serving on the staff, was sent forward to procure quarters for Wellington himself. Apparently, after riding for many a mile he could only find a simple hut whereupon a fire was made and a suitable message scrawled upon the door. When Freemantle returned to the hut, however, he found an officer warming himself by the fire and refusing to move, 'not even for Lord Wellington or Old Nick himself.' The officer was threatened with arrest and surrendered, and was never seen at headquarters again. The story was repeated at White's whereupon the celebrated Beau Brummel exclaimed "If I had been in your place, Freemantle, I should have rung the bell, and desired the servants to kick the fellow downstairs."[23]

During Massena's sojourn in front of the lines of Torres Vedras in the winter of 1810-11 the Guards slept fully clothed in anticipation of an enemy attack. When it became clear, however, that such a course of action was beyond the French, so impregnable were the lines, the Guards set about improving their billets while their owners were away. Chimneys were constructed 'by the ingenious bricklayers', doors were repaired and window-frames constructed and filled with oiled paper. Portable tables and chairs were constructed and stretchers used as beds. However, after three months of sleeping in their clothes they found it difficult at first to adjust to their new-found comfort. As Stepney Cowell was moved to write:

I shall never forget the comfortless feeling experienced in confiding my person, for the first time, to a pair of cold stark naked sheets. I could not sleep a wink. But at length we accustomed ourselves to repose in our beds, although all were prepared, at a moment's notice, to turn out of them.[24]

Stepney Cowell found himself in a variety of billets and bivouacs in the Peninsula, from monasteries to muddy cabins, and filthy windowless cottages to ice-filled trenches and on many occasions had to share his bed with unwelcome guests. On one occasion he was billeted in a stable:

Some husks of Indian corn occupied the corner on the left of the door; two others were filled by large wooden chests, formerly enclosing the worldly goods of the poor proprietors, but now made to serve us as table and bed; a knapsack was our pillow, and our cloaks our covering. A whole army of fleas in close column were in previous possession of this apartment; they took up an imposing position under the corn-husks; we were determined to dislodge them. They disputed the point inch by inch, and the encounter with so formidable a phalanx was not ended without the loss of blood on both sides; and, although the main force had been routed, night after night much desultory skirmishing ensued.[25]

In the summer of 1811 the Coldstream Guards found themselves at St Oloia. On this occasion huts had been constructed for the battalion. Such was the heat that the men were obliged to remain inside, a common practice during the extreme heat of the Spanish summer. However, still unable to master the art of constructing huts from branches, the huts had the adverse effect and the Coldstreamers soon found themselves cooking inside:

The heat was excessive, our shelter from its intenseness inadequate; large plains, dotted and interspersed with olive-trees, afforded more dust than shade; our huts were not constructed of the best materials to defend us from the sun's scorching blaze; soon after daybreak they became little hothouses, or rather ovens, from whence came forth for parade an almost *baked* battalion.[26]

Many a Guards officer brought with him to the Peninsula a tent or purchased one on arrival. John Rous paid fifteen guineas for one during an auction in November 1812, probably during the sale of effects of a dead officer. Although officers were able to purchase tents for themselves they were not made standard issue until March 1813 at the rate of one for each field officer, one for the company officers, one each for the adjutant, quartermaster, the medical staff and the paymaster while for the NCOs and men three tents per company were issued.[27] No matter how bad the billet most Guardsmen would have considered it more preferable to spending the night in the open without any shelter at all, as was often the case during the war. As well as tents many Guards officers brought umbrellas with them to the Peninsula that made good sun shades. One hot July day an officer of the 53rd Regiment recalled seeing a Guards officer, 'just from the shady side of Pall Mall, reposing under the shade of a green silk umbrella, and coiling up his legs that they might partake of the benefit of the shade.'[28]

During the pursuit of Soult's army in June 1809 following the passage of the Douro, John Aitchison, of the 3rd Foot Guards, spent several nights in the open air in incessant rain, sometimes accompanied by hail,[29] and John Mills, echoing these thoughts said:

The periodical rains have begun. Fireplaces built out of windows, of stone and other rude, unfashioned materials, cemented with mud; and roofs which despite the vulgar accomplishment of keeping out rain, do not inspire the same sensations of comfort that a comfortable fireside, and the certainty of no trickling of water upon the head, are accustomed to do in England - added to this I am afraid we are about to move and as I reckon a bird in the hand equal to two in the bush, I had rather brave all the aforesaid dangers than hazard the chance of no roof at all - therefore I fear the move.[30]

And when circumstances dictated, even general officers had to spend the night lying on the ground in the open as Henry Mackinnon did, wrapped in a blanket, on May 16th 1809 following the crossing of the Douro.[31]

The most famous night spent out in the open was, of course, the night of June 17th-18th 1815, on the eve of Waterloo. Almost every soldier who wrote an account of the campaign recorded his experiences of the night before the battle - perhaps this was because of the dreadful conditions at the time, considered by many to be a good omen as it had rained on the eve of many of Wellington's victories in the Peninsula. Private William Pritchard, of Lieutenant Colonel Bywater's company, Third Guards, wrote:

We lay in a bean field that night [the 17th-18th June] and it rained it torrents, we being all so fatigued we were forced to lie down and in less than an hour we were almost drowned in water and in that condition we laid all night.[32]

The night was indeed a terrible one. There was little shelter to be had and all got a good soaking. However, spirits were not dampened to the extent that the Guards lost their sense of humour. When Ensign Rees Gronow joined his comrades of the 2nd Battalion First Guards on the morning of the battle he found them breakfasting on cold pie, ham, wine and champagne.[33] Others, like Private Matthew Clay, of the Third Guards, found it hard to raise a smile after falling into a ditch waist-deep in water:

On arriving at an opening in a fence, on the inside of which was a deep ditch, and the ground being wet, I could distinguish that my company had gone that way; in making a spring to leap the ditch, the ground being slimy and the increased weight of my wet blanket caused me to slip into the same, which being neck deep I found very great difficulty in getting out.[34]

There was, of course, some shelter to had inside Hougoumont but the Guards there were kept so busy constructing firesteps and barricades that little rest was had by anyone. On the ridge behind Hougoumont, meanwhile, men were trodden on by frightened horses that ran about in the dark as flashes of lightning provided a spectacular illuminated backdrop to the miserable, wet scene.

Of course, in spite of the comradeship and friendships formed and home comforts procured by the Guards on campaign, a soldier's life was a hard one and in some cases too hard for those concerned. Ensign Gronow recalled the tragic story of a fellow officer of the First Guards on campaign in the Peninsula. The officer in question was Sir Thomas Styles, a young man who had gone to school at Eton with the poet Shelley. As Gronow says, Styles would have, 'shone to advantage on parade and at the mess-table,' but on campaign it proved a different story. Styles arrived in Lisbon in 1813 to find that his battalion was in the Pyrenees. Styles then had to undergo the long journey through Portugal and Spain, all the time in extremely hot weather, and by the time he reached his battalion was in a poor state. His brother officers congratulated him on his safe arrival but Styles was exhausted and said he had not slept for half-an-hour since leaving Lisbon and added that he was in such a state that he thought he could not survive for much longer. Gronow goes on:

Observing that something extraordinary had happened, he was pressed to be more explicit, and to tell what had occurred to make him so miserable. He replied, with a very grave countenance, that the fleas and vermin on the march had nearly driven him mad and that when the peasant girls observed him scratching himself, they would laugh, and shaking their petticoats over pails full of water, tell him how much more they were to be pitied than he.

The regimental doctor, Bacot, thought that Styles was suffering from 'brain fever' and confined him to his bed where he placed wet towels over his head and told his servant to keep watch over him. During the night, however, he fell asleep at which Styles got up, unlocked his trunk and took out his razors. He then cut his own throat from ear to ear. For some, obviously, campaign life was just too much.[35]

NOTES

[1] For a definitive study of the pastimes and indulgences of Wellington's men one cannot do better than read Anthony Brett-James' *Life in Wellington's Army*, (London, 1972).

[2] Ibid. 204.

[3] The Earl of Malmesbury, *A Series of Letters of the First Earl of Malmesbury, His Family and Friends, from 1745 to 1820.* (London, 1870), ii. 240.

[4] John Rous' brother, Admiral the Honourable Henry John Rous was instrumental in setting up the Jockey Club and was often referred to as 'The Dictator of the Turf.'

[5] Malmesbury, *A Series of Letters*, ii. 233-234.

[6] Ibid. ii. 300.

[7] Ian Fletcher (Ed), *A Guards Officer in the Peninsula: The Peninsular War letters of John Rous, Coldstream Guards, 1812-1814.* (Tunbridge Wells, 1992). 48.

[8] John Raymond (Ed), *The Reminiscences and Recollections of Captain Gronow, being Anecdotes of the Camp, Court and Society, 1810-1860.* (London, 1964). 32-33.

[9] John Lucie Blackman, August 7th 1812. 8807-052. NAM

[10] Fletcher, *A Guards Officer*, 51-52.

[11] Raymond, *Captain Gronow*, 366.

[12] John Stepney Cowell, *Leaves from the Diary of an Officer of the Guards*, (London, 1854), 38. Wellington set himself against the practice of officers writing home to their friends and families as these then published the letters and thus betrayed the movements of the army to the French. Indeed, he later claimed that the French gleaned more information from the British press than they did any other source.

[13] Ibid. 271.

[14] Lt. & Capt. G.H. Percival, June 18th 1811. 8208-8 NAM

[15] Fletcher, *A Guards Officer*, 121.

[16] Ibid. 109

Sir John Moore, commander of the British Army during the ill-fated Corunna Campaign. Painting by Sir Thomas Lawrence.

An Officer of the First Regiment of Foot Guards, 1808.

An Officer of the Coldstream Guards, 1808. Painting by H. Edridge.

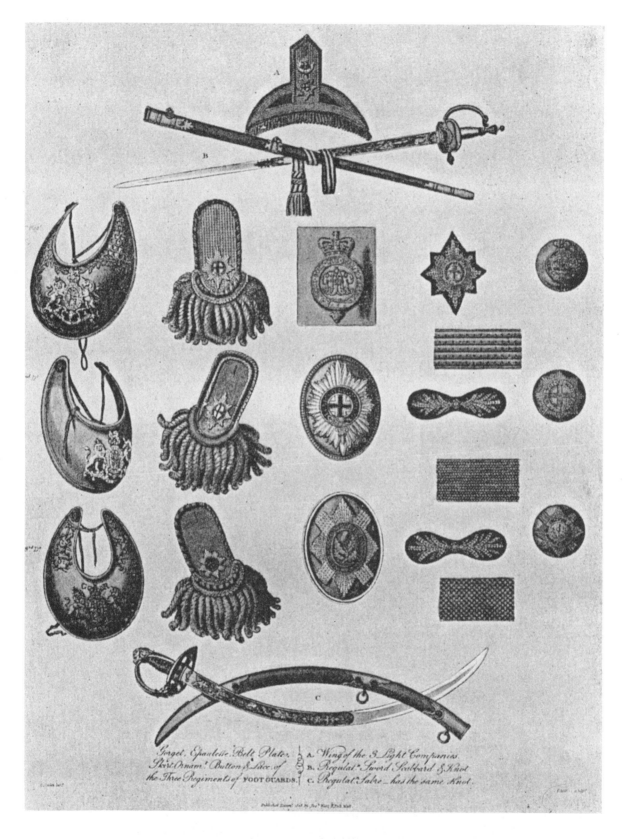

Epaulettes, wings, gorgets, badges, etc of the Foot Guards, 1808.

Mark Burns, strikes an heroic pose as Colonel Lord Russell of the Coldstream Guards, in the film *The Adventures of Gerard*. Burns gave a wonderful depiction of the typical aristocratic Coldstream Officer as he may well have appeared in the Peninsula.

Two more views of Mark Burns as Colonel Lord Russell in the film *The Adventures of Gerard*, as he leads a squadron of British Light Dragoons, (above), and (left) a unit of Scottish infantry.

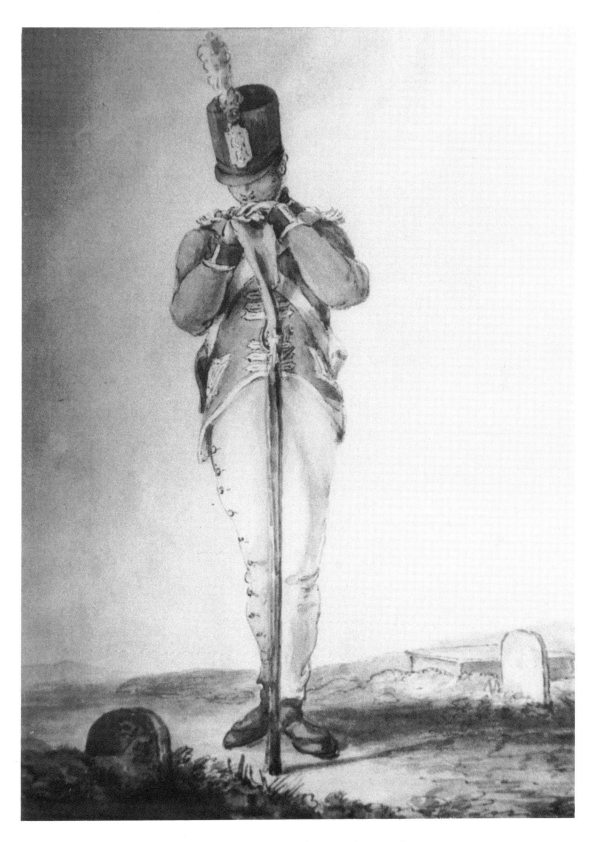

Private, Third Foot Guards, 1807, by J. Atkinson.

Rear view, Private, Third Foot Guards, 1807. Print by J. Atkinson.

Wellington in the Peninsula, depicted on campaign in the Pyrenees. Painting by T.J. Barker.

(Left); Ensign Noel Long, Coldstream Guards. Long died in April 1809 before he had even set foot in Portugal, following a tragic accident. He drowned whilst trying to change boats during the disembarkation of his regiment. (Below); Wellington's men cross the Douro at Oporto in May 1809.

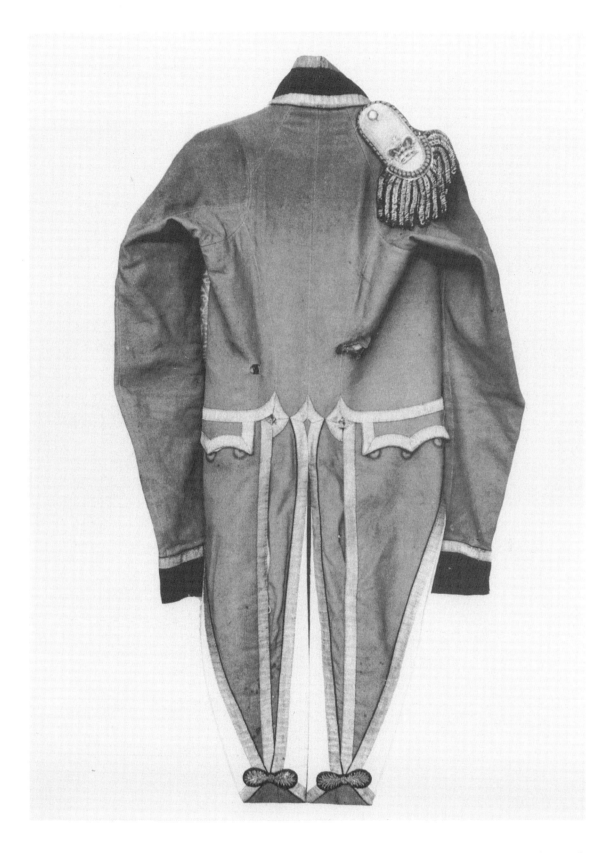

The coat worn by Ensign William Scott, of the Third Guards, when he was wounded at the Battle of Talavera in July 1809. The epaulette has probably been added at a later date. Note the bullet hole.

Captain Robert Dalrymple, Third Guards, in undress ensign's uniform. He was killed at the Battle of Talavera, July 28th 1809 and is the bareheaded officer featured in the Lawson's painting of the battle, which is reproduced in the colour section of this book. Painting by Angelica Kauffman.

(Right); A miniature of an Officer of the First Foot Guards, 1810.

(Bottom left); A miniature of an Officer of the Coldstream Guards, 1810. By Faulkiner.

(Bottom right); the gorget, shako plate and shoulder badge worn in the Peninsula by John Rous, Coldstream Guards, 1812-1814. The gorget and shoulder badge can be seen on the portrait of Rous on the following page.

John Edward Cornwallis Rous in the uniform of the Coldstream Guards. Painting by Thomas Beach. As the son of the 1st Earl of Stradbroke, Rous could indeed be said to be the typical `Gentlemen's Son.'

This painting is titled, `An Officer, Coldstream Guards.' However, when one compares this with the painting opposite it is almost certainly that of John Rous' brother, William Rufus Rous, Coldstream Guards, who joined the regiment in December 1812. He wears the uniform of the light infantry company as it was called.

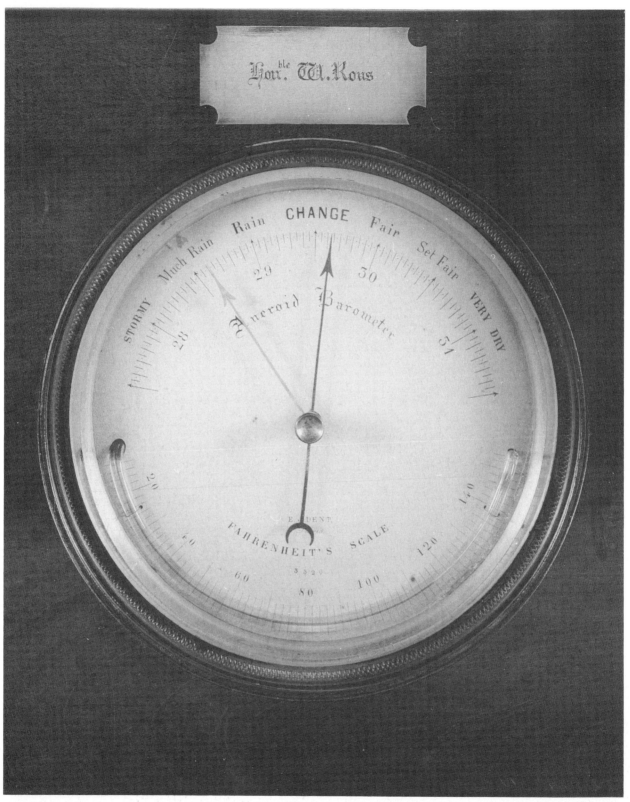

The portable Aneroid Barometer used in the Peninsula by William Rufus Rous and now in possession of his family. This is an example of the superfluous type of equipment carried by the Guards Officer when on campaign.

[17] Stepney Cowell, *Leaves from the Diary*, 191.

[18] Fletcher, *A Guards Officer*, 121.

[19] Stepney Cowell, *Leaves from the Diary*, 191.

[20] Ibid. 7.

[21] John Mills, April 21st 1811.

[22] Major General Henry Mackinnon, *A Journal of the Campaign in Portugal and Spain, containing remarks on the Inhabitants, Customs, Trade and Cultivation of those Countries, from the Year 1809 to 1812.* (Bath, 1812). 39.

[23] Raymond, *Captain Gronow*, 23-24.

[24] Stepney Cowell, *Leaves from the Diary*, 34-35.

[25] Ibid. 26.

[26] Ibid. 133.

[27] S.G.P. Ward, *Wellington's Headquarters: A Study of the Administritive Problems in the Peninsula, 1809-1814.* (London, 1957) 200.

[28] Brett-James, *Wellington's Army*, 32.

[29] J.W.F.K. Thompson, (Ed). *An Ensign in the Peninsular War: the Letters of John Aitchison.* (London, 1981), 43.

[30] John Mills, October 30th 1811.

[31] Mackinnon, *Journal of the Campaign*, 15.

[32] Private William Pritchard, July 12th 1815. 6807-157. NAM.

[33] Raymond, *Gronow*, 141.

[34] Private Matthew Clay, *A Narrative of the Battles of Quatre Bras and Waterloo, with the Defence of Hougoumont.* (Bedford, 1853), 9.

[35] Raymond, *Captain Gronow*, 331-332.

MILITARY DRESS

The subject of military dress is a study in itself and for this reason this particular chapter is confined to some of the non-regulation and more unusual items of dress worn by the officers and men of the Foot Guards during the Peninsular and Waterloo campaigns.[1] Apart from the colours of the lace and facings the uniform worn by the Guards, according to the official dress regulations, was no different from that worn by the ordinary line regiments, namely, a red jacket with either grey or white breeches or trousers. The Guards officers wore blue facings and gold lace while the other ranks wore white lace. However, as the non-practicalities and deficiencies of some items of the uniform became apparent, a great deal of improvisation began to occur, so much so that Robert Mercer, of the Third Guards, wrote on December 22nd 1810 - still at an early stage of the Peninsular War - 'Every person here dresses as he likes. These fancy dresses occasion much surprise and horror to the martinets who arrive from London.'[2]

We may like to begin with footwear, for it was during the first campaign in the Peninsula, the ill-fated Corunna campaign, that the wretched boots issued to the army were exposed for what they were - miserable, cheap and totally inadequate, so much so in fact that some soldiers said they broke up on the first day of the campaign. During the retreat of Sir John Moore's army through the bleak, snow-covered mountains of Galicia, the British army endured terrible deprivations, made worse by the poor footwear worn by the men. Boots and shoes were simply sucked off in the slushy, muddy roads and hundreds of men were forced to march bare-footed, their sore, bleeding feet leaving bloody red trails as a testament to their boots' inadequacies. The First Guards suffered along with the rest of the army but owing to their superior discipline and *esprit de corps* they were one of the few units to maintain discipline and as we shall see later, Moore were moved to remark upon their splendid appearance when they arrived at Corunna. However, this was not accomplished without pain and suffering and there were more than a few barefooted Guardsmen when the ships of the Royal Navy spirited them away safely to England.

When the battered wreckage of Moore's army reached England there was one particularly interested spectator standing on the dock watching in horror as the dishevelled, ghost-like figures dragged themselves along the quayside, their lacerated and festering feet swathed in tattered bloody bandages. The shocked onlooker was Marc Isambard Brunel, the father of the great engineer, Isambard Kingdom Brunel. Marc Brunel was an inventor in his own right and when he saw the miserable wretches coming off the ships he immediately began to enquire as to just how many men had been lost or had suffered due to poor footwear. The results of his enquiries came as something of a shock as figures revealed that as many men were lost through faulty footwear as from enemy action.

Upon examining the boots Brunel found that between the thin inner and outer soles there was a layer of clay. Needless to say, as soon as the boot was emersed in water they dissolved. Brunel set to work designing a new improved boot for the army and the following year filed a patent for it. It was to be a further two years, however, before the British government decided to place an order for Brunel to supply all boots for the army but once this had been done production climbed to some 400 pairs of boots per day. The issuing of the new boots came towards the close of the Peninsular War, by which time Wellington's men had resorted to several different alternatives to the standard issue army boot, but when Wellington's Foot Guards stood up to defeat the Imperial Guard at Waterloo in 1815 they were wearing the Brunel boot.[3]

Footwear was a major problem for Wellington's army and his men would try anything to ease the problem, ranging from the wearing of captured enemy footwear to the wearing of cow hides cut to the shape of the feet. On March 28th 1812 Ensign John Lucie Blackman, of the Coldstream Guards, wrote from Abrantes:

Our reason for staying here so long is that the men may get new shoes and other necessities they may be in want of as they will not have another opportunity till we arrive at Elvas.[4]

Following the battle of Salamanca the Guards had 'marched their shoes off,' and with no prospect with replacements forthcoming, they adopted the mode of footwear used by the Spanish muleteers. The raw hides of freshly killed bullocks were laid flat and the man's foot placed on it. A sufficient piece of hide was then cut to cover the foot whereupon a sandal was made. This was most comfortable to wear, so much so that when the Guards entered Madrid many of them could not be persuaded to use captured French shoes that were found in the Retiro, so well-fitting were they.[5] Many of the Guards were still lacking shoes the following year when they began to embark

(Left), An Officer of the Coldstream Guards, 1807, after a watercolour by Robert Dighton.

upon the Pyrenees campaign. Fortunately, they were provided with light hempen sandals which were made and worn by the local people and these were well suited to the steep and slippery slopes of the mountains.[6]

Perhaps the flimsiness of contemporary boots can be

illustrated by an anecdote from Ensign Rees Gronow, of the First Guards. When Sir John Shelley went into Hoby's the bootmaker of St James he complained that his boots had split in several places and upon being asked how this had happened, Shelley replied, "Why, in walking to my stable." Hoby was taken aback. "Walking to your stable! I made the boots for riding not walking." On another occasion Hoby was visited by Ensign Horace Churchill, of the First Guards, who said that his boots were so ill-made that he would never use Hoby again. Churchill must have previously spent a large sum of money in Hoby's shop for when he left Hoby said to his assistant, "John, close the shutters. It is all over with us. I must shut up shop; Ensign Churchill withdraws his custom from me."[7] Other evidence for the short life-span of army boots can be found in various references in the letters of Guards officers requesting new boots from England, amongst whom were Ensigns John Lucie Blackman and John Rous, both of the Coldstream Guards.[8]

As befitted the Foot Guards the officers and NCOs took great pride in their appearance but the rigours of the Peninsular campaign took their toll and before long their uniforms were quite different from those worn in St James' Street and along Pall Mall. Indeed, the overall appearance of the Guards was such that Ensign John Stepney Cowell, of the Coldstream Guards, was moved to write in 1812 that, 'in the haberdashery line we were all a little like those troops with which Falstaff, from a delicate sense of propriety, would *not* march through Coventry.'[9]

Changes to the regulation uniform were made purely out of necessity and although the NCOs of the Guards did their best to ensure the men looked their best even they, after a couple of Spanish summers and Portuguese winters, were forced to accept that non-regulation items of clothing were part and parcel of campaign life. Indeed, Wellington himself said he cared little what his men looked like provided they came into battle, 'well appointed and with sixty rounds of ammunition...he never looked to see whether their trousers were black, blue or grey....scarcely two officers were dressed alike.'[10] Wellington himself was considered a dandy and rarely wore his full uniform, choosing instead to don civilian garb, usually a blue coat and buff breeches.[11]

During the cold winters in the Peninsula many of the Guards took to pulling down the sleeves of their long Welsh flannel shirts over their hands which were then tied to form a sort of crude glove. The officers could not do this and so instead a number of them had 'muffatees' sent out from England which were normally knitted by 'the prettiest ladies we know,' according to Ensign John Rous, of the Coldstream. When he wrote home on September 17th 1813 to ask for some muffatees, he said they were worn by a few officers but said that the ladies should not knit any for the soldiers as it would make them too tender and added that they would not keep them more than six hours![12] When he received the muffatees he wrote home saying:

You may depend on my taking the greatest possible care of the Muffatees, which will be of great use in the winter, at the same time you may be assured that the soldiers will never keep anything that they are not obliged, nor are they permitted on service to have anything in their possession which is not a regimental necessary. One would easily be lost, but to replace it would be difficult, and every soldier has a long welsh flannel waistcoat, with sleeves, and does not suffer at all from cold in the wrist.[13]

Nevertheless, a great deal of non-regulation clothing was worn by both the officers and men, particularly following a battle or successful storming of a town when captured French clothing and equipment would often be taken in large quantities.

The extremes of the Iberian weather also caused both officers and men to adopt suitable measures. Umbrellas, for instance, were very fashionable amongst the officers of the Guards, not only to keep themselves dry, as witnessed in the celebrated 'incident of the umbrellas' before Bayonne in December 1813, but also to provide shade beneath the blistering summer sun. The weather, of course, paid scant regard to rank or social standing and when Moore's army retreated through the mud and snow to Corunna in the terrible winter of 1808-09 one soldier, of the 71st Regiment, made note of a Guards officer, struggling through the appalling weather:

The officers, in many points, suffered as much as the men. I have seen officers of the Guards, and others, worth thousands, with pieces of old blankets wrapped round their feet and legs; the men pointing at them, with a malicious satisfaction, saying, 'There goes three thousand a year,' or, 'There goes the prodigal son, on his return to his father, cured of his wanderings.' Even in the midst of all our sorrows, there was a bitterness of spirit, a savageness of wit, that made a jest of its own miseries.[14]

Of course, as the war proceeded, and Wellington's army advanced towards northern Spain, the army was able to be supplied by the ports on the northern coast, rather than from Lisbon with its

1815
Sergeantmajor in 3 Reg des
Garelis.

1815
'Clairen des Com in legires du
3 Gards à Pues

(Above) Sergeant Major and Bugler, Third Guards, Paris 1815, after sketches by W. Aertes.

consequential long trek across hundreds of miles in order to reach the marching army. This meant that they men could be better supplied and clothing and equipment issued far more regularly.

One wonders what those Guards who had been at Barrosa looked like by the end of the 1812 campaign in the Peninsula. The Brigade of Guards consisting of the six companies of the 2nd Battalion First Guards, and three companies each of the

Coldstream and Third Guards, was part of the Allied force defending Cadiz and in 1811 the accoutrements and arms which were new in 1809 were still being worn. The jackets of the Coldstream were said to be 'very short in the waist...and not very well fitted.....First Guards also rather short in waist and wear the clothes of last year.'[15] Their caps were also in poor condition and when a supply of new ones were ordered only 102 arrived. When the siege of Cadiz was raised the Guards then marched to Seville, on to Talavera, and reached Madrid before retiring to Salamanca, a total of some 640 miles. They then took part in the retreat to Portugal. One shudders to think how they must have looked after the rigours of this particular campaign, first in the blistering Andalucian sun, across the plains of Leon, and then in torrential rain and mud of the retreat to Portugal.

As befits the 'Gentlemen's Sons' there was a great deal of excess campaigning kit and items of clothing sent out from England to the officers of the Guards during the Peninsular and Waterloo campaigns but one of the more unusual items worn belonged to the Honourable Orlando Bridgeman, a captain in the First Guards. The garment in question was a fine red silk cloak to which is attached a remarkable story which is worth recalling.

Bridgeman was serving with the 1st Battalion First Guards who were at the time defending Cadiz. However, following Soult's retreat from Andalucia the Guards, under General Sherbrooke, marched nearly 400 miles to take Seville in August 1812. After Sherbrooke's men had captured the city Bridgeman was placed in charge of a group of French prisoners amongst whom was a wounded captain of Chasseurs, named De Marbot. Bridgeman spoke good French and De Marbot told him that he was due to marry a Mademoiselle de Casteja, her mother being French and her father a Spaniard. He had arranged to meet her in Madrid but now, of course, this was impossible. De Marbot asked Bridgeman that if he was ever in Madrid would he find the lady, tell her of his circumstances and if possible do what he could to help her. Bridgeman agreed and when he found himself in the Spanish capital in November of that year he did indeed manage to find Mademoiselle de Casteja. She begged Bridgeman to help her escape from the city which he did, delivering her safely into the hands of some Spaniards who promised to get her to France. As Bridgeman helped her onto her horse at the outskirts of Madrid she took off her small black velvet jacket and her red silk cloak and wrapped herself in clothing more suited to her journey. She asked Bridgeman to accept the jacket and cloak as a token of her appreciation saying it was all she had to give him. Bridgeman duly accepted and no doubt wore the cloak during the rest of the campaign.[16] Bridgeman was later wounded at Waterloo and one wonders whether Bridgeman wore the cloak during that campaign.

As we will see later in this book, the Waterloo campaign opened in dramatic circumstances with the officers dashing away from the Duke of Richmond's Ball to rejoin their battalions but such was the speed in which the army assembled and marched off to Quatre Bras that many officers found their uniforms packed up and the baggage already strung out along the road and as a result many of them had to fight in their Ball dresses. However, it was not only their dress that gave cause for comment. Indeed, this hasty commencement of operations caused personal hygiene to suffer also as there was little time to wash or shave and when Captain George Bowles, of the Coldstream Guards, wrote to Lord Fitzharris on June 19th, the day after the battle of Waterloo, he said he had not washed his face or taken off his boots since the 16th.[17] Beards were also in abundance and two days after the battle, when the Guards were on the road to Paris, the order to halt was given and every officer and soldier set to work getting rid of the beards that had grown over the last few days. As Ensign Gronow, of the First Guards relates, this task quickly sparked off the sporting instincts of the Guards officers:

During this not very agreeable duty, a shout was heard from Lord Saltoun, who called us to witness a bet he had made with Bob Ellison, that he, Ellison, could not shave off his beard in one minute. Preparations were made, Ellison taking care to bathe his face for a considerable time in water. He then commenced operations, and in less than a minute and without the aid of a looking glass, actually won his bet, (a considerable one,) to the astonishment, and I must add, the satisfaction of his comrades. This feat appeared to us all perfectly impossible to accomplish, as he face was covered with the stubble of a week's growth of hair, so dark that it procured for him in the regiment the sobriquet of Black Bob.[18]

A final note on military dress also relates to the Waterloo campaign. When the Peninsular War ended the Guards could look forward to receiving an issue of new clothing upon their return to England. However, if we are to believe that the they wore new clothing during the Waterloo campaign we must think again. The 2nd Battalion Coldstream Guards had sent six companies to Holland in November 1813 and were joined in Brussels the following year by a further four companies. They were still stationed there at the outbreak of the Waterloo campaign following Napoleon's escape from Elba. The battalion had received an issue of new clothing in 1814, whilst the First and Third Guards were still wearing their 1813 issue in May 1815. By then, of course, the men's clothing was in a very poor condition, particularly the greatcoats which prompted the Quartermaster of the Coldstream Guards to write, 'we shall be very fortunate if they will hang on the men's backs two months longer. It is impossible to make them last near the summer....Many of the men have got them very much patched already.'[19]

By early May 1815 the much needed new clothing for all four battalions of Guards in Brussels had still not been packed ready for transportation to Brussels. The Quartermasters of the Coldstream had every confidence in being able to supply the 2nd battalion of their regiment before hostilities broke out but by June 5th the ships had still not sailed and it was not until the last day of July that the clothing finally arrived. The Guards certainly cut fine figures in Paris during the occupation but on the great day of June 18th they defeated Napoleon's men wearing the old, much patched clothing of the year - and in some cases two years - before.

NOTES

[1] For a detailed study of the uniforms, equipment, Colours, etc. of the Foot Guards at Waterloo, one can do no better than to consult the four excellent volumes by Bryan Fosten, published by Almark Publications. For the wider study of military dress one should consult *Military Dress of the Peninsular War*, (London, 1974) by Martin Windrow and Gerry Embleton, and almost anything by Philip Haythornthwaite.

[2] Captain Robert Mercer, Third Guards, December 22nd 1810.

[3] Paul Johnson, *Marc Isambard Brunel*, (London, 1970). 52-54.

[4] John Lucie Blackman, March 28th 1812. 8807-052. NAM.

[5] John Stepney Cowell, *Leaves from the Diary of an Officer of the Guards*, (London, 1854), 181.

[6] Anthony Brett-James, *Life in Wellington's Army*, (London, 1972), 82.

[7] John Raymond, (Ed), *The Reminiscences and Recollections of Captain Gronow, Being Anecdotes of Court, Camp and Society, 1810-1860.* (London, 1964), 192.

[8] John Lucie Blackman, March 28th 1812. See also, Ian Fletcher, (Ed), *A Guards Officer in the Peninsula: the Peninsualr War letters of John Rous, Coldstream Guards, 1812-1814.* (Tunbridge Wells, 1992), 80.

[9] Stepney Cowell, *Leaves from the Diary*, 253.

[10] William Grattan, *Adventures with the Connaught Rangers, 1809-1814.* (London, 1847), 50.

[11] In the Wellington Museum in the village of Waterloo, there is even a

buff coat said to have been worn by Wellington during the Peninsular War.

[12] Fletcher, *A Guards Officer*. 76. The Rous family story has it that the ladies of Henham Hall, Rous' home, would only knit the muffatees for him on condition that he allowed his men to wear them also.

[13] Ibid. 7.

[14] Christopher Hibbert, (Ed), *A Soldier of the 71st*, (London, 1975), 33.

[15] WO27/102 Brigade of Guards at Isla de Leon, April 1811.

[16] In September 1815, during the Allied occupation of Paris, Bridgeman men an officer from De Marbot's regiment who was able to tell him that the French captain was living at the village of Lariviere in the department of Correze. In November Bridgeman visited De Marbot at his home where he was delighted to find that Mademoiselle Casteja, after many adventures, found her way to Paris and had since become Madame de Marbot, having married her French captain. Whilst Bridgeman was staying at their house he noticed a pair of gilded lamps, similar to others he had seen in Madrid at the Casteja's house. Madame de Marbot's lamps were exactly the same and had come from her grandmother's house in Venice. Both the captain and Madame de Marbot begged Bridgeman to take the lamps to remind him of the visit which he did. Today, the cloak is on display in the Guards Museum, London. The lamps, featured in a photograph elsewhere in this book, were also displayed until a few years ago when a workmen, thinking them to be worthless, threw them away!

[17] The Earl of Malmesbury, *A Series of Letters of the First Earl of Malmesbury, His Family and Friends, 1745-1820.* (London, 1870), ii. 441-442.

[18] Raymond, *Gronow*, 157.

[19] G.A.Steppler, *The Coldstream Guards at Waterloo; A Quartermaster's Tale.* JSAHR, Summer, 1989, lxvii. 66.

CORUNNA

On October 19th 1807 Marshal Andoche Junot, at the instigation of the Emperor Napoleon, crossed the Franco-Spanish border with 28,000 men with orders to be in the Portuguese capital of Lisbon by December 1st. Napoleon had commanded this course of action in response to Portugal's defiance of his decree forbidding the countries of Continental Europe to carry on any trade with Britain, the intention being that she would be subsequently starved into submission. This move precipitated the flight to Brazil of the Portuguese Royal Family, which set sail just as Junot's remaining 1,500 exhausted troops entered Lisbon after a most fatiguing march across the Iberian Peninsula.

A week after Junot's men set out for Lisbon Napoleon concocted the joint Franco-Spanish Treaty of Fontainebleau whereby he was able to march some 75,000 troops into Spain, without notifying the Spanish authorities, at the beginning of 1808. This move naturally outraged the Spanish people and on May 2nd riots broke out in Madrid where Frenchmen were hunted down and killed on the streets. And when Marshal Joachim Murat, commanding at Madrid, subsequently installed Napoleon's brother Joseph on the Spanish throne by way of reprisal, a rebellion broke out in earnest throughout the entire country. Spanish troops pulled out of Portugal, that country declaring its independence, and soon the 'Spanish Ulcer', as the war in the Peninsula was to become known, was created.

Dubbed a 'running sore' by Napoleon himself, the Peninsular War - or War of Independence as the Spaniards called it - proved to be a turning point in the history of Europe and was a major factor in Napoleon's ultimate downfall. It was a massive drain on French arms, armour and, more important, manpower. Thousands of French troops were tied down in the Peninsula, troops who might otherwise have been employed elsewhere in Europe, as what seemed like yet another Napoleonic conquest turned into a savage conflict, fought not only between the armies of France and Britain and her allies, Portugal and Spain, but also between the French invaders and guerrilla armies of both of the Iberian nations.

Unlike the people of other European nations that had crumbled beneath the power of French arms the people of Spain and Portugal were not prepared to simply lie down and become yet another French satellite state. The risings in both Spain and Portugal that followed the rebellion in Madrid were remarkably successful at first, particularly in Spain where a French force surrendered at Baylen, prompting an appeal to Britain for help, as a result of which the British government decided to act to help the two countries.

They had at their disposal a force of trained troops, mainly in Ireland, which was placed under the command of Sir Arthur Wellesley. Later to become the Duke of Wellington, Wellesley had already displayed his prowess in the field during the Mahratta Wars in India where he had led his men to numerous outstanding triumphs including a magnificent victory at Assaye, fought in 1803, which he later claimed was his greatest achievement. This 'Sepoy General', as Napoleon called him, was to follow up his Indian victories on the battlefields of the Peninsula where he proved himself to be a master not only of strategy and tactics, but also organisation and preparation.

On August 1st 1808, Wellesley's force of some 9,500 men landed on the Portuguese coast north of Lisbon with the Atlantic to the west and the wide estuary of the Tagus to the south-east. Wellesley aimed to trap Junot on the peninsula and was aided by Major-General Sir Brent Spencer who had sailed from Cadiz with a further 5,000 men. Moving inland, the British clashed with the French, under General Delaborde, at Roliça on August 17th. The French defended a strong position atop a mountain-like ridge with four distinct defiles. A planned pincer movement went awry when Colonel Lake led his battalion straight up one of the defiles and was quickly cut off, a mistake that cost him his life. Wellesley was then forced into launching a full scale assault on the French position which Delaborde, after some hard fighting in the rocky gullies, was forced to abandon.

Four days later Junot himself marched from Lisbon to attack the British at Vimeiro, a few miles south of Roliça. Again there was hard fighting, this time amidst the gentle slopes and vineyards that led up to the village and along the foot of a long, tall ridge to the east of the village. By the end of the day the French had lost 1,000 men as well as 14 of their 23 guns as the British tactics of steady musketry against mass French charges again gave Wellesley victory. The road to Lisbon now lay open, a fact that should have spelt the end for Junot and his army but an elderly general, Sir Harry Burrard, a former commander of the First Brigade of Guards, had landed in Portugal to supersede

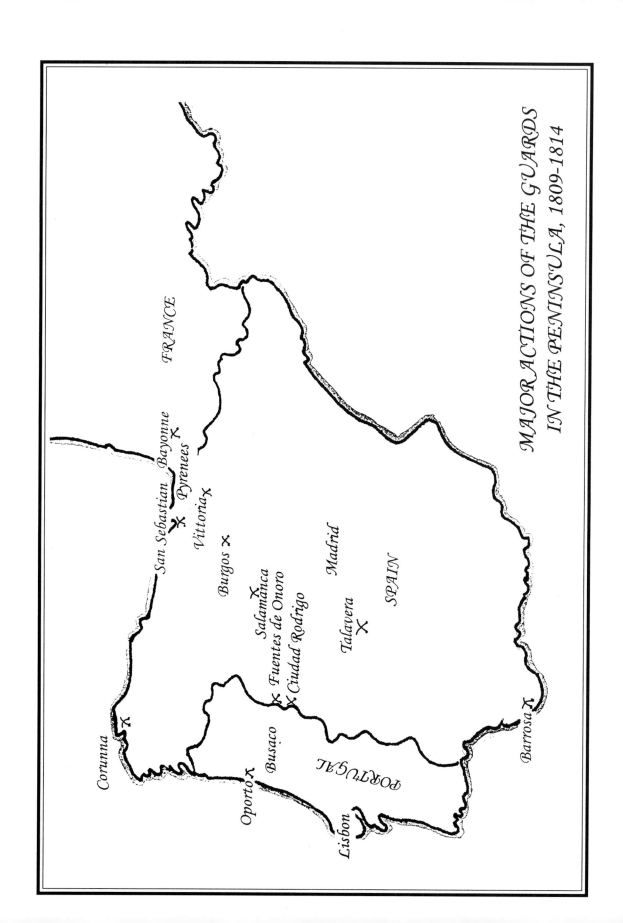

MAJOR ACTIONS OF THE GUARDS
IN THE PENINSULA, 1809-1814

FRANCE

Bayonne
San Sebastian
Pyrenees
Vittoria
Burgos
Salamanca
Fuentes de Onoro
Ciudad Rodrigo
Madrid
Talavera
SPAIN

Corunna
Busaco
Oporto
PORTUGAL
Lisbon
Barrosa

Wellesley and the next day an even older general, Sir Hew Dalrymple, in turn took over from Burrard and decided that any further action was unnecessary. Upon being asked what they should do next Wellesley, extremely irritated, turned to his confused officers and replied, "We shoot partridges," and while the army was left chaffing at a lost opportunity the two elderly generals agreed to the notorious Convention of Cintra, whereby it was agreed that Junot and his army, along with their arms and accumulated plunder, would be given free passage back to France unmolested aboard ships of the Royal Navy. Following this, all three generals were recalled to England to explain before a Court of Enquiry how they had allowed the French army to escape back to France.

Meanwhile, the British army in Portugal was put under the command of Sir John Moore who had been instrumental in re-modelling the British army at Hythe and Shorncliffe in new tactics based upon improved musketry and individual drill, and on placing less reliance on the lash, preferring instead to mould his men into an effective fighting force based upon a mutual respect between officers and men. In August 1808 the British government had decided to send a reinforcement of 10,000 men from Britain to Spain. This reinforcement included a Brigade of Guards consisting of the 1st and 3rd Battalions of the First Guards under Lieutenant Colonels Cocks and Wheatley respectively and on September 8th the battalions embarked at Ramsgate bound for the Peninsula.[1] The brigade, placed under the command of Major General Warde, was of the following strength:[2]

	Capts	Subs	Staff	Sgts	Drms	Ptes
1st Batt.	7	32	5	80	26	1361
3rd Batt.	9	28	5	67	21	1113
Total	16	60	10	147	47	2474

The ships carrying the Brigade of Guards sailed from England on October 8th and five days later anchored off Corunna in the north-west of Spain. Leaving behind 10,000 troops to defend Portugal Moore planned to march into northern Spain in order to join up with the 15,000 troops under Sir David Baird which included the Brigade of Guards. Once accomplished Moore intended to co-operate with the Spaniards, his plan being largely based upon assurances given by the Spaniards that all Spain was ready to rise against Napoleon - who had by now come in person to enforce his brother's authority and drive the

British into the sea - provided substantial British help was to be had. Moore, however, did not know the Spaniards. They were very brave, proud and touchy and very dilatory, never doing today what they could leave until tomorrow. Moreover, there was no effective insurgent Spanish government. The *juntas* or committees which sprang up everywhere claiming to act in the name of the absent king were composed of jealous local magnates; each appointed his own general, while all Spanish generals considered it as beneath their dignity to accept orders from an English heretic. They would discuss Moore's suggestions and then carry out what they had already determined upon without any consideration of Moore's plans. In spite of this Moore left Lisbon on October 26th and began his march north towards Salamanca where he hoped to concentrate his army.

Meanwhile, at Corunna, the local *junta* had refused Baird permission to land, claiming that they could not allow him to do so until they received authority from the Central *Junta* which would take several days. Therefore, it was not until October 28th that the 1st Battalion First Guards was able to disembark, the 3rd Battalion doing so the following day. Once ashore, Warde reminded his brigade that his men were now in a foreign country and that of an ally and pointed out, as Baird had done to the rest of his force, the need for the British troops to act in harmony with the Spanish people. Warde also asked his men to remember:

the very honourable position they hold, both as His Majesty's Guards and the Right Brigade of the British Infantry; that it will not only be necessary for them to behave well, but by their uniform good conduct he hopes and trusts they will set an example worthy of imitation.[3]

As we shall see the Guards were not to let him down when, during the retreat to Corunna, the brigade was one of the few units to maintain its discipline as the army virtually disintegrated in the Galician snows. Indeed, the high morale and level of discipline was evident from the moment the Guards landed at Corunna, as the historian of the First Guards pointed out:

The conduct of the officers and soldiers of the Guards was highly to their credit from the time they disembarked; fewer excesses were committed by those men than many regiments of similar numbers, and their officers preferred sharing with them their quarters, to profiting by the billets offered out to them. Out of 2500 men, when they were put in motion, they only left 20 sick at Corunna: other regiments not half their number left twice as many.[4]

Once Baird had completed the disembarkation of his force he began to set about getting his men forward, not an easy task as he had problems with transport and supplies. The Spaniards themselves suggested that he move his men forward in groups of 2,000 in order to ease the burden on the Commissariat, as a result of which his force became spread out along the whole length of the road from Corunna to Astorga. The Guards themselves marched by way of Corral and Ordinez to Santiago where they arrived on November 2nd, more often than not being quartered in convents where they were well received by the locals.

By November 19th the brigade had reached Villafranca and four days later reached Astorga. It was here that Moore received the bad news of the Spaniards' defeat at Espinosa on November 11th. With no Spanish army covering him Baird was now exposed to two French corps under Soult and Lefebvre who, if they continued westward, would intercept Baird as he marched across their front at Salamanca. On November 24th, as Baird contemplated his next move, he received a message from Moore ordering him to fall back towards Corunna. Baird now decided to divide his force into two and while the cavalry and Light Brigade covered the retreat the rest of Baird's force began to fall reluctantly back towards Villafranca. Command of the Brigade of Guards, meanwhile, evolved upon Colonel William Anson while six flank companies were formed into a battalion under Colonel John Lambert. Baird had been only a few days at Villafranca when, on December 6th, he received further orders from Moore countermanding his earlier order to retreat. This time a despairing Baird was forced to turn his men around and march towards Benavente.

With Spanish resistance in the country virtually at an end Moore, waiting at Salamanca, had to decide whether to retreat, which would leave a hopeless situation, or to advance which might force Napoleon to move against him and thus take the pressure off Madrid and allow the Spaniards to reorganise their revolts against the French. He chose the second course and so began his bold march across Napoleon's front. It was a brave move as he knew that should Napoleon turn on him the consequences for him and his army would be disastrous. What he did not know was that Madrid had already fallen, the news not reaching him until December 9th. Undeterred, he decided to continue his bold move and on December 11th began his march forward from Salamanca. It is recorded that while Moore was waiting for news at Salamanca one of his staff officers, Lord Proby of the 1st Battalion First Guards, was out on reconnaissance at Tordesillas when the town was entered by a patrol of French cavalry. The knowledge of Proby's presence in the town was widespread and yet even though he was forced to remain there for quite some time, not a single Spaniard betrayed him and he was able to rejoin Moore when the enemy had left.

On December 20th the junction on Moore and Baird took place at Mayorga. This brought the total number of his army to 25,000 men including 2,450 cavalry and 66 guns. The Brigade of Guards occupied Sahagun where Lord Paget led the 10th and 15th Hussars to a victory over a superior body of French cavalry on the 21st, following which, on December 23rd, orders were given for the army to advance. Paget's success had come as cheering news to the British but even as Moore contemplated his next move French troops were pouring out of Madrid towards the passes over the Guadarrama as Napoleon turned his attention towards them and began his advance north from Madrid against the British rear. If Napoleon could reach Benavente before Moore the British troops would be cut off from their ships at Corunna. One can imagine the disgust, therefore, felt by the British soldiers whose orders to advance were yet again countermanded by orders for a retreat, given on December 24th. They were understandably dismayed as they longed to turn and fight the French but were denied the chance by Moore's order to begin the retreat to Corunna, the most suitable Spanish port where transports could be assembled to withdraw British army.

Baird's division, including the Brigade of Guards, began to retreat on Christmas Day 1808, by way of Valencia and San Juan and the next day the Guards occupied Villa Manian. On December 29th they reached Astorga where they were billeted in the magnificent episcopal palace, the exhausted Guardsmen throwing themselves down amidst the numerous splendid galleries and corridors and in the large courtyard. As the year 1808 ended so the first signs of indiscipline began when the troops, drained, weary and hungry, broke into the wine-cellars at Bembibre and generally acted with great licentiousness.

It was at Astorga that Moore detached Craufurd's Light Brigade to retreat to Vigo in order to cover his left flank whilst the main body of his army continued its retreat to Corunna. The retreat to Corunna was carried out in terrible conditions and matters were made worse by the total breakdown of the Commissariat which in turn led to widespread indiscipline amongst the men. The roads quickly turned into quagmires and the troops suffered dreadful hardships in the bitterly cold winter weather, hundreds of them giving up the will to live and, unable to go on, simply lay down to die in the bleak Galician mountains or were captured by the pursuing French. Quite often those in the rear, and in particular the men of Robert Craufurd's Light Brigade, tired of running from an enemy they considered well within their power to beat, would turn about and face their tormentors and deal them a bloody nose, but more often than not they would be hacked down by French sabres or trampled beneath the hooves of the enemy cavalry. Hundreds of those who survived the ordeal suffered terrible mutilations from French sabres during these attacks.

On New Year's Day 1809 some 70,000 French troops, with Napoleon at their head, were just two days behind Moore's army but shortly afterwards the emperor - considering the defeat of the British just a formality and with events in Germany threatening his grip on that country - left the pursuit of Moore to Soult and departed for Paris.

There was no let up in the terrible weather, however, as the British army continued its retreat along appalling roads strewn with the carnage and debris that becomes the all-too familiar trade mark of a retreating army - dead horses and mules, discarded arms and ammunition and the bodies of the dead and dying who could go on no more. These, of course, included many women and children, and babies too, who had considered themselves lucky enough to have been allowed to come out to the Peninsula but who now paid the price of their loyalty to their menfolk. Indeed, such was the need for haste that on January 5th the military chests containing some 90,000 dollars were thrown headlong down a precipice. That same evening Moore's army arrived at Lugo where it grabbed some much-needed rest and it was here that Moore decided to halt and await the French attack. A few miles before Lugo, Lieutenant Robert Blakeney, with the 28th Regiment, passed through the Brigade of Guards as it camped by the roadside, unaware of the close proximity of the French, as he later recalled:

We marched through the brigade of guards, who were for the most part in their shirts and trousers, and in the act of cooking. All their appointments swung airily from the branches of trees. As we passed, some of the officers asked Major Browne if we had heard anything of the French. "I'll tell you what, my honest lads," replied Browne, "you had better take down your pipeclayed belts from those trees, put them on, eat your dinners, if you have any, as quick as you can; otherwise you may not have the opportunity of finishing them." The guards laughed with an air of incredulity. We marched on, but had not proceeded half a mile when we heard our guns, which were placed in the position mentioned, open on the advancing enemy. We now laughed in our turn at the guards, and continued our march to Lugo.[5]

Moore had his 19,000 men under arms early on the morning of January 7th and when he rode down their ranks he saw his men were quietly confident of defeating the French. This confidence was borne out by the re-appearance of many of those men who had left the ranks to plunder the wine-cellars and hovels of the Spanish peasants along the route of the retreat. Stragglers appeared from all directions as news spread of the impending fight. Marshal Soult's guns opened fire at about midday and after making a feint on the right, a French column moved against the British left. This, however, was repulsed by some companies of the Guards and Leith's brigade. Following this repulse, Soult decided to make no further attempt on the British line until the arrival of Marshal Ney who was fast approaching with his troops. Lieutenant Colonel Donaldson, Captains Packe and Latour, of the 1st Battalion First Guards, and Ensign Blunt of the 3rd Battalion, distinguished themselves during the fight, and the First Guards as a whole received the thanks of Major General Warde, who issued the following complimentary order:

Major General Warde takes the earliest opportunity of thanking those officers, and the part of the brigade who were engaged in the affair of yesterday for their very cool and gallant conduct.[6]

The following morning Moore's army waited in vain for Soult to attack, but even with numerical superiority he refused to do so. Moore was left, therefore, with little choice but to continue the retreat. On January 9th he issued a further order pointing out to his men the dangers of straggling behind and for the need to keep discipline. However, it was becoming increasingly difficult for many of the men to keep up as conditions grew worse. The blizzards that blew into the despairing faces of the British troops grew stronger and more biting each day and it was noted that many cavalrymen and mounted officers had difficulty even in staying in the saddle. The bedraggled infantry, meanwhile, sought shelter in ditches and each night were forced to endure the biting cold conditions as the bleak and barren Galician mountainsides afforded little protection or shelter from the elements. And yet in spite of their sufferings the men longed to turn and fight the enemy and achieve the victory they considered well within their grasp. Moore, however, was determined to continue the retreat and considered as his priority the safe deliverance of the army to

England, after all, it was the only army Britain had.

On the evening of January 9th the Guards reached Betanzos and on the 10th halted for the day before resuming their march at dawn on the 11th. As discipline and order worsened it was noted that only the Guards, the artillery and the rearguard managed to maintain discipline:

The corps in which there was the least straggling were the artillery, the Guards, and the reserve. The Guards were the strongest body of men in the army, and consequently suffered least from fatigue; besides, they are strictly disciplined, and their non-commissioned officers are excellent.[7]

When the army resumed its march on January 12th it did so with a marked improvement in the men's step as they realised that after days of inexpressible misery this was to be the final day's march. Some semblance of order began to re-appear and the sagging spirit of many a soldier was restored by the prospect of release from their sufferings. They trudged the few final miserable miles through the snow and slush before suddenly and mercifully, in the distance, there appeared the wide bay of the port of Corunna. The sight hardly prompted a dash for the port - the men were far from in condition to do that - but the feelings of relief were indescribable. And yet little did they know they would be called upon to turn and fight at the moment of their re-embarkation. For now, however, thoughts turned to England and although the transports that would spirit them away to safety had not yet arrived the army could look forward to a couple of days of blissful rest.

Throughout the next few days it was a strange and terrible collection of ragged, unshaven and tattered creatures that cascaded down from the hills around Corunna as Moore's army arrived above the town. Moore himself stood watching this harrowing spectacle as the remnants of his army marched in when suddenly over the hill there came the 1st and 3rd Battalions of the First Guards, marching in sections with their drums beating and the drum major brandishing his baton. At their head marched the sergeant major and on the flanks were the drill sergeants, keeping the men in step as if they were drilling on their own parade-ground in England. Next to Moore stood Sir Robert Arbuthnot and as he watched the two battalions of men come in Moore turned and said, "Arbuthnot, look at that body of men in the distance; they are the Guards, by the way they are marching."[8] As J.W. Fortescue, the great historian of the British army wrote;

He [Moore] can hardly have failed.....to point out that the senior
regiment of the British infantry had set an example to the whole army,
and that it was only vicious systems and neglectful officers that had
prevented every battalion from behaving as the Guards.[9]

As the transports had not yet arrived at Corunna Moore's troops,
by now totalling 14,500, were able to grab two days' much-needed
rest. However, it had become obvious to everyone that the re-
embarkation would not be possible without first making a fight of
it as Soult's army closed in on the town. On the 14th, therefore,
after embarking the sick into those supply ships that were in the
harbour, Moore's troops began to march out of Corunna to take
up their battle positions upon a ridge about two miles from the
town. A chain of heights - Mesoiro, Peñasquedo and Palavea -
dominated the town but with such a small force available to him
Moore was unable to hold these and was forced instead to take up
a position further to the north, commanding the road running to
Corunna from El Burgo, the route by which Soult had to approach.
Moore based his main position upon a hill known as Monte Mero
with Hope's division covering the left flank and Baird's the right.
The left flank was secured by the estuary of the Rio Mero but
Moore's right flank hung precariously around the village of
Elvina and could easily be turned. It was here that the Brigade of
Guards was placed in reserve.
As the anxious British troops scanned the horizon for the
approaching French on the evening of the 14th the ships of the
Royal Navy finally slipped into the harbour and the operation to
evacuate the town got into full swing with the embarkation of all
but nine of Moore's guns, his cavalry and as much of his stores as
he could find room for. Any such stores and ammunition that
could not be loaded aboard the ships was piled up to be blown up
at the point of embarkation. The operation went on throughout
the night and was still going on the next morning when the first
grey shafts of light streaked through the sky, revealing to the
British troops the approaching French battalions in the distance.
The re-embarkation of stores continued throughout the 15th with
even greater haste, brawny sweating sailors working furiously as
they tossed stores and equipment into the holds of the waiting
ships, while up on the hills around Corunna the vanguard of
Soult's army set about driving Moore's outposts from the heights
of Peñasquedo to be replaced by French gunners who dragged
their guns into position for the coming contest.
When noon came on January 16th the French attack had still
not materialised but around 2pm the village of Elvina was assaulted

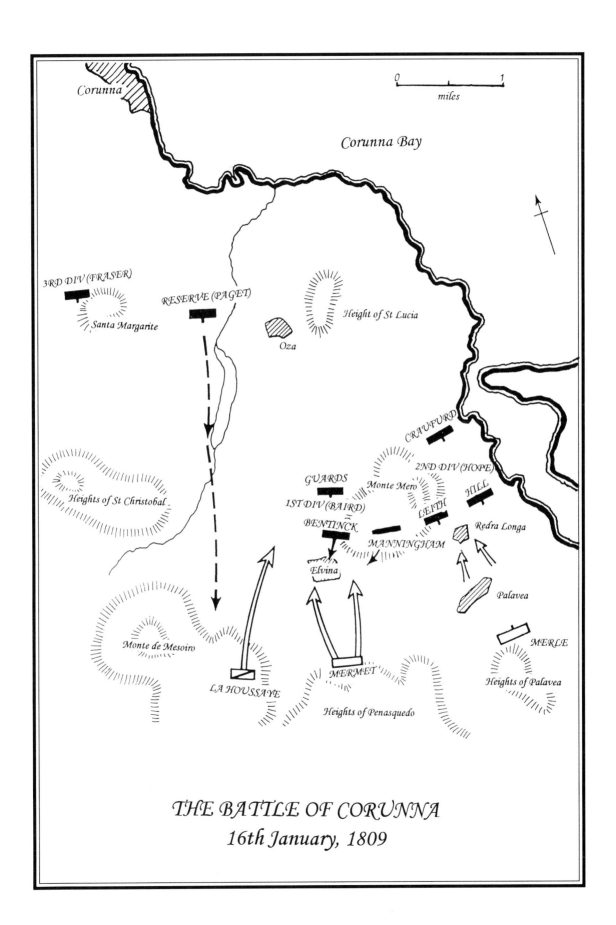

THE BATTLE OF CORUNNA
16th January, 1809

by Mermet's division and as the British troops were driven from it Moore's right flank was put under severe pressure. To counter this threat Paget's division was brought forward whilst Baird was ordered to retake the village, a battalion of Guards being pushed forward in support. But even as Moore's troops struggled to hold back the French on the right flank Merle's division came forward to throw its weight behind the French attack while Delaborde's division advanced along the main road against Hope. The fighting in Elvina ebbed and flowed and at one point Moore himself led the 42nd Highlanders, shouting, 'My brave Highlanders! Remember Egypt! Think of Scotland!' before clearing the village of the French. However, although the French were driven from it by British bayonets their artillery pounded away causing heavy casualties amongst the rest of Baird's division while Baird himself was badly wounded by grape shot that cost him an arm and forced him to leave the field.

With the French attack on the right seemingly thwarted, at least for the time being, Moore brought up the second Guards battalion to join in the counter-attack. Moore himself was always in the thick of the action as the battle raged around him and whenever a crisis loomed at any given point he could be seen, rallying his troops and urging them on. During the afternoon Captain Hardinge, having returned from ordering the second Guards battalion to advance, was pointing out the battalion to the commander-in-chief when suddenly Moore was wrenched violently from his horse by a round shot that thudded into him, sending him spinning backwards to the ground.

At first, it seemed as though no great harm had been done as Moore lay on the ground, quite still and not making a sound, his face not betraying a sign of pain. But when his aides rushed to his assistance they saw just how serious the wound was. As they turned him on his back the full damage caused by the round shot was revealed. The left side of Moore's body was covered in blood that seeped from a deep hole that gaped open, exposing part of his lung. His ribs and part of his collar-bone had been shattered and his chest muscles torn apart and twisted back together in a thick, sickly mess. His left arm, in fact, was attached to his body by the thinnest of sinews, by some tattered pieces of skin and by a piece of his shredded uniform, parts of which had been driven deep into the wound by the shot. He was still conscious, however, and as he was carried away he smiled as the 42nd Highlanders advanced to attack the French.

With Moore badly wounded and Baird already off the field, command of the army devolved upon Sir John Hope. It was a crucial stage of the battle for shortly after the French once again entered Elvina and were stopped from advancing any further only by a few well-drilled volleys from the Guards. Also, British reserves had been thrown into the fight but by 5pm, with the French unable to make any headway against the rest of the British line, Soult's men began to withdraw under cover of a cannonade and by 6pm, with the light failing, the fighting had all but ceased and the British were left in possession of the field. Although the French would re-occupy their positions the next morning Moore had defeated them and he would die that evening content in the knowledge that he had saved the army from destruction.

Moore had been carried from the field by six soldiers of the First Guards and the 42nd Highlanders and taken to a house in Corunna. The house had long since been deserted and Moore was laid carefully down with the thundering sounds of the battle fading in the distance as the fighting came to a close. Those with him were grief-stricken and many a tear was shed as Moore's life ebbed away. 'It is great uneasiness. It is great pain.' he whispered and about 8pm he spoke his last words as, pressing the hand of his close friend Robert Anderson tight to his body, he died.

With Soult's forces checked the British troops were able to begin their withdrawal from the battlefield in order to board the waiting ships in Corunna's harbour. Picquets were left behind to keep campfires burning whilst throughout that night and well into the morning of the 17th a frightening and macabre collection of dishevelled shabby shapes shuffled along the streets to the harbour where they clambered aboard ships bound for England. Of course, it must not be forgotten that the French were equally exhausted by their efforts in pursuing Moore's retreating army and they were unable to press in on the town until the morning of the 17th when at about noon they had brought forward six guns that fired defiantly on the ships as they departed.

As the clocks in Corunna struck eight o'clock on the morning of January 17th a small group of British officers and workmen shuffled sadly around a freshly dug grave, situated in the northern bastion of Corunna's citadel. The four officers had carried Moore's body there from the house in which he had died and after wrapping it in his blood-stained cloak they lowered it slowly into the grave where he would rest alongside General Anstruther, formerly of the Third Guards, who had died of dysentery in Corunna two days earlier.

The service was performed by the Rev. H.J. Symonds, one of the chaplains of the First Guards, who was forced to hurry the ceremony owing to the close proximity of the French gunners, now firing from the heights above the southern end of the bay. When the sad service was complete the small congregation departed in haste for the harbour where they joined the last ragged British troops who had come in from the heights around the town to board the waiting ships. These were the men of Hill's and Beresford's brigades who had remained as long as possible to cover the embarkation.

Moore's losses during the campaign were put at around 7035[10] although some 800 men managed to find their way to Portugal where they were formed into battalions of detachments. The 1st Battalion First Guards lost five men killed and the 3rd Battalion eight men during the battle of Corunna, although it is estimated that during the next couple of weeks following their return home the 1st Battalion suffered 86 deaths and the 3rd Battalion 54, mainly due to fatigues of the whole campaign.[11] Apart from these later deaths total losses of the First Guards during the whole campaign were 74 for the 1st Battalion and 66 for the 3rd Battalion.[12]

The ordeal for Moore's soldiers was not quite over yet, however, as a storm blew up shortly after the ships had departed, scattering the fleet of transports and even wrecking some of them. In the end the storm proved to be mercifully beneficial as some of the transports were driven home in four to five days. In many cases the storm went unnoticed as it is said that such were the rigours and fatigues of the Corunna campaign that many men fell asleep as soon as the ships weighed anchor and did not wake until they reached England.[13]

Throughout late January and early February the inhabitants of Portsmouth, and those of many other ports along the south coast, were treated to a harrowing spectacle as the men from Corunna disembarked from their ships. In most cases the troops were disembarked during the hours of darkness so as not to alarm the local people too much. The transports carrying the Brigade of Guards had anchored in Portsmouth harbour on January 25th, and following their disembarkation the men were marched off to Chatham where they arrived on February 8th for a few days' rest.

Along with Robert Craufurd's Light Brigade and Paget's rearguard the Brigade of Guards could pride itself as being one of the very few units to maintain discipline and order during the Corunna campaign, a conspicuous performance that has been universally acknowledged by past and present historians. As

Fortescue wrote, 'they had faced the high ordeal of the march as disciplined men.'[14] Much of the credit for this has to go to the Guards' *esprit de corps*, borne out of their system of training which was devoid of the harsh brutalities inherent in many of the ordinary line battalions. The Guards' officers and NCOs were of a different bearing and did not need to resort to the lash as did many of their contemporaries. This is also reflected in the fact that Moore's own system of training - which also relied less on the lash and more upon building a closer relationship between officers and men - had moulded the Light Brigade into a fine fighting force and it too was one of the few that came through the traumas of the retreat with great honour and credit.

But these were just the early days of the Peninsular campaign and the full benefits of Moore's methods had yet to be felt. When Wellington himself returned to the fray in the spring of 1809, however, his own reforms - along with Moore's - would fashion the British army in the Peninsula into one of the finest ever put into the field, and one with which Wellington himself would later say he 'could do anything and go anywhere.'

NOTES

[1] Lieutenant General Sir F.W. Hamilton, *The Origin and History of the First or Grenadier Guards*, (London, 1874), ii. 379.

[2] Ibid. ii. 379.

[3] Ibid. ii. 383.

[4] Ibid. ii. 383.

[5] Robert Blakeney, *A Boy in the Peninsular War; The Services, Adventures and Experiences of Robert Blakeney, Subaltern in the 28th Regiment*, (London, 1899), 86.

[6] Hamilton, *Grenadier Guards*, ii. 389.

[7] Ibid. ii. 391.

[8] Ibid. ii. 392.

[9] J.W. Fortescue, *History of the British Army*, (London, 1910-1930), vi. 375.

[10] Sir Charles Oman, *A History of the Peninsular War*, (Oxford, 1902-1930), i. 647.

[11] Hamilton, *Grenadier Guards*, ii. 395.

[12] Oman, *Peninsular War*, i 646. Oman erroeously lists the 2nd Battalion as being present instead of the 3rd.

[13] Fortescue, *History of the Army*, vi. 393.

[14] Ibid. vi. 375.

THE CROSSING OF THE DOURO

Even as Sir John Moore's army was struggling and slithering along the snowy, slushy roads of Galicia plans were already afoot to send reinforcements to the Peninsula. These troops were to form a division to be commanded by Major General Sherbrooke and consisted of the 1st Battalion Coldstream Guards and the 1st Battalion Third Guards, along with the 2/87th Regiment and the 1/88th Regiment.[1]

	Lt.Col	Capts	Sub	Staff	Ptes
1st Batt. Colds. Guards	7	7	14	5	1120
1st Batt. Third Guards	7	14	16	3	1361
Total	14	21	30	8	2481

The Coldstream were to be commanded by Lieutenant Colonel Richard Hulse and the Third Guards by Colonel the Hon. Edward Stopford. The two line battalions totalled a further 1,711 officers and men.

Preparations for the expedition began towards the end of December 1808 and as the year came to a close Kentish roads resounded to the crunching of boots as the Foot Guards marched to Ramsgate from their quarters in Chatham. As the Guardsmen clambered aboard the ships there were the usual distressing scenes at the quayside as those women not lucky enough to be taken along sobbed helplessly. No more than six wives per company were allowed to go abroad with their husbands and these were chosen by drawing lots. Pieces of paper marked 'to go' or 'not to go' were placed into a hat and lots were drawn. The lucky ones would shriek with joy whilst the less fortunate were left to contemplate an uncertain future; a hard time lay ahead of them and with no-one to support them they faced possible starvation and deprivation. Those who were to accompany their men would have to endure a hard and strenuous life but they were prepared to suffer even the rigours of the campaign that lay ahead of them rather than the bleak, uncertain prospects that faced them if they remained at home. The Coldstream Guards took 17 women along with them while a further 19 accompanied the Third Guards.

Sherbrooke's force set sail from Spithead on January 15th but had hardly got out of the Solent when a violent storm blew up scattering the ships and the fleet did not reassemble until February 24th at Cork. During the storm Assistant Surgeon Good, of the Third Guards, on board the *Shaw*, said in his diary that many of the ship's company received great help from the Guardsmen:

The ship's company are but a poor set, but they received great assistance from some of our men, who are very good sailors and were selected for the purpose, the rest of the troops being shut down between decks. It was some time before we could get the pumps to work, the sucker being out of order and the Quartermaster a great bungler. However, it was not of much consequence as we found but little water in the hold.[2]

The Guards sailed from Cork on March 2nd but their troubles were not over yet, for on March 7th the transport ship *Prince George* - also the headquarters ship of the Coldstream - ran down an American brig which had been detained the day before by the *Isis*. This latter ship hurried to assist her prize but collided with the *Prince George* as she did so. As the two ships closed with each other two officers and 50 men of the Coldstream jumped into the *Isis* but as they did so Ensign Noel Long, in attempting to do likewise fell into the sea and drowned along with a drummer boy.[3]

Sherbrooke's original destination had been Corunna but in the wake of Moore's retreat and with other political factors to be considered, this was changed to Cadiz. However, when the flotilla arrived there the *junta*, their faith in their British allies apparently at an end, refused Sherbrooke permission to land, and the flotilla was diverted to Lisbon, where the force disembarked on March 13th. The Brigade of Guards was quartered in and around the Convent of Belem which, despite the filthy state of the barracks, came as a welcome relief for them having been cooped up aboard ship for the past eleven weeks. Only nine companies of the Coldstream Guards disembarked at Lisbon, however, as the light company's transport had been driven into the Waterford river during the storm and only landed on April 6th, marching the very next day to join its battalion which had already began its march to Saccavem on March 22nd. Once established ashore, the first problem to be encountered, apart from the dirty state of the barracks, was drunkenness, as Ensign George Bowles relates:

Those only who are acquainted with the dirt and stink of the middling and lower orders of the Portuguese, more especially at

Belem, can form an opinion of the comfort of such quarters. This was much increased by the gross intemperance of the troops, who being for the first time in a wine country, and where they could get dead drunk for a few *vintems*, exhibited the most distressing proofs of ill-conduct; and this was not confined to the bad characters, but entirely pervaded the brigade, and I believe there was hardly a non-commissioned officer or private who was not brutally intoxicated once or twice during the first week. The greater part were constantly so, and it was not till the end of the month that we could get the better of this practice, although the severest examples were constantly made, and no less than 27 men were actually flogged one morning for being drunk on duty.[4]

The British forces in Portugal were, at this time, under the command of Sir John Cradock, but on April 22nd the frigate *Surveillante* arrived in Lisbon with Sir Arthur Wellelsey on board. Having been cleared of all charges arising from the Convention of Cintra he had returned to the Peninsula to assume command of the army in place of Cradock who was to travel to Gibraltar to take up the governorship there.

As Wellesley rode to join the army the Brigade of Guards found itself marching along sandy roads and across the white-tipped Junto mountains to Batalha where the magnificent convent there played host to the Guards. Colonel Henry Mackinnon thought there was not such a specimen of gothic architecture in all of France or England but its occupants may have shuddered somewhat when it was promptly taken over by nearly 2,500 of His Majesty's Foot Guards who clattered through its cloisters to be allocated quarters by the NCOs and sergeants. Nevertheless, the Guardsmen seem to have treated the convent with suitable reverence and respect and that night the monks treated a party of thirty officers to a dinner.[5] Indeed, such was the splendid dinner given by the monks that Mackinnon relates that he returned to Batalha six days later to dine with them once again!

After its departure from Batalha the Brigade of Guards marched through a countryside covered with olive and vine groves and thick with gumcestus, and the although the temperatures were nowhere near those yet to come the march was, nevertheless, a sticky one, the only shade being afforded by cork and fir trees that covered the hillsides. The conditions were not made any easier by the poor state of the roads. The best road, which was supposed to link Lisbon with Oporto, had only reached as far as Redinha and from then onwards became narrow and poorly paved. Nevertheless, on May 1st the Brigade of Guards reached Coimbra and as the men marched through the town they were received with shouts of joy by the locals:

The balconies were filled with females; embroidered and damask cloths, as is customary in Catholic countries on great festivals, were suspended from the windows; sweetmeats, sugar-plums, and orange flowers, were showered on the soldiers in great profusion during their passage through the town; in the evening the city was illuminated.[6]

According to his orders Wellesley was to defend Portugal but, as the old adage runs, 'attack is the best form of defence,' so it was to be on this occasion for within just two weeks of his return to the Peninsula Wellesley had formed his plan which involved a direct advance upon Oporto, at the time occupied by Marshal Soult. To the south lay other French forces under General Lapisse, at Ciudad Rodrigo, and Marshal Victor, at Talavera and Wellesley naturally resolved to strike against Soult before the others, separated by geographical barriers, could unite against him. He had at his disposal some 24,000 British troops as well as 9,000 Portuguese. These latter troops were as yet untried in battle but were undergoing re-modelling under the command of Major General William Carr Beresford. He decided to divide his force into three; General Mackenzie was left to defend Lisbon with 12,000 men, Beresford would lead 6,000 towards Amarante to cut off Soult's line of retreat eastward, whilst Wellesley himself would command the main body of the army, consisting of 16,000 British and 2,400 Portuguese and would advance directly on Oporto.

On May 8th an advanced guard of Wellesley's army moved out of Coimbra and the following day the main body of the army, including the Brigade of Guards, followed. Three days later French picquets were driven from the hills above Grijon and as they retreated upon Oporto they destroyed the bridge of boats - the only bridge still standing - behind them. Having done this Soult felt confident of being able to withstand Wellesley's attack which, with all the bridges across the Douro now destroyed, he was convinced would have to come from the west and be made with the assistance of the Navy. Accordingly, his defences were organised to face this direction, never for one moment believing that Wellesley would be so bold as to cross the river in broad daylight. He was in for a rude awakening.

Shortly after dawn on May 12th British troops entered Villa Nova on the left bank of the Douro whilst Wellesley himself rode forward to the hill upon which was situated the Monastery de Serra do Pilar. While the army remained out of sight behind the hill Wellesley set up an observation post at the monastery. As he scanned the right bank through his telescope he could see, below him, several French picquets guarding the quayside and the barges moored there whilst to the north-east two columns of French infantry were preparing to move off as escort for Soult's sick, wounded and reserve artillery. As he looked to the right, however, a very different picture emerged. There appeared to be no activity here and in fact the streets and houses seemed deserted. Also, the Bishop's Seminary, a large building at the bend of the river, not only appeared to be unguarded but seemed to be out of sight of the majority of the 11,000 French troops stuffed into Oporto. This careless oversight, and Soult's over-confident conviction that the British attack must come from the west, was to prove his downfall. As Wellesley considered his next move he was informed that the sunken ferry boat at Barca d'Avintas, four miles above Oporto, was not seriously damaged and that local people were repairing it. Two battalions of King's German Legion infantry and some cavalry under Major General Murray were despatched to cross there but it was the discovery brought to his attention by Colonel John Waters, commanding Wellesley's scouts, that cheered him most of all. Ensign William Scott, of the Third Guards, wrote:

We had in our army a very clever fellow, Waters by name, better known as Billy Waters. He had been educated in Portugal for the wine trade, but he had too much spirit for that and entered the army and became aide-de-camp to Sir Arthur. When Sir Arthur gives an order you had better say nothing, but go and do it. So thought Billy Waters. His orders were go and get boats. You may call for spirits but will they come. It so happened that as he was walking along the river bank Waters fell in with one who is in general the cleverest man of a village, the barber. The barber knew where there was a small boat and Waters, seeing two large ones on the opposite side, induced the barber to get into it and they secured the two large ones and brought them safe to Sir Arthur.[7]

The barber had, in fact, rowed across in his own boat to tell Waters that there were four undamaged wine barges moored on the right bank and, more important, they were unguarded. As soon as Wellesley was given this information he ordered Waters to cross the river and bring them across to the left bank. Soon, Waters, and the barber, along with four peasants and a priest - 'as strange a force as ever won a battle'[8] - were stealing silently across the river to bring back the barges. Once secured, Wellesley drew breath and said simply, 'Well, let the men cross,' and at that the daring operation to cross the Douro got underway.

Each of the barges was only large enough to ferry across one officer and twenty-five men but the first, carrying a party of the 3rd Foot (The Buffs), was soon gliding gently out into the river with the three others close behind. As soon as the barges touched the opposite bank the men leapt from them and dashed excitedly into the grounds of the Seminary which they secured by closing the iron gate which formed the only landward exit while others constructed crude firesteps from piles of wood and earth. The barges now began their return journey and soon reinforcements were crossing the river, all the time under the watchful but apprehensive gaze of Wellesley and his staff who could not believe their good fortune. And so it went on for almost an hour, the barges criss-crossing the Douro in silence as more and more redcoated British infantry were ferried across to bolster the defences at the Seminary. When the barges made their third crossing they carried across General Edward Paget who commanded the whole movement.

By the time the French finally realised what was going on some 600 British troops were firmly established on the right bank of the Douro. At about 11.30 a rider galloped breathlessly into Soult's headquarters with the news that British troops were crossing the river. Soult himself was in bed, having been up all night, and his staff were still at breakfast but all was soon frantic activity as the stunning truth finally dawned on them. General Foy was the first to attack the Seminary with three battalions of infantry but these were beaten back and when he brought guns up to the water's edge to open fire these too were silenced by the British batteries situated high above them at the convent. French efforts to dislodge the British cost them dear - they had to cross an open space which was swept by musketry from behind the garden walls and from the roof and windows of the Seminary.

In despair, Soult now threw Reynaud's brigade into the fight. This brigade had until now been guarding the barges at the quayside and no sooner had they been marched hastily off towards the Seminary than the Portuguese inhabitants came tumbling from their houses and ran to the river to ferry the remaining barges across to the British, waiting on the opposite shore. Within minutes the Portuguese had scrambled into them and soon a small flotilla of barges was wafting easily across to the left bank. The Brigade of Guards, under Sherbrooke, should have been first to cross but word came back from the river that the 29th Regiment, already waiting at the water's edge, was unable to make room for the Guards and would therefore be the first to cross. They were closely followed by the

Guards who crossed under the direction of Colonel Donkin of the Headquarters Staff. Amongst the first to cross was Captain Robert Dalrymple of the Third Guards:

The scene was altogether most beautiful and perfectly unique. The day was very fine, and, the tide being in, the river was quite full. Immediately opposite Oporto is the town of Villa Nova, where we embarked to cross the river. Here on the beach was raised an immense standard of white cloth, on which the sign of the cross was embroidered; the opposite walls of Oporto were lined with people waving white handkerchiefs to us, expressing, by their signs and gestures, their extreme anxiety for our crossing the river: the Portuguese rowed their own boats, and the animation these poor fishermen displayed, and their exertions to get us quickly over, were very striking. The houses in Oporto are very lofty, and there is a range of balconies to each floor; as we passed through the streets, the houses were chiefly shut, from fear of being pillaged by the French in their retreat; but the balconies were full of people, chiefly women, and from one end of the street to another there was a continued line of white handkerchiefs waved to us from the balconies.[9]

As the barges touched the opposite shore the Guards leapt into the water and with their sergeants bawling at them to get forward they dashed into the streets with fixed bayonets. However, as Assistant Surgeon Good of the Third Guards wrote, they were frustrated to find no French troops waiting to greet them:

the Brigade of Guards....loaded and advanced up the town, but the devil a Gaul would wait for us, they were all out, except some few dead and wounded lying in the streets at the upper end of the City. Indeed, they went away in such a hurry that they left the streets blocked up with artillery, ammunition wagons, etc. Some of these had broken down and the horses of others had been shot. We pursued the fugitives through the town, but they would not stop for us, however we should soon have got up to them, had we not been ordered to halt; so that we could not get one shot at them.[10]

George Bowles, of the Coldstream, was one of the first across in a small boat filled with the mixed companies of his battalion:

We landed on nearly the centre of the quay, and although the companies had been completely mixed in getting into the boats, yet the brigade was formed on landing without the smallest confusion and in almost an instant, in a manner which I cannot even now comprehend, as of all the possible situations this appeared the most likely to cause delay and confusion. We instantly moved in column up the principal street, through the centre of the town of Oporto....the street being full of dead and dying Frenchmen and horses together with guns, tumbrils, &c. Our movement through Oporto presented a most interesting and animating spectacle. The windows, balconies, and tops of houses were crowded with men, women, and children, who by huzzaing, waving their hats, handkerchiefs, &c., testified their joy and anxiety for our success. Even the latticed windows of the nunneries were thrown open and the sacred, though certainly not very fascinating, visages of their antiquated inhabitants exposed to view for our encouragement. The streets were filled with dead and dying, a sharp action in which we were hoping soon to bear a part was going on a few hundred paces in front, and altogether it was certainly a most glorious moment, the remembrance of which will never be effaced from the minds of those who were present.[11]

The Guards stormed through the narrow streets but found the French in full retreat. Soult, realising that he could not dislodge the British and with Murray threatening his right flank, ordered a general withdrawal and in so doing precipitated a panic-stricken rout as the French soldiers fought to extricate themselves from the streets of the city. Such was their haste that they abandoned a number of ammunition wagons as well as 70 guns and when Wellesley sat down to dinner that evening in the Palacio das Carrancas he ate the supper that had been ordered for Soult.

When the Guards marched through Oporto they were greeted with the same enthusiastic welcome as they had received at Coimbra. Once again they were showered with roses by women who crowded the balconies waving their handkerchiefs while the rest of the inhabitants spilled out onto the streets crying "Viva os Ingleses" and "Viva o Grand Britania", and brought out hogsheads of wine for the troops.[12] The daring but hazardous crossing of the Douro was accomplished by Wellesley at the cost of just 23 killed and 98 wounded whereas the French lost some 300 men killed and wounded as well as 1,500 taken prisoner.

Wellesley decided not to pursue the defeated French as his men were tired having marched eighty miles in just four days, three of which had seen action. However, as he took stock of the situation he received dramatic news that Beresford had seized the bridge over the Tamega at Amarante, severing Soult's line of retreat. The French commander was forced to destroy his baggage and 58 guns and continued his retreat by way of a track through the Tras os Montes towards Braga. Murray was hastily sent forward in pursuit with some cavalry whilst Wellesley marched out of Oporto on the 14th with the main body of the army.

The good weather of the last few days turned and the men of both armies were quickly soaked by heavy rain that lashed down on them and made conditions treacherous underfoot. The exhausted and defeated French soldiers found their retreat slowed down by the bad state of the roads which turned to muddy quagmires and the pursuing British troops found the roads littered with the bodies of murdered French stragglers who had been unable to keep pace with the main body of their army any longer. As well as these corpses the route of the French retreat was marked by burning villages strewn with the dead bodies of their inhabitants who the French had murdered after destroying the houses and plundering anything of value.

In spite of the stinging rain and biting cold wind that had got up, Wellesley's troops were in good spirits and were driven on by the desire to overtake the French and sure enough on May 16th the British advanced guard, which was the Brigade of Guards, came up with the rear of the French column at Salamonde. The French position was a strong one with their right protected by a deep ravine. On the left was a steep hill whilst it was difficult to make a frontal approach as the road was open and exposed to heavy enemy fire. Wellesley decided to turn the French left by attacking with the light companies of the Coldstream and the Third Guards, as well as the 5/60th Rifles, under Lieutenant Colonel Fuller of the Coldstream. These were covered by two 3-pounders which ceased fire as they closed on the French. At this the rest of the Brigade of Guards advanced but after firing one volley the French - the 4th Léger, considered to be one of the best French regiments - broke and fled in disorder. The French were chased over the Ponte Nova, a narrow bridge with no parapets and in the chaos and confusion of the retreat, as the panicking French fought and struggled with each other to cross the bridge, a great number of them were either crushed or fell into the torrents below and were drowned. The carnage was increased when the British brought their guns to forward to open fire with deadly effect and the French were saved from further punishment only when nightfall brought the curtain down on the fighting. In a despatch written on May 18th Wellesley said:

The Brigade of Guards were at the head of the column, and set a laudable example; and in the affair with the enemy's rearguard on the evening of the sixteenth they conducted themselves remarkably well.[13]

When the Guards settled down for the night many of them passed the time examining a large number of knapsacks and a good deal

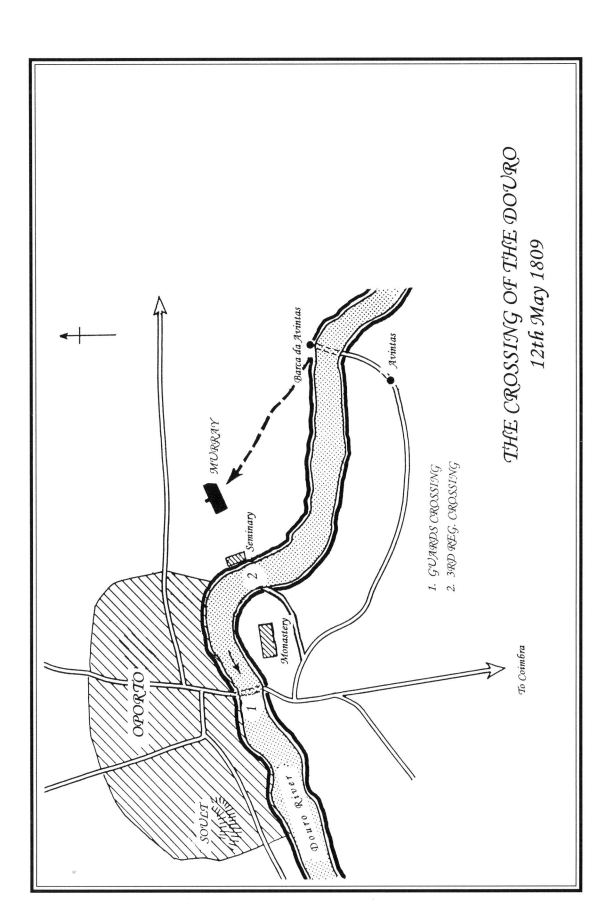

THE CROSSING OF THE DOURO
12th May 1809

OPORTO

SOULT

Douro River

SEMINARY

MURRAY

Barca da Avintas

Avintas

Monastery

To Coimbra

1. GUARDS CROSSING
2. 3RD REG. CROSSING

of baggage, left behind by the French, and which were full of all kinds of accumulated plunder, 'the produce of the jewellers' and other shops at Oporto.'[14] That night was spent in the open but the fires that the French had abandoned enabled the Guards to cook their dinners and dry their clothes which, after the recent heavy rains, came as a welcome relief.[15] Soult continued his retreat on the 18th, closely pursued by the Guards who crossed the bridge at Ruvaens and halted at Scavessa de Rio after a long and unpleasant march. The following day Wellesley gave up the pursuit and, concerned as to the actions of the French under Victor, decided instead to return to Oporto which was reached May 24th. By the beginning of June Wellesley had returned to Coimbra and marching through Leiria and Thomar the army reached Abrantes on June 10th where the it concentrated.

NOTES

[1] Colonel Daniel Mackinnon, *Origins and Services of the Coldstream Guards*, (London, 1833), ii. 103.

[2] Major General Sir Frederick Maurice, *The History of the Scots Guards, 1642-1914*, (London, 1934), i. 294-295.

[3] The Earl of Malmesbury, *A Series of Letters of the First Earl of Malmesbury, His Family and Friends, from 1745 to 1820*, (London, 1870), ii. 88-89.

[4] Ibid. ii. 91-92.

[5] Major General Henry Mackinnon, *A Journal of the Campaign in Portugal and Spain from the Year 1809 to 1812*, (Bath, 1812). Mackinnon's journal is a remarkable work and reads like a travelogue, describing the agriculture, geography and architecture of virtually every town and city he passed through with the Guards. George Bowles was amongst the diners with Mackinnon and he contrasted the red coats of the officers with the white gowns of the monks, adding that it formed a very striking scene. Malmesbury, *A Series of Letters*, ii. 93-94.

[6] Mackinnon, *Coldstream Guards*, ii. 108.

[7] Maurice, *Scots Guards*, i. 297-298.

[8] Major H.L. Aubrey-Fletcher, *A History of the Foot Guards to 1856*, (London, 1927), 219.

[9] Maurice, *Scots Guards*, i. 300-301.

[10] Ibid. i. 301.

[11] Malmesbury, *A Series of Letters*, ii. 101.

[12] Mackinnon, *Coldstream Guards*, ii. 111. See also Maurice, *Scots Guards*, i. 301.

[13] Mackinnon, *Coldstream Guards*, ii. 113.

[14] Malmesbury, *A Series of Letters*, ii. 106-107.

[15] Mackinnon, *Coldstream Guards*, ii. 15-16.

TALAVERA

With Marshal Soult having been driven from Oporto Wellesley turned his attention towards Marshal Victor, whose 25,000 men lay in the region around Talavera having withdrawn from Estremadura owing to a shortage of supplies.

When the British army left Abrantes on June 27th it was already lacking many essentials such as money, boots, horses and other stores and provisions. The most serious deficiency, however, was transport. The army was caught between two stools as the Portuguese muleteers, at this stage of the war, would not leave their own country while the Spaniards, on the other hand, would not come forward. The best that could be found were a few pack-mules and a train of bullocks that dawdled after the army.

As the weather was very hot the marches took place during the early morning before the sun had become too hot. 'At half-past 1 on the 28th,' wrote Captain William Stothert, of the Third Guards,

the general beat and by 3 the column was formed on the road leading to Castello Branco. At 9 the troops halted in a wood of pines near the village of St Domingo. June 29th the troops advanced at the same early hour as on the preceding day; and about 4 halted in the little town of Costacada. This day's march was six leagues, the road very hilly and the troops in consequence much fatigued. About 2 o'clock a tremendous thunderstorm came on accompanied with lightning and heavy rain. The Coldstream and General Cameron's brigade halted at Cordagos, seven miles in the rear.[1]

When the brigade had halted on the 28th the Guards found the ground already marked out for them by the Quartermasters and the men set about constructing huts.[2] At Cordegos where, as Stothert correctly states the Coldstream halted on the 29th, huts were again constructed. On July 3rd the Brigade of Guards reached the village of Ladciro, one quarter of which was accidentally destroyed by fire when the Guardsmen lit fires to cook their meat. The next day the same thing happened, this time at Zibreira. On July 5th the Guards crossed into Spain and during the next two weeks marched up to thirteen hours a day across wide open cornfields as the weather grew hotter each day. In fact, when the Guards reached Malpartida on the 17th they had to spend the whole day in the open beneath the blazing sun in a ploughed field, there being no means of constructing huts. On July 19th Wellesley's men finally reached Oropesa and two days later Cuesta's Spaniards began to file into the town. The junction of the British and Spanish armies was therefore accomplished but relations between the two Allied commanders were strained to say the least. General Gregorio Cuesta was a stubborn old general, 70 years old, and was most indignant at having to listen to, let alone heed, any advice given to him by an English heretic, namely Wellesley, some 30 years younger, and a mutual distrust quickly developed between them.

As well as having to cope with someone described by Colborne as 'a perverse, stupid, old blockhead', Wellesley had to come to terms with the ineptitude of the Spanish *Junta* whose assurances that supplies would be forthcoming and transport provided went miserably and despairingly unfulfilled. The British troops suffered great provisions as a result and inflated prices were paid in order to secure even the most basic of items.[3]

In spite of the problems, however, the two commanders linked up at Oropesa in order to advance on Victor before he could be reinforced from Madrid by General Sebastiani and King Joseph. With the Allied army now totalling around 55,000 Wellesley proposed a joint attack on Victor for the 24th but when the morning came the Spaniards, in spite of their earlier enthusiastic promises, were nowhere to be seen. Wellesley was naturally furious as a good opportunity to strike a blow had been lost and when Cuesta recommended following the French, who withdrew that evening, Wellesley refused to move and even went so far as to threaten to return to Portugal if rations and transport were not forthcoming for his near-starving troops. And so while Wellesley's men halted - the Brigade of Guards being quartered in a deserted convent - Cuesta decided to go it alone and attack the French. He advanced to Santa Olalla but was attacked himself and was forced to retreat in disorder to the Alberche where his men rejoined their British allies on the 25th. Two days later the British withdrew - as did Cuesta after pleas from Wellesley - to a position about three miles north of Talavera.

The position, upon some heights known as the Sierra de Segurilla, followed the line of the Portina brook which flowed south into the Tagus at Talavera. The Spaniards themselves were positioned on the right amongst the vineyards and orchards around Talavera where natural obstacles would provide a stiff challenge for the French should they attempt a frontal attack. Next to them was Sherbrooke's 1st Division - the Brigade of Guards, and the brigades of Cameron, Langwerth and Low - and Campbell's 4th Division. The left flank around the Cerro de Medellin, a prominent ridge and the key to Wellesley's position, was entrusted to Hill's 2nd Division.

The failure of Cuesta to join Wellesley in attacking the French on the 24th became all the more critical because by the time the Allies were finally in a position to attack Victor, as Wellesley feared, was joined by King Joseph and Sebastiani giving the French an overall strength of around 46,000, all of whom were tried and tested soldiers, and 86 guns. Wellesley himself commanded around 23,000 British troops and 30 guns whilst Cuesta's Spaniards numbered 40,000.

The battle of Talavera was fought over two days and was one of the fiercest of the Peninsular War. Although the main fighting took place on July 28th some fighting occurred on the 27th, the most notable incident happening towards evening when four battalions of Spanish infantry, on seeing some French cavalry close to the town, let loose a shattering volley at the extreme range of no less than 1,000 yards. The noise of their own volley was such that the Spaniards panicked at the sound of it and fled in disorder, stopping to plunder the British baggage train on their way. Elsewhere, Donkin's brigade held the Casa de Salinas, a fortified building on some heights on the left of the British line. His men were unable to defend so large a space and were overrun, losing 440 men in the fighting. He was reinforced by Hill, however, and the situation was restored and the French driven from the summit.

There were other alarms during the evening as the French stole forward in the darkness to attack the Medellin in preparation for the main battle the following day. As the firing developed along the British line the Coldstreamers came into action and in the ensuing fighting Lieutenant Colonel Ross and two men were killed. Captain Bryan was wounded and later died as a result of them. When the fighting finally died down for the night Wellesley wrapped himself in his cloak and laid down, his army having sustained about eight hundred casualties.

The main French attack got underway shortly after dawn on the 28th, forcing the British troops on the Medellin to lie down behind the crest as a torrent of shot and shell came raining in on them from some 53 enemy guns positioned upon the heights of Cascajal opposite. The British infantry could do little for the moment but lie down and hope that the incoming shells that thudded into the earth around them would not strike home. Every now and then, however, a scream would indicate that a shell had found its target and turned a living being into a bloody mess. An onslaught by French infantry, therefore, was seen as a release from their ordeal. Ensign John Aitchison, of the Third Guards, carried the King's Colour, and was naturally a prime target, and he gives us a graphic account of the Third Guards under shell fire:

Till about two o'clock on the 28th our men from daybreak were for the greater part exposed to a tremendous cannonade - shots and shells were falling in every direction - but none of the enemy were to be seen. The men were all the while lying in the ranks, and except at the very spot where a shot or shell fell, there was not the least motion. I have seen men killed in the ranks by cannon shots - those immediately round the spot would remove the mutilated corpse to the rear, they would then lie down as if nothing had occurred and remain in the ranks, steady as before. That common men could be brought to face the greatest danger, there is a spirit within which tells me it is possible, but I could not believe they could be brought to remain without emotion, when attacked, not knowing from whence. Such, however, was the conduct of our men (I speak particularly of the Brigade) on July 28th, and from this steadiness so few suffered as by remaining quiet the shots bounded over their heads.[4]

As the shells streamed in the steady drumming from the valley below heralded the start of the French infantry assault as 4,300 troops from Ruffin's division tramped across the battlefield to attack the Medellin. The scenario was to become typical of the battles in the Peninsula between the British and French infantry; the French advanced in columns as they came forward, their officers shouting at the men, keeping them in order with the flats of their swords; the British skirmish line pulled back, firing as it went; and then, just when it seemed as though the French attack had succeeded, the British infantry, drawn up in lines, sprang up from the ground to repulse them with steady, controlled musketry. On this occasion it is was the 29th and 48th Regiments that delivered the blow, and within just three minutes their 2,000 Brown Bess muskets had blasted away the front ranks of the French columns which, owing to their formation, could only bring about a fifth of that number to bear on the British. The French were stopped in their tracks and retreated to their original position beyond the Portina brook, chased all the way by angry, bayonet-wielding British infantry.

Following the repulse of Ruffin's division there was a lull, lasting for about four hours, during which there were remarkable scenes as troops from both sides drank from the Portina to slate their thirst. It was still only 7am but the day was already very hot. The men chatted and even shook hands and the wounded were gathered and brought away. There was no love lost between the French, Spanish and Portuguese troops - the British also had little love for their Spanish allies - but there was a mutual respect between the French and British and the scenes would be repeated several occasions during the war. As William Stothert, of the Third Guards wrote:

The firing ceased as if by mutual consent, for nearly three hours, during which interval the French appeared to be employed in cooking and the British reposed on the ground, seemingly regardless of the enemy's presence. It was at this time also that the wounded were carried to the rear, and while engaged on this duty the British and French soldiers shook hands with each other and expressed their admiration of the gallantry displayed by the troops of both nations.[5]

After a diversionary attack upon Campbell's 4th Division on the right of the British line a terrific bombardment by 80 guns opened up on Sherbrooke's 1st Division and as the guns pounded away the divisions of Sebastiani and Lapisse began to make their way forward. In front of them lay the Brigade of Guards. Stothert again:

several heavy columns advanced upon this point and deployed with the utmost precision as they entered the plain, which lay between the heights occupied by the rival armies. This was the grand attack, and on the first indication of the enemy's intention, General Sherbrooke gave directions that his division should prepare for the charge. At this awful moment all was silent, except for a few guns of the enemy, answered by the British artillery on the hill. The French came over the rough and broken ground in the valley, in the most imposing manner and with great resolution, and were met by the British with their usual undaunted firmness.[6]

The Brigade of Guards formed with the Coldstream on the right and the Third Guards on the left and they waited in silence with a grim determination as the French came on. When they were just fifty paces away a British voice cried out "Present! Fire!" and all at once the head of the French column disintegrated as the Guards unleashed a devastating volley, blasting the leading files into eternity whilst the rear of the columns began to melt away in panic. One French source says the regiments of the French 4th Corps lost a third of their number in about ten minutes. John Aitchison, of the Third

Guards, later recalled the moment:

This coolness on our part staggered the resolution of the enemy, and instead of being the assailants they *by it* became the assailed, and the confidence this gave to our men of their superiority over the enemy had the same effect as addition to their numbers; in short, the enemy in every attack was repulsed with prodigious slaughter.[7]

As the flight of the French began Sherbrooke's men charged to follow up their success but whereas Cameron's brigade was halted at the Portina brook the Guards and the Germans of Langwerth's and Low's brigades could not be restrained and charged far into the plain in front of them where fresh French reserves were waiting. Aitchison again:

The eagerness of *our* men in advancing without support, beyond the distance intended, had nearly proved fatal, for we had no sooner passed the ravine in our front than the enemy [having] perceived the troops on our left halted, took us in our left flank by his retiring columns and the columns which he posted in a front in a wood behind the bank of a vineyard. Thus gaining confidence, nearly turning our right, they stood till the grenadiers were actually within double musket length, but they then retired in great confusion. At this point of the action our numbers were diminishing very fast, and it being impossible to maintain this advance position we were ordered to be withdrawn. Accordingly we faced about, retired to the ravine, slower and in better order than we advanced. Here we made a stand and did considerable execution, but the enemy having come on with all those troops that had been flying, supported by strong columns which [were] concealed in the wood, it was deemed necessary to order another retirement, and we once again faced about - the enemy by this time having advanced within a few yards, the havoc was great, and we were thrown into momentary confusion.[8]

The Guards and the Germans were soon exhausted by their reckless advance beneath the shimmering July sun and when the French reserves turned on them they were swept back, fighting desperately as they went. As the Guards were pushed back they lost all cohesion and formed themselves into small units to fight off the overwhelming numbers of enemy infantry that tore into them with their bayonets, killing and wounded hundreds of them. Of the 2,000 or so that had chased the French no less than 611 had fallen killed or wounded but not one had been taken prisoner. As the Guards fell back John Aitchison, carrying the King's Colour, received a musket-ball in the right shoulder blade, as he later recalled:

It was in this retrograde movement that I was wounded and I was shortly after obliged to quit the field. It was not, however, until our men had formed round their colours in a drill and had opened a most destructive fire on the enemy who, notwithstanding our misfortune, was not able to gain one inch of ground even by redoubling efforts with fresh troops.[9]

Ensign George Bowles, carrying the colours of the Coldstream, was also wounded during the battle, but enjoyed a lucky escape when a musket ball buried itself in a half-loaf of bread that was in his pocket, saving his life.[10] Not so fortunate, however, was 29-year-old Captain Robert Dalrymple who found himself in the thick of the fighting. Dalrymple stood bare-headed before his men, sword in hand, cheering them on, when he suddenly struck by a musket ball which killed him.[11]

When the Guards re-crossed the Portina they were joined by the 61st and 83rd Regiments but still the French came on. Wellesley quickly saw that he had a potential disaster on his hands for not only was in danger of losing two battalions of his Guards, as well as four KGL battalions, but there absence from the line had left a gap which about 15,000 enemy troops waited to exploit. At this moment of crisis Mackenzie's brigade - the 2/24th, 2/31st and 1/45th - was brought forward to plug the gap left by the Guards who now passed bruised and battered through the Mackenzie's troops as they opened to let them through. In spite of their losses, however, they were unbowed and as the Earl of Munster later wrote, 'their good humour and determination after such dreadful losses was shown by their giving a loud hurrah as they took up their new ground.'[12]

Once the Guards had returned to the Allied line their skirmishers engaged in a sporadic fire-fight with their opposite numbers from the French army. One anonymous sergeant left us a vivid account of this fight and of his narrow escape from death afterwards:

The skirmishers on both sides singled out their objects, and thus for 10 or 15 minutes were amusing ourselves shooting at one another as deliberately as if we had been pigeon shooting. I cannot resist telling you that the object I had singled out, and myself exchanged three rounds each, the second of his, hit me slightly on the right shoulder and after my third he disappeared, therefore I conclude he went home!.....Shortly after this, they collected again in considerable numbers in the wood and drove us out and during this time I thought it impossible I should have escaped unhurt but thank God it happened. Two men and myself of the same company having stayed behind the

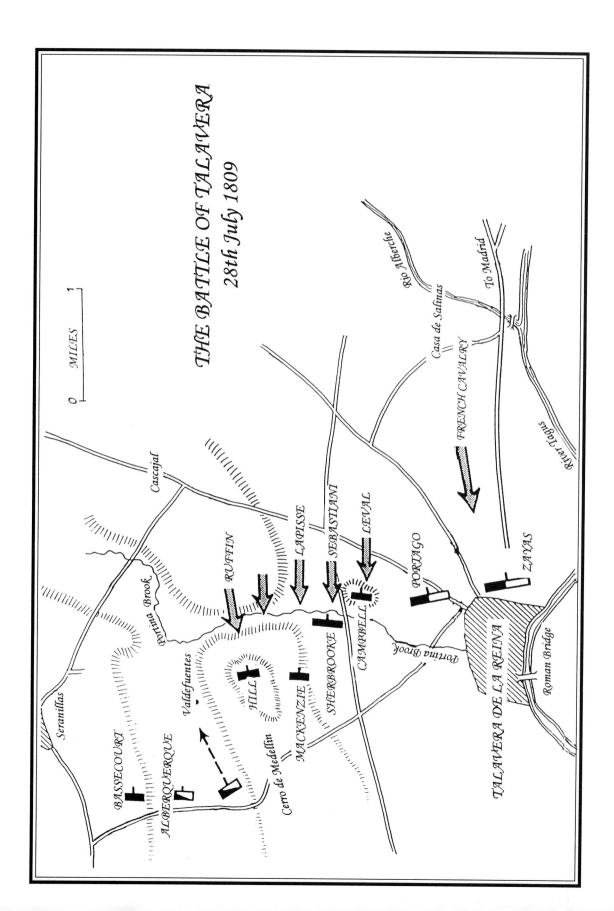

THE BATTLE OF TALAVERA
28th July 1809

MILES
0   1

Seranillas
BASSECOURT
ALBERQUERQUE
Valdefuentes
Cerro de Medellín
HILL
MACKENZIE
SHERBROOKE
CAMPBELL
Portina Brook
Cascajal
RUFFIN
LAPISSE
SEBASTIANI
LEVAL
PORTAGO
ZAYAS
Portina Brook
TALAVERA DE LA REINA
Roman Bridge
FRENCH CAVALRY
Casa de Salinas
Rio Alberche
To Madrid
River Tagus

rest not hearing the bugles sound the recall, were within 20 or 30 paces of the enemy ere we perceived the others had gone in, therefore nothing but flight could prevent us falling into their hands, and facing about away we started and were instantly saluted with a shower of musketry and which was continued without intermission until we reached our line . Nothing less than a miracle could have saved us, balls were lodged in our clothes and knapsacks, yet unhurt![13]

Mackenzie's troops, meanwhile, opened fire on the oncoming French and although he himself was killed his men stemmed the tide. After a fire-fight of about twenty minutes the French could take no more and Sebastiani was forced to withdraw having lost 70 officers and 2,100 men killed or wounded. However, just as the crisis in the right-centre had been avoided another loomed on the left-centre.

The other brigades of Sherbrooke's division, under Cameron, Low and Langwerth, were desperately weakened after the fighting of the previous night and of the day itself, and were in serious danger. Two French divisions, under Ruffin and Villatte, were attacking in strength and there were now no reserves left behind the left centre. It was now that he sent forward the 1/48th Regiment, one of his strongest and best Line battalions, that hurried forward from their position on the Medellin to meet the mounting crisis. While the broken remnants of Cameron's and Langwerth's brigades passed around its flanks to form up in its rear, the men of the 48th stood firm and rigid - the outcome of the battle depended on them. As the French columns neared them the 48th quickly got into position, loaded and opened fire, clouds of smoke pouring out as a rolling fire rang out from the ranks of redcoats to shove French shouts of 'victory!' back down their throats. The defeated British brigades rallied behind them and after another fearsome fire-fight the French broke and fled back across the Portina, the Guards reformed and the British line was restored.

There was still fierce fighting to come during the day but the pressure on that part of the line held by the Guards was off. A third French attack on the Medellin, by Victor, failed and when dusk brought a close to the proceedings the British still stood on the ground they had occupied that same morning. The fighting was over but just as the light began to fade the battle of Talavera suffered a grisly finale as fires, accidentally started when the tinder-dry brush caught alight, consumed many of the wounded as they lay helpless in the grass. Hundreds of men on both sides were to die in agony this way as their comrades looked on unable to do anything, as our anonymous sergeant recalled:

Shot and shells were not the only dangers presented to the contending armies for the intermediate space of ground between the lines was covered partly with standing corn and high stubble which from the incessant firing kept up on both sides, was set in a blaze several times during the day, and lines of running fire half a mile in length were frequent and fatal to many a soldier, some by their pouches blowing up in passing the fire, other wounded unable to reach their respective armies lying weltering in their gore with the devouring element approaching and death most horrid staring them in the face.[14]

Our sergeant went on to say that Captain Beckett, of the Coldstream died in such a manner after being knocked from his horse after rallying his brigade following their disorderly retreat earlier in the day and was consumed by flames before help could be got to him.[15]

The British army suffered 5,363 officers and men killed and wounded during the course of the two-day battle. The Third Guards, who had gone into action 1,019 strong, lost 54 killed and 267 wounded. Officer casualties were Captains Walker, Buchanan and Dalrymple, Ensigns the Hon. E.M. Irby and Ram killed, while Lieutenant Colonel Gordon, Major Fotheringham, Captain Geils, Ensigns Aitchison, Towers and Scott were wounded. Coldstream casualties were 3 officers and 33 men killed and 10 officers and 253 men wounded. The dead officers were Lieutenant Colonel Ross, Captain Beckett and Ensign Ross. The wounded were Lieutenant Colonels Stibbert and Sir William Sheridan, Captains Bouverie, Collier, Milman, Christie, Wood, Jenkinson, and Bryan, and Ensign Sandilands. Bryan was taken prisoner and later died of his wounds.

The dawn of the following day showed that the French army had retreated leaving only a thin screen of cavalry to act as rearguard. Wellesley's army, meanwhile, was in no condition to pursue it. Supplies were scarce and the army half-starving and he decided, therefore, to halt for a short period of recuperation. However, on August 2nd he received news that Soult was at Plasencia with just 15,000 men. Leaving Cuesta and his Spaniards at Talavera - along with some 4,000 British wounded - Wellesley resolved to march against Soult but no sooner had he set out than he received news that there were in fact 54,000 Frenchmen, Soult having been joined by Ney and Mortier. And as if this were not bad enough the exasperated British commander learned that Cuesta, on being threatened by Joseph, had hurriedly left Talavera having first abandoned all the British sick and wounded.

These soldiers had been left in the care of Colonel Henry Mackinnon of the Coldstream, who wrote in his journal:

The sick were principally placed in the large convents in the town, some in deserted houses. The confusion and scenes of death can scarcely be described: many men till this day never having had their wounds dressed. As far as I could ever collect, the number of men attached, and forming part of this hospital, could not have been far short of 5,000.[16]

However, as George Bowles relates, it was not only the British wounded that needed care after the battle;

The cowardice of the Spaniards when engaged, and their excessive cruelty afterwards, make one hate and despise them to the greatest degree. I was actually obliged, several times, to send a force to save the lives of many wounded Frenchmen in our front the morning after the battle of Talavera, from whom these wretches had run away the day before, but *then* wished to murder in cold blood, and were beyond measure astonished at being prevented.[17]

Upon the approach of the French, Cuesta had decided to withdraw his army and advised Mackinnon to leave also as soon as possible. Hastily assembling his officers and surgeons, he gave orders for all those men able to walk to assemble at three o'clock on the afternoon of August 3rd in order to march to Calera that evening. The wounded needed transport, of course, and it was only with the greatest difficulty that Mackinnon persuaded Cuesta to let him have seven waggons. At five o'clock the column began to move off, Mackinnon himself leaving at eight. When Marshal Victor arrived at Talavera on August 7th just over two thousand British soldiers, still either sick or wounded in the hospitals and convents, were taken prisoner. Amongst them were Lieutenant Colonel Sir William Sheridan, Captains Christie, Milman and Bryan, Ensign Sandilands and Assistant Surgeon Whymper, all of the Coldstream, and Colonel Gordon, Major Fotheringham, Ensign Scott and paymaster Captain Geils, of the Third Guards. Fortunately for the prisoners, they were treated with great kindness by their captors, as Ensign Scott recalled:

It is impossible to conceive the attention paid us by the French officers. Not a thing has been touched, so we have all our baggage and servants as if the English were here instead of the French. The King has ordered everything possible for our accommodation and, as little can be done here, he has ordered the officers to proceed to Madrid, the men to Segovia, many of whom are gone. In short there never has been such treatment shown. Many officers have already been exchanged. There is a regular post to France, some French officers have had the goodness to take charge of letters to Versailles. About the end of this month I expect to receive answers and establish a regular correspondence.[18]

The real strength of the French having now been discovered, Wellesley decided to fall back across the Tagus, crossing at Arzobispo. By now his army was suffering from a severe shortage of food and provisions, the Spaniards having been found wanting yet again when it came to the subject of supplies. Relations between Wellesley and Cuesta having evaporated the former decided to establish his headquarters at Badajoz from where he could defend the main route to Lisbon. The Brigade of Guards reached here on October 20th marching by way of Merida and Talavera Real, where the men constructed huts to protect themselves from the intense heat.

Whilst at Badajoz the officers of the army found little with which to amuse themselves although one or two houses opened up to entertain them. During the course of the war Badajoz was often suspected of harbouring pro-French sentiments and coupled with the poor Spanish sanitation and bad quality water - which resulted in an epidemic of fever which filled the hospitals - few soldiers were left with a favourable impression of the place. Just two weeks after they arrived in Badajoz the Third Guards, for instance, could muster only 654 men for duty whilst 362 of them were sick.[19] Overall, the army were not treated with the sort of regard they might otherwise expect from an allied town, something which undoubtedly contributed to the notorious events that followed the storming of the place two and a half years later.

Following the victory at Talavera Sir Arthur Wellesley was made Baron Douro of Wellesley and Viscount Wellington of Talavera, the name which we shall call him from now on. It was during October 1809 that Wellington travelled to Lisbon with his Chief Engineer, Colonel Richard Fletcher, in order to plan the famous Lines of Torres Vedras, a series of three defensive lines, natural and man-made, that stretched from the Atlantic coast to the Tagus. The construction of these lines was one of the greatest achievements of the war. Thousands of Portuguese labourers worked on the lines, constructing them in total secrecy. In fact, the French knew nothing of their existence until they came up against them the following year, stopping their advance dead in its tracks. The construction of the lines represented Wellington's only realistic course of action at this time as he knew he could no longer rely on

Spanish promises of co-operation. The people might play havoc with the French as guerrillas but the regular army was weak, ineffective and disorganised. Many considered the poor quality of the Spanish army to be the fault of its officers and of the Spanish nobility:

Nothing more is to be expected from the Spaniards - they will not make the sacrifices and exertions which are absolutely necessary to oppose the invading army. I ascribe it all to the nobility - they really are a despicable set. The men composing the Spanish army are remarkably fine and I am yet persuaded that if they were well officered they would fight. But they have no example shown them - their officers are miserable beyond conception and they were always the first to desert.[20]

Whatever the reason, Wellington knew that he dare not risk his army any longer and decided to move his army into Portugal. On December 8th therefore, his army began to move out of Badajoz. The Brigade of Guards led the way, marching by way of Portalegre, Abrantes and Coimbra until on New Year's Eve they reached Vizeu where the army went into quarters for the winter.

NOTES

[1] Captain William Stothert, *The Narrative of the Principle Events of the Campaigns of 1809, 1810, and 1811.* (London, 1812), 63.

[2] Colonel Daniel Mackinnon, *Origins and Services of the Coldstream Guards*, (London, 1833), ii. 25.

[3] According to Mackinnon one officer of the Coldstream paid a dollar for a small loaf the day before the battle of Talavera. *Coldstream Guards*, ii. p.116.

[4] W.F.K. Thompson, (Ed), *An Ensign in the Peninsular War; the Letters of John Aitchison*, (London, 1981), 57.

[5] Stothert, *Narrative*, 88.

[6] Ibid. 90.

[7] Thompson, *Ensign in the Peninsular War*, 58.

[8] Ibid. 58.

[9] Ibid. 56.

[10] The Earl of Malmesbury, *A Series of Letters of the First Earl of Malmesbury, His Family and Friends, from 1745 to 1820*, (London, 1870), ii. 129.

[11] Dalrymple is the central figure in Lawson's painting of Talavera, reproduced in this book.

[12] Major General Sir Frederick Maurice, *The History of the Scots Guards, 1642-1914*, (London, 1934), i. 309.

[13] Philp Haythornthwaite, *Uniforms of the Peninsular War*, (Poole, 1978), 172.

[14] Ibid. 173.

[15] Ibid. 173.

[16] Mackinnon, *Coldstream Guards*, ii. 36.

[17] Malmesbury, *A Series of Letters*, ii. 148.

[18] Maurice, *Scots Guards*, i. 311.

[19] Ibid. i. 312.

[20] Thompson, *Ensign in the Peninsular War*, 61.

RETREAT TO PORTUGAL

On January 13th 1810, Wellington wrote to Colonel Edward Stopford, commanding the 2nd Brigade of Guards, from his headquarters at Vizeu:

I have taken frequent occasions of stating publicly the great satisfaction which the conduct of the Guards has invariably given me; which satisfaction has been renewed on the recent march through Portugal; in which, as they were the head of the column, they set the example to the other troops, of the most orderly and regular behaviour. I am anxious to testify this satisfaction in a manner which shall prove to them that the attention which they pay to their duty is not unobserved by their superiors; and if the commanding officers of the two battalions will be so kind as to recommend a sergeant each, will recommend them to vacant ensigncies in the army.[1]

This was a great compliment from Wellington and came just one month after he had appointed Sergeant Major Fleming, of the Third Guards, to be adjutant of the 2/24th Regiment.[2] However, it is noticeable that none of the three were promoted to vacant ensigncies within the Guards themselves and one wonders just how they would have fared - and how the other officers of the Guards would have reacted - had they been so.

For the Guards, therefore, the year of 1810 had started on a high note but if things had begun well for his senior regiments it was not quite the same for Wellington himself. In fact, he was entering what was for him the most difficult period of the war. The months following the battle of Talavera had been spent retreating to the Portuguese frontier and it was to be many more months before he achieved another major victory. In Wellington's eyes there seemed little other course to take but sit tight on the border and wait for the completion of the Lines of Torres Vedras. After all, the Spanish army had all but been destroyed and there seemed little hope in continuing co-operating with them, the more so as his was the only army Britain possessed at the time and as he himself put it, he had to take great care of it. This caution was all part of his strategy but others, less far-sighted than him, did not see it this way. Indeed, the politicians at home were sceptical of this negative approach and soon became very anxious, not only for the safety of Britain's army but also to get their money's worth as they were only too wary of the expenditure involved in keeping an army abroad. And with this cost being almost as high as the general air of pessimism then prevailing, the rumblings of discontentment and dissatisfaction began to resound not only in the corridors of power but amongst the Opposition who began to demand the immediate evacuation of Portugal. There was also widespread doubt and suspicion amongst many of Wellington's own officers who had become disgruntled at the lack of progress so far in the campaign. Much of this disquiet emanated from the 'coffee houses', as Wellington called them, of the army, which seemed to form wherever and whenever the army halted for any given period of time.

The year of 1810 was a particularly bad one in this respect and the 'croakers' - those officers were seemed to spend their time back-biting and conspiring against Wellington - had a field day. Wellington was well aware of this talk but had no option but to suffer it. After all, Wellington 'knew his business best', as he said on another occasion, and if he was wont to keep his plans to himself the 'croaking' was something he simply had to put up with. Moreover, he had great confidence in himself and his plans and was helped by the Prime Minister, Spencer Percival, who remained unruffled and free of the anxiety that seemed to grip many of his ministers.

During the first half of 1810 the Brigade of Guards saw little action. Indeed, the army as a whole spent the period standing on the Portuguese frontier as the French prodded and probed at Wellington's line of outposts, Robert Craufurd's newly-created Light Division, the only unit to see continual action throughout the spring and summer of that year as the 'Light Bobs' clashed time and again with Massena's advanced troops. Craufurd, however, was buying time for his commander for while Wellington and his army maintained their defensive posture guarding the frontier, the Lines of Torres Vedras neared completion. There had been much sickness amongst the Brigade of Guards and the army in general and this sojourn in Vizeu, situated as it is on a high plateau, gave the men time to recover and restore their health, as Ensign John Aitchison noted in one of his letters:

The bracing air of Vizeu has been of great service to the army and our men are now very healthy and stout - our brigade is again respectable in numbers. We are now going on quietly as if at Chatham. The men are remarkably clean and we have field days; indeed, were it not for the convoys of provisions and stores which are continually passing, and detachments of convalescents which often arrive, we might suppose

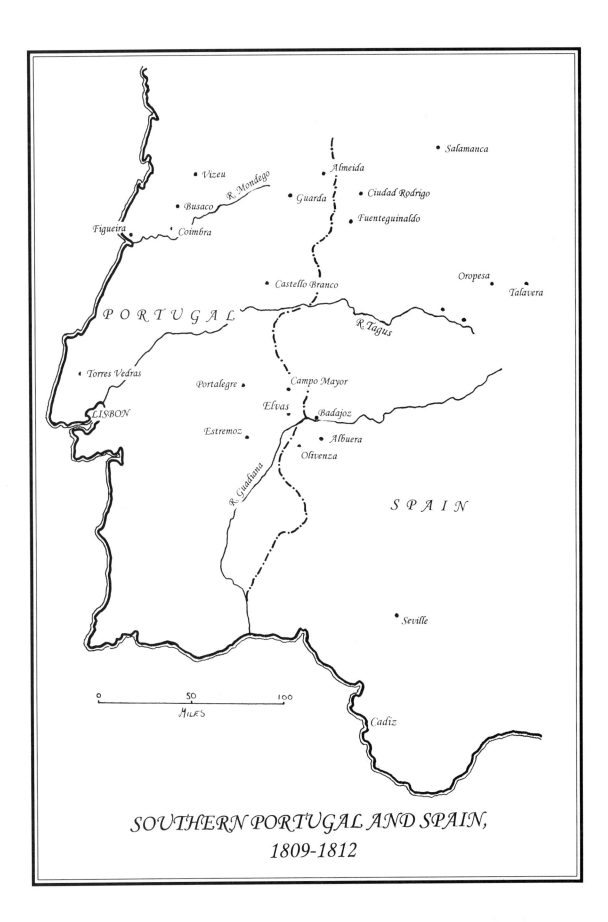

SOUTHERN PORTUGAL AND SPAIN,
1809-1812

ourselves at peace. I ride and walk every day when the day is fine - my stud at present consists of a horse, one small mule, a donkey and a goat.[3]

In England, meanwhile, plans were afoot to send a composite battalion of Guards to the Peninsula to assist in the defence of Cadiz. This came about following the disintegration of the Spanish armies which allowed Napoleon's brother Joseph to invade Andalusia with some 60,000 French troops. He met with hardly any opposition and his march turned into a 'triumphant tour'[4] as one by one the important towns of the region fell to him. On February 1st 1810 he entered Seville after first taking Jaen, Andujar, Cordoba and Grenada, all of which fell without any effort whatsoever. When he entered Seville he was greeted by the sardonic cheers of a populace who were delighted to see the back of the despised Supreme *Junta* which had done little to co-ordinate national resistance against the French. Joseph's conquest of southern Spain had been accomplished without a struggle but so simple had it all been that due to an oversight by the careless Marshal Victor, the Spanish commander, Alburquerque, managed to slip into the important port of Cadiz with about 15,000 men. It was a move that was to cost the French dear for, as one historian put it, 'Cadiz was destined to hold many thousands French soldiers in fruitless inactivity before its watery ramparts for months and even years,'[5] troops which the already stretched French could ill-afford to waste.

The British government - which had for a long time sought to get a body of troops into Cadiz but which had been denied access by the Spanish authorities - cobbled together a force of 3,000 men to sail for the town in order to support Alburquerque and the Spaniards who, faced with the prospect of a siege, now clamoured for the British help they had earlier scorned. The composite battalion of Foot Guards, totalling about 1,300 in all, consisted of six companies of the 2nd Battalion First Guards, under Colonel Sebright, two companies of the 2nd Battalion Coldstream Guards, under Lieutenant Colonel Jackson, and three companies of the 2nd Battalion Third Guards, under Lieutenant Colonel Onslow. Brigadier General Dilkes, of the Third Guards, commanded the brigade which also included two weak Line battalions and half a battalion of the 2/95th Rifles. During the second week of March the Guards marched from London to Portsmouth where transports were waiting to ship them to Cadiz where the brigade arrived on March 24th. These troops joined some 4,000 other British and Portuguese troops that had arrived at Cadiz on February 11th, sent there by Wellington who, with his usual foresight, had recognised that a successful and protracted defence of the town would hold down many French troops who would otherwise be used against him elsewhere in the Peninsula.

The British and Portuguese troops in Cadiz were placed under the command of Lieutenant General Thomas Graham who set his men to work on strengthening the town's defences. Cadiz, standing as it did on a narrow peninsula, was strong in natural defences and was virtually unassailable except by way of the marshy Isle de Leon. Also, the town was out of range of the French guns on the mainland and because of this the siege did not take the same form as those of Ciudad Rodrigo, Badajoz and San Sebastian, for instance, but instead turned into a long and desultory siege. It was never attacked but served only to pin down thousands of French troops and because of this we will leave Cadiz for the time being and return to events in Portugal.

The Brigade of Guards was still in its quarters around Vizeu and had been enjoying the pleasant surrounding countryside and the hospitality of the local people and in particular the Benedictine nuns who seemed to be very excited by the arrival of the British army whose officers were frequent visitors to the nunnery and were given refreshments whenever they did so. The nuns, far from being afraid of the soldiers, were apparently very unreserved in their manners, according to Stothert, and were 'sufficiently talkative and old and young had a wonderful share of curiosity to know what was passing in the world.'[6]

Wellington, meanwhile, was forming his plans for the coming campaign. He knew that a French invasion of Portugal was imminent and that the likely route for such an event was via Ciudad Rodrigo and Almeida where, as we have seen, Robert Craufurd's Light Division was positioned along the line of the Coa river in order to screen the main body of Wellington's army from the preying eyes of the French. There was little activity for the Guards, although Sir John Sherbrooke, commanding the 1st Division, went home on leave and was succeeded by Lieutenant General Sir Brent Spencer, the Brigade of Guards itself remaining under the command of Stopford.

On July 9th Ciudad Rodrigo fell to Massena in spite of appeals from the Spaniards for Wellington to come to their assistance. However, he would not be drawn across the frontier, and thus caused his allies much anguish. Two weeks later, Craufurd dallied too long on the right bank of the Coa in the face of overwhelming French superiority and nearly paid the price for it when he almost lost his Light Division to Ney during the infamous 'combat of the Coa' on July 24th. This left the way clear for the French to begin the investment of Almeida, the twin fortress of Ciudad Rodrigo, standing on the Portuguese side of the frontier. Wellington had hoped that a protracted defence of this place would delay the French approach by at least four or five weeks but a freak accident meant otherwise. The French siege guns opened fire on August 26th and had only been firing a short time when a stray shell rolled into a magazine in the town and exploded killing nearly 500 Portuguese and flattening most of the houses. Almeida, was held by Portuguese garrison commanded by an Englishman, Brigadier William Cox, who still thought the place to be defensible. His officers, however, thought otherwise and the town was surrendered to Ney.

The fall of Almeida was a blow to Wellington but he could at least take some comfort from the fact that Massena was unable to move his forces until the middle of September as he was having difficulty in feeding his men and was forced to wait until sufficient supplies could be collected. However, when all was ready Massena began to move forward into Portugal and soon French troops were advancing inexorably along the valley of the Mondego whilst Wellington's men fell back slowly and steadily before them. On September 20th the French began to concentrate around the Guards' old quarters at Vizeu where one of their convoys was attacked with great daring by the renegade Colonel Nicholas Trant and his Portuguese militia. Trant captured two officers and a hundred men and caused the French artillery to retreat, delaying Massena for a further five days.

As Wellington continued his retreat he had to decide whether to keep going all the way to the Lines of Torres Vedras or to make a stand. He had no need to take the latter course and as Aubrey-Fletcher has pointed out, there was no real military necessity for him to do so.[7] After all, the Lines would stop Massena just as well, after which - if the Lines proved to be as effective as expected - Wellington would simply wait for starvation to set in. However, there were other factors, both political and moral, to be taken into account, not least of which was the need to prove to his Portuguese allies that he intended to remain in Portugal and that he did not propose, as some people widely believed, to re-embark his troops as soon as he reached Lisbon. The Portuguese - and the British government - were convinced that Wellington would do this, particularly after the unwillingness he had shown to help both Ciudad Rodrigo and Almeida. It was important, therefore, that Wellington restore the confidence not only of the British government but also the Portuguese nation, both shaken and disturbed by his army's continued retrograde movements. Moreover, William Beresford had been working tirelessly to fashion the Portuguese army into an effective fighting force and there would be no better opportunity for their 'baptism of fire' than at the position he now decided to occupy, some five miles east of the main Coimbra to Oporto road on the heights of the Serra de Busaco.

The ridge at Busaco runs north from the Mondego river for about ten miles. It is a steep and commanding ridge that rises to a height of between 1,300 to 1,600 feet on both sides and for an attacking force it represented a daunting task; a difficult, exhausting climb in order to face a confident and fresh enemy waiting at the top. In fact, Wellington's position at Busaco has been called one of the finest defensive positions in Europe, a position from which he was certain that not even Massena's veterans would be capable of dislodging him, and he realised he would never again have such advantageous conditions in which to 'blood' his Portuguese troops.

Wellington began to deploy his troops on the ridge at Busaco on September 26th. Cole's 4th Division held the left flank, with Craufurd's Light Division on his right directly in front of Wellington's command post. The 1st Division, under Spencer - with the Brigade of Guards on the right, - held the centre, to their right was placed Picton's 3rd Division and Leith's 5th Division, whilst Hill's 2nd Division held the extreme right flank of the line. Altogether, Wellington's force numbered about 52,000 and the French about 65,000.

The ridge of Busaco was and still is one of the most picturesque parts of Portugal and as the sun beat down on September 26th it must have been a colourful sight as the troops of both armies deployed. Apart from some very light skirmishing between the light troops of the respective armies there was no fighting that day. Surgeon Good, of the Third Guards wrote later:

It is impossible to describe the beauty of the scene. The day was lovely. We had a little exchange of shot on the right and left between the sharpshooters. When the night drew on, it became damp and foggy. The men remained under arms each officer with his company. Jeffreys[8] and myself took post about one hundred yards in rear of the battalion and got under the lee of a large stone, making our saddles our pillows. Rodney[9] having joined during the day and having brought with him some cooked poultry, I partook of the same, which was made the better by a glass or two of Malmsey Madeira he had with him.[10]

Dawn broke on the morning of the 27th to the unmistakable sounds of a French advance. It was still quite foggy but from beyond the grey mist could be heard the unmistakable thumping of enemy drums, the shouting of officers and the cheering of the men themselves who, instead of saving their breath for the arduous climb ahead of them, felt the need, perhaps, to reassure themselves with their customary noisy approach. The shouting might have frightened their adversaries in the past but on this occasion Wellington's men held all the aces and must have felt supremely confident as they lay in wait in strong positions atop the ridge.

The Brigade of Guards played little part in the battle of Busaco as the French attacks, by Ney's corps and Reynier's corps, were directed against those parts of the line held by Craufurd's Light Division and Picton's 3rd Division, ironically either side of Spencer's 1st Division. As Aubrey-Fletcher wrote,

It was a tantalising day for the Guards. Perched in the centre upon the topmost point of the ridge, they had watched column after column of the French, first upon their right and then upon their left, hurled backwards from the ridge without their being able to share in the triumph even to the extent of one round of ammunition. It was the fortune of war.[11]

These two attacks were met by a destructive fire of grape shot and musketry which decimated the attacking columns and sent them tumbling back down the hillside with the red-coated British infantry hot on their heels. The fighting was over an hour before mid-day when the battered and beaten French columns withdrew to their original positions beyond the villages of Moura and San Antonio de Cantaro. The day ended in a most complete victory for Wellington, the French suffering some 4,600 casualties which included 5 generals and 300 other officers and were the highest casualties sustained by the French in the war so far. Wellington's casualties amounted to 1,252.

Wellington saw little to be gained in following up his victory - as we have already seen, it was just a delaying action - and his troops spent the night in their positions on top of the ridge. At dawn the following morning, however, patrols of Massena's cavalry had discovered a route that outflanked Wellington's position to the north and which he hoped to exploit by feeding through his cavalry, thus giving rise to the theory that the French had at least 'drawn' the battle, having forced Wellington to retreat. However, Wellington had already begun to pull back his troops as part of the withdrawal to the Lines of Torres Vedras.

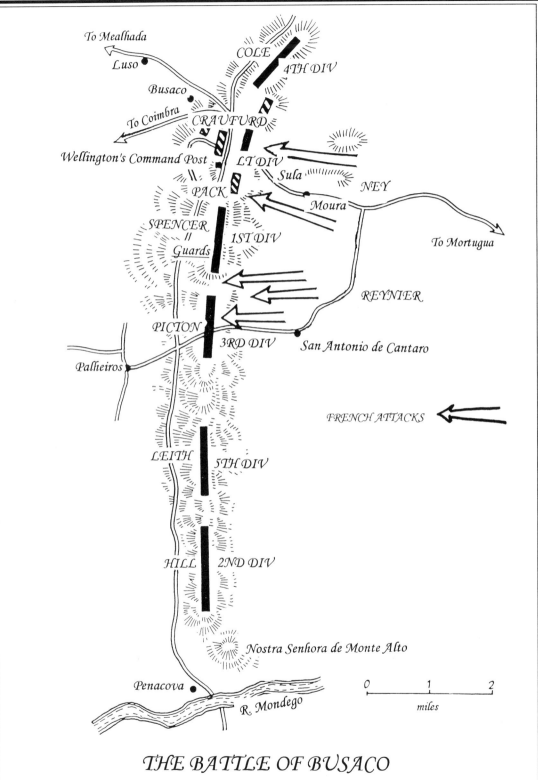

THE BATTLE OF BUSACO
27th September 1810

Apart from realising the next stage of his plan the battle had two other important and significant consequences; first, that the Portuguese army 'came of age' and gained the respect not only of their British comrades but of the French, and second, that from now on Massena would be apprehensive and most cautious about making a frontal attack on Wellington's forces.

The Brigade of Guards moved off of the ridge at Busaco at ten o'clock on the morning of September 28th and forded the River Mondego two days later as the march towards the Lines continued. It was here that a detachment of Guards that had recently arrived in Portugal, joined the rest of its battalion. Amongst their number was Ensign John Stepney Cowell who recalled the moment he joined his battalion of the Coldstream:

After delivering over the detachment of our men to the commanding officers of the regiments which formed our brigade, and the officers being posted to the different companies of our battalions, our next step on joining our corps was making the acquaintance of those of our future comrades to whom we were as yet unknown. Amongst them I remember well being struck by the appearance of an intellectual-looking, high-spirited, laughing little fellow, agreeably lounging in a many-coloured bed-gown out of a cottage window in the main thoroughfare of our village. He seemed to stand in high popular estimation, and was warmly greeted by all who passed.....We were quartered together, and after the evening's refreshment, such as it was, we partook of the same mattress laid on the mud floor of our cabin, sleeping in our clothes and in our cloaks, divesting our feet only of our boots. This was a new situation; a wakeful night ensued, and I had ample time to ponder on the starry sky through the glassless and shutterless window. My more veteran comrade however slept soundly.[12]

The following morning Cowell was roused long before daylight by the blare of bugles and the rattle of drums and with the stars still shining brightly in the sky his company was marched to an olive grove outside the village in response to an alarm.[13] It proved false, however, and the men marched back to their camp where, as the flickering light of the night's dying fires danced upon the men, their arms and accoutrements, their rations were issued. At daylight the Brigade of Guards was on the move once again, along with the rest of the army. The spectacle of the whole army in retreat left a vivid impression on Cowell:

For miles, over hill and dale, through heath and wood, clouds of dust betrayed their direction and line of movement; and even amidst the dark pine forests, the masses were to be detected by the glancing of the sun upon their arms, which, according to Horse Guards' regulations, it was thought necessary to keep as bright as the brass knocker of a suburban villa.[14]

Wellington's army continued its retreat at a steady pace, the right of his army marching by way of Thomar and Santarem, the centre through Batalha and Rio Mayor, and the left by way of Alcobaça and Obidos. As the army trudged south to the Lines the weather turned cold and heavy rain began to fall, which for many rekindled painful memories of the retreat to Corunna the previous year. On this occasion, however, the army was able to maintain discipline and with the French army following but never really threatening it was only the weather that caused any misery.

On October 10th Wellington's army began to enter the Lines which formed a series of natural and man-made fortifications which stretched across the Lisbon peninsula between the Tagus and the Atlantic. The system comprised mainly of three separate Lines; the first, to the north, ran inland from the Atlantic to the town of Torres Vedras and then on to the Tagus. The second Line, ran almost parallel to the first but five miles further south. The third lay west of Lisbon and enclosed an area from which a re-embarkation could be made if it became necessary. The system included the damming of streams and rivers to make inundations, castles in towns were protected by earthworks and every hill along the first two Lines was crowned with a defensive work or redoubt. Coupled with the naturally rugged terrain the Lines of Torres Vedras were an almost impregnable system of fortifications.

The area enclosed by them was over five hundred square miles and although a large portion of the Portuguese population had come into the area there was still plenty of food for both them and the Allied army. Another feature of the defensive system was that the Lines and fortifications were held only by secondary troops, about 2,500 Portuguese militia, 8,000 Spaniards and 2,5000 British artillerymen and marines. This meant that Wellington's British and Portuguese regulars could be placed in positions from where they could be quickly concentrated to oppose any French thrust. All was co-ordinated by a series of telegraphs and signalling stations, the highest of which was situated upon the top of Mount Socorro, Wellington's 'eagle nest', from where he could see the movements of any enemy force for miles around. Wellington established his headquarters in the centre of the Lines, at Pero Negro, a short distance behind the second Line. Spencer's 1st Division,

(Left); A Grenadier of the First Foot Guards, 1812. Artist unknown.

(Right); A Grenadier of the First Foot Guards, 1815. By J.A. Atkinson.

(Above); The Battle of Fuentes de Onoro, May 3rd-5th 1811. The wounded are carried from the field, in foreground, and prisoners taken away. In the centre of the picture, Norman Ramsay's Horse Artillery escapes by riding through the French cavalry.

(Left); Sir Duncan Campbell, Third Guards, 1808. Campbell served from 1804-1811. Painting by Raeburn.

(Left); Major General John Freemantle, Coldstream Guards. Freemantle, or Fremantle as it is often spelt, was ADC to Welington in the Peninsula. He is pictured here in civilian dresss. Painting by Margaret Carpenter.

(Above); A miniature of an extremely young looking ensign of the First Foot Guards, 1812.

(Left); Thomas Powys, Coldstream Guards. Painting by William Bradley.

(Right); Lieutenant & Captain Charles
Mackenzie Frazer, Coldstream Guards,
1810-14.

(Below); An Officer of the Third Guards,
1810.

(Right); John Aitchison, Third Guards, 1807,
by George Engleheart. Aitchison saw action at
the siege of Copenhagen in 1807 before depart-
ing in 1809 for the Peninsula where he served
with distinction until the end of the war in
1814. He was badly wounded at Talavera while
carrying the King's Colour. His letters are
featured in WFK Thompson's *An Ensign in the
Peninsular War*. He is pictured here in civilian
dress.

(Above); A typical camp scene in the Peninsula. At left, a barber cuts hair, whilst others cook their meals, see to the horses and mules, milk the goats and generally relax or go about their duties.

(Left); Lord Charles Vere Ferrar Townshend, 2nd son of the Marquis Townshend, in the uniform of the Third Guards, 1815. Painting by Thomas Hudson.

(Opposit page); The cloak given to The Hon. Orlando Bridgeman, First Guards, by Mademoiselle de Casteja for helping her to escape from Madrid to join her French fiancee, then a prisoner of war. The coach lamps, given to Bridgeman by the lady and her husband, Captain de Marbot, in 1815, can be seen on either side of the cloak.

(Left); Major Sir John Guise, Third Guards, 1815. Guise served with the Third Guards from 1795 to 1821 and saw active service in Egypt and the Peninsula.

(Opposite); Francis Wheler Hood, also of the Third Guards.

(Right); The Honourable Orlando Bridgeman, First Guards, wearing his Waterloo Medal. Bridgeman was just eighteen years old when he joined his regiment in Spain and stayed with it until the end of the Peninsular War. He was ADC to Lord Hill and Waterloo where he was wounded. His adventures ith Mademoiselle de Casteja are recalled elsewhere in this book.

Three young Coldstream Guards Officers. (Top); An unknown Officer of the Coldstream Guards, by George Engleheart.

(Centre); Lieutenant Thomas Gore, Coldstream Guards, 1813, by Andrew Palmer.

(Left); A Captain of the Coldstream Guards by George Engleheart, 1808.

This very angelic looking ensign of the Coldstream Guards is John Stepney Cowell, to whom we are indebted to so many splendid vignettes in his *Leaves from the Diary of an Officer of the Guards*. Cowell was commissioned in May 1809 and saw service in the Peninsula from 1812. He was present at Waterloo and rose to the rank of lieutenant colonel. He was created baronet in 1871 and died six years later.

(Above); The Guards entering France towards the end of 1813. (Below); The bridge of boats across the Adour, where the Guards crossed in February 1814, following a bold initial crossing by some of the Guards on rafts.Both drawings are by Captain Robert Batty, First Guards.

Lieutenant Colonel Sir Henry Sullivan, Coldstream Guards. Sullivan was killed during the sortie from Bayonne in April 1814. In this aquatint by Edridge he has gold lace binding around his shako which was replaced later by black tape. Sullivan is buried in the Coldstream Guards Cemetry at Bayonne.

(Above); The sortie from Bayonne, April 14th 1814, a needless and costly attack by the French Governor Thouvenot two days after peace had been declared.

(Left); Lieutenant Colonel George Collier, Coldstream Guards. Collier died of wounds sustained during the sortie as is buried in the Coldstream Guards Cemetery Bayonne.

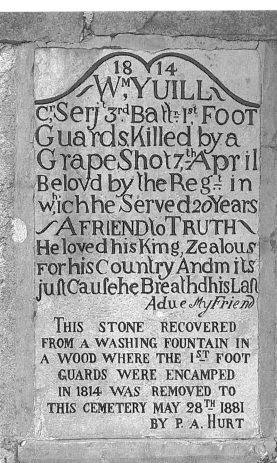

18 14
Wm YUILL
Cr Serjt 3rd Battn 1st FOOT
Guards Killed by a
Grape Shot 7th April
Belov'd by the Regt in
which he Served 20 Years
A FRIEND to TRUTH
He loved his King, Zealous
For his Country And in its
just Cause he Breath'd his Last
Adue My Friend

THIS STONE RECOVERED
FROM A WASHING FOUNTAIN IN
A WOOD WHERE THE 1ST FOOT
GUARDS WERE ENCAMPED
IN 1814 WAS REMOVED TO
THIS CEMETERY MAY 28TH 1881
BY P. A. HURT

Gravestones in the Guards Cemeteries. (Left); An original headstone of Colour Sergeant Yuill, First Guards, killed on April 7th 1814. The stone is now inside the Coldstream Guards Cemetery, Bayonne. (Below); The grave of Captain Luke Mahon, Third Guards, who died of his wounds following the sortie from Bayonne. Mahon lies in the Third guards Cemetery, deep in the heart of some woods which was the site of their camp in April 1814.

To the Memory
of
Captain Mahon
Third Guards
who died of wounds received
in action before Bayonne
on the 14 April
1814

(Right); Ensign William Pitt, Coldstream Guards. A miniature by Thomas Heaphy. Pitt was mortally wounded during the sortie from Bayonne. He is buried in the Coldstream Guards Cemetery, Bayonne.

(Below); This stone marks the site of the small but very poignant Third Guards Cemetery at Bayonne. As the inscription says, the graves were looked after for many years by the sister of one of the officers who lies here, Captain Holbourne, Third Guards, killed during the French sortie on April 14th 1814.

took up a position in the Lines around Sobral before marching to Zibreira situated at the right centre of the defences.

As the weeks passed it became clear to the despairing Massena that he could no longer afford to just sit and wait as his army starved. The French lived off the land and the surrounding countryside was quickly stripped bare of all food and forage and it became increasingly difficult even for the resourceful French to find food. They would scour the countryside for miles around for just a bushel of corn or a few potatoes. By the middle of November Massena's generals told him they could remain in front of the Lines no longer and when Wellington's outposts looked out on the morning on November 15th they saw not French troops manning their outposts but straw dummies, with old hats and muskets placed on them to make them look real. The French had gone.

Massena's army had begun to retreat up the Tagus towards Santarem where the countryside was a little more fertile. Trailing cautiously behind them was Wellington and on the 17th the Brigade of Guards passed through Alemquer and Cartaxo where, on the 19th Wellington formed his men as if to make an attack across the Rio Mayor. The Guards were to lead the way across a long causeway which crossed an extensive marsh but as the artillery were late in arriving the attack was put off until the following day.[16]

The bugles sounded early the next morning and the Guards fell in at their assembly points. Apparently there was a touch of jealousy amongst the brigades of the 1st Division because Brigadier General Cameron, who commanded the second brigade of the division, said that if the Brigade of Guards was to lead the attack, 'there would be very few of His Majesty's Guards left to tell the tale.' However, both brigades of the 1st Division were to be disappointed as the country in front of them had been flooded by heavy rain during the night and the attack was called off. Also, it was discovered that the enemy was in front of them and in strength and as a result the Guards were withdrawn and went into cantonments at Cartaxo where they remained for the remainder of the year.

NOTES

[1]Colonel Daniel Mackinnon, *Origins and Services of the Coldstream Guards*, (London, 1833), ii. 130. See also Major General Sir Frederick Maurice, *The History of the Scots Guards from 1642 to 1914*, (London,

1934), i. 313.

[2] General Orders, December 12th 1809.

[3] W.F.K. Thompson, (Ed), *An Ensign in the Peninsular War; the Letters of John Aitchison*, (London, 1981), 93.

[4] Major H.L. Aubrey-Fletcher, *A History of the Foot Guards to 1856*, (London, 1927), 240.

[5] Ibid. 240.

[6] Captain William Stothert, *The Narrative of the Principal Events of the Campaigns of 1809, 1810, 1811*, (London, 1812), 154.

[7] Aubrey-Fletcher, *Foot Guards*, 249.

[8] Surgeon Jeffreys, Third Foot Guards.

[9] Ensign the Honourable J.B. Rodney, Third Foot Guards.

[10] Maurice, *Scots Guards*, i. 330.

[11] Aubrey-Fletcher, *Foot Guards*, 253.

[12] John Stepney Cowell, *Leaves from the Diary of an Officer of the Guards*, (London, 1854), 13-14.

[13] Ibid. 14.

[14] Ibid. 16-17.

[15] Ibid. 19-21.

[16] Mackinnon, *Coldstream Guards*, ii. 141. See also Stepney Cowell, *Leaves from the Diary*, 31.

BARROSA

While Massena's half-starving army pulled back to the northern bank of the Tagus between Santarem and Thomar another French army, some 25,000 men under Marshal Victor, was besieging the important Allied port of Cadiz, garrisoned by an equal number of British and Spanish troops, well ensconced behind strong defences and well supplied by the Royal Navy. In mid-January Massena's appeals to Napoleon for reinforcements resulted in Soult having to leave Andalusia in order to lay siege to Badajoz. Soult, in turn, began to draw heavily on Victor's troops around Cadiz which consequently reduced the number of his men to around 15,000.

With the news of Massena's withdrawal and encouraged by the subsequent reduction in Victor's troops the defenders of Cadiz resolved to make an attack which involved the shipping of 10,000 Spanish and 4,000 British troops some 50 miles to the south to Tarifa who would then march north and attack the French from the rear. At the same time 4,000 Spaniards under General Zayas would make a sortie from Cadiz.

The first problem the Allies encountered was, predictably, the question of who would be the overall commander. As the majority of the force consisted of Spaniards they insisted that General Manuel La Pena be placed in command. Known to the Spaniards themselves as 'La Donna Manuela', La Pena was considered by the British to be totally inept, an opinion soon to be proved all too true. The British commander in Cadiz, meanwhile, was Major General Thomas Graham, at 62 one of the British army's eldest generals, but a fervent anti-Francophile who, from the days during the Revolution when French guards had opened the coffin of his dead wife to search for arms and ammunition, had embarked on a personal crusade to bring about the downfall of Napoleon and had even raised a regiment at his own expense for the purpose. Graham had specific orders from Wellington not to serve under La Pena but as the Spanish *Junta* insisted that La Pena command, and for the sake of Anglo-Spanish relations, Graham agreed to serve under the Spaniard, a decision which almost proved catastrophic.

Graham set sail from Cadiz on February 21st but the bad weather prevented the force from landing at Tarifa and instead the force sailed on to Algeciras where the troops disembarked on the 23rd, marching to Tarifa the following day. On arrival, Graham organised his force into two brigades, one of which was a Brigade of Guards under General Dilkes, the first battalion of which consisted of six companies of the 2nd Battalion First Guards, under Colonel Sebright, whilst the second battalion consisted of two companies of the Coldstream and three companies of the 2nd Battalion Third Guards under Colonel Onslow. Two companies of the 2/95th Rifles were added to this second battalion. The other brigade, under Colonel Wheatley, consisted of three Line battalions. Two other composite Line battalions were present also.

When Graham's men arrived at Tarifa there was no sign of La Pena's Spaniards who had endured a rough passage and it was two days before they finally arrived, during which time the British troops wandered around the town's narrow streets and explored the ancient ramparts of the most southerly town in Europe. On February 28th, the Spaniards having arrived, the Allied force marched out of Tarifa and for the next five hours trudged across wild and rocky countryside before camping for the night amongst olive groves, the men taking out their hatchets and bill-hooks to build crude shelters. The march towards Chiclana was painfully slow mainly due to La Pena's insistence on making night marches. Added to this was the fact that the guides were unreliable and the troops usually lost their way in the darkness.

La Pena's punishing schedule also meant that the troops rarely had time to cook a decent meal. This strained relations between La Pena and Graham to breaking point and at one point Graham himself, convinced that La Pena was taking the wrong route, rode to head of the column to point out the correct route. His observation was quickly dismissed, however, it being pointed out to Graham that a lake in front of them would be impracticable for artillery, the more so since the recent heavy rains had submerged part of the causeway across it. However, a British engineer reported the causeway passable and the advance along the route continued. There was still a hold-up to be endured, however, for the Spaniards, not wishing to get their feet wet, stopped to take off their shoes and socks whilst many of the officers insisted on being carried across! One wonders what the fiery Robert 'Black Bob' Craufurd, the commander of Wellington's Light Division, would have made of the situation had he seen these effeminate Spaniards picking their way across. It was part of his code of conduct that no man was ever to stray from the path of the march no matter what the reason. This whole ridiculous situation caused yet another hold up, causing Graham to ride up to see what was going on. The sight of the Spaniards reluctantly crossing the causeway contrasted sharply with the British who plunged into the water waist-deep, each man supporting the next as they crossed. At one point, one of the guns became stuck amongst some rocks and the Spaniards were shamed by the sight of Graham himself who leapt into the water to put his shoulder to the gun's wheel to help free it. The entire march was altogether most stressful and exhausting but by daylight on March 5th the Allied column found itself marching along the beach near to the tower of Barrosa.

Later that morning La Pena's advanced guard clashed with Villatte's Frenchmen and whilst the fighting here developed the garrison of Cadiz made its sortie, crossing a bridge of boats to attack Villatte's flank and rear, forcing him to withdraw. By now Graham was positioned upon the ridge of Barrosa, which stretches for about a mile and a half from the coast with the beach on the left and the thick pine forest of Chiclana to the right. His men had just settled down when a messenger arrived with an order from La Pena who, after his success against Villatte, told Graham to join him. Graham was reluctant to leave the ridge as he knew it would be an important position in the fight which now seemed inevitable. However, he relented and after leaving a British composite battalion, under Colonel Browne, on the ridge along with five Spanish battalions he marched off with Dilkes' Brigade of Guards and Wheatley's brigade.

Graham had not long departed from the ridge when two animated Spanish guerrillas rode up and informed him, breathlessly, that a French division, under Leval, was moving menacingly through the forest towards the ridge, just as he had predicted, and that further to the south another French division, under Ruffin, was closing on the ridge. In fact, when Ruffin's column marched into sight the Spanish troops on the ridge panicked and quickly abandoned the position, leaving Browne's battalion all alone. This latter incident was unknown to Graham, of course, but the reliability of the other information was never in doubt because no sooner had the Spaniard ridden off than a round shot came bouncing through the trees and killed an officer of the Guards. Dilkes' Brigade of Guards was immediately ordered to face about and there was some confusion and much shouting and shoving as the Guards, as always claiming the right to lead the attack, pushed their way through the ranks of the 87th Regiment which was right behind them. The forest was thick with firs, 'so thick as to be nearly impracticable for the guns and mounted officers,'[1] which added to the initial confusion. As the Guards debouched from the forest, with the 2nd Battalion First Guards leading the way in line, they came under a heavy fire from the French who were already on the ridge having forced the outnumbered Browne to retire.

As Graham rode to the edge of the wood to see what was happening he noticed Leval's division moving towards him on his left and Ruffin's men already taking up positions on the ridge itself. Of the Spaniards he could see nothing. As he rode forward Graham was spotted by Browne, who had been forced off the ridge and had taken up a position at the edge of the forest. Turning to his men Browne shouted, 'Hurrah, flankers! Here comes Graham and the Guards. I'll insure you all now for half a dollar, by God!'[2] But if Browne was pleased to see Graham, the latter was none too pleased to see that Browne had disobeyed his orders to remain on the ridge. Browne, however, replied, 'But you would not have me fight the whole French army with 470 men,' and added ruefully that the Spaniards had all ran away. This left Graham in a desperate situation. If he chose to retreat he faced the prospect of being trapped on the beach by a much larger enemy force.

With the situation deteriorating rapidly, Graham decided that the only way of saving the day was to attack without delay and drive the French off of the ridge. Therefore, he ordered Wheatley to attack Leval whilst Dilkes' Brigade of Guards would make a frontal attack on the ridge. In the meantime, Browne's battalion was sent forward in order to gain time for the Guards to deploy. The cheerful and charismatic Browne returned to his men and said, 'Gentlemen, I am happy to be the bearer of good news. General Graham has done you the honour of being the first to attack these fellows. Now follow me, you rascals', and pointing to the enemy on the ridge he gave the order to advance, breaking into his favourite song, 'Hearts of Oak', at the same time.[3] The British started up the hill in a two-deep line, struggling over the scrubland in the teeth of a withering fire from the French. The first salvoes from the enemy guns caused havoc amongst Browne's men and with little or no cover to be found casualties increased with each blast that exploded amidst their ranks. As the British infantry got within range of their assailants they prepared to fire but before they could do so another salvo swept away fifty more men and with two-thirds of his officers either killed or wounded and having lost half his men, Browne ordered his men to throw themselves down to take what cover they could find. They could do little from here but annoy their tormentors on the ridge by firing independently as round shot ploughed up the ground around them. Any minute now Browne expected the inevitable French counter-attack that would surely mean the end for him and his men. But just as Ruffin began to deploy his men for the coup de grace he was checked by the sight of Dilkes' Brigade of Guards which suddenly emerged from the woods 'in fighting mood'.[4]

While the gunners of Major Duncan's artillery sweated away as they worked their ten guns, the First Guards began the long climb up the ridge with Colonel Sebright at their head whilst the three companies of the Third Guards, under Colonel Onslow, formed the second line. Unlike Browne's battalion, the Guards took a route which afforded more protection, the Guardsmen making the best use of every bush, rock and tree along their way. The march proved a difficult one, the more so since the Guardsmen had been marching most of the night and had had no time to prepare any food. They advanced up the hill in skirmishing order and before the French could bring their guns to bear on them the Guards neared the summit of the ridge. At this point Ruffin ordered four battalions to charge down the hill to drive them back but the Guards, struggling wearily up the hill, would not give way and when Onslow brought the Third Guards up on the right to form a line with the First Guards the French were driven back as the dusty, red-coated infantry continued their relentless drive to the top, halting once to deliver a storm of lead into the massed ranks of wavering Frenchmen. By now, Graham himself was at the head of the Guards, riding his horse and waving his cocked hat in the air, cheering his men on. French reserves were thrown into the fray by a despairing Marshal Victor but these too were thrown back by Browne's men who had returned to the fight and when the Guards reached the summit of the ridge Graham shouted, 'Now my lads, there they are. Spare your powder, but give them steel enough.'[5]

A bitter fight now ensued during which Ruffin was badly wounded. Sebright himself was also struck down and carried off the field, Colonel Sambrooke Anson assuming command of the First Guards. Dilkes himself had his horse shot dead under him but in spite of the hard fighting the Guards held firm and slowly but steadily began to drive the French from the ridge. Part of Dilkes' report ran as follows:

Our army still advanced, bringing up their right shoulder, and threatening his left, so that at last he formed that flank *en masse*, continuing his retreat down the hill, and ascending another rising ground, halting occasionally and keeping up a severely destructive fire. When fronted at one time, I perceived him push forward two or three divisions from the *masse*, as I conceived, to charge our line, whose well-directed fire still advancing, obliged him to desist. Unfortunately, our men were so completely exhausted by their march, &c. &c. as to be quite unable to return the compliment.[6]

On the left of the British line, meanwhile, Wheatley's brigade had been equally successful when a bold charge by the three companies of the Coldstreamers - who had originally been left to protect Duncan's guns - and the 87th Regiment sent Leval's division reeling. During the attack, Sergeant Patrick Masterman, of the 87th, launched himself into the fight for the eagle of the French 8th Regiment. In a furious struggle some seven French soldiers were killed and Lieutenant Gazan, severely wounded, was forced to relinquish his hold on the eagle, leaving a triumphant Masterman to claim the distinction of capturing the first eagle to be taken by the British in the Peninsula. Soon afterwards the French broke and withdrew from the field, leaving the victorious British soldiers exhausted and drained but victorious upon the summit. They were too tired to continue after the retreating French but simply dropped down upon the beach to grab some much needed and well-deserved rest.

Of some 5,000 British troops engaged 1,238 became casualties. French losses were 2,062 including Ruffin who was wounded as was one of his brigadiers, Rousseau, who later died. As well as the eagle, the French lost five guns of which the Guards took two of them.

Casualties amongst the Guards were heavy. The 2nd Battalion First Guards lost two ensigns, two sergeants and thirty-one rank and file killed, with one lieutenant colonel, three captains, four ensigns, eight sergeants and 169 rank and file wounded, a total of 216 casualties. The dead officers were Ensigns Commerell and Eyre, and the wounded officers Lieutenant Colonel Setbright, Captains Colquitt and Stables, and Ensigns Sir H. Lambert, Cameron and Vigors. Captain Adair and Ensign Field were slightly wounded.[7] The 2nd Battalion Coldstream Guards had one officer and eight men killed and two officers and forty-six rank and file wounded. The dead officer was Ensign Watts, and those wounded were Ensigns Talbot and Bentinck.[8] The 2nd Battalion Third Guards lost one officer killed and fourteen other ranks, and three officers and eighty-four rank and file wounded. The dead officer was Captain Swann and the wounded were Colonels Onslow and Hepburn and Ensign Watson.[9]

The British army at Barrosa had achieved a notable victory and as Graham said in his despatch it was almost impossible to

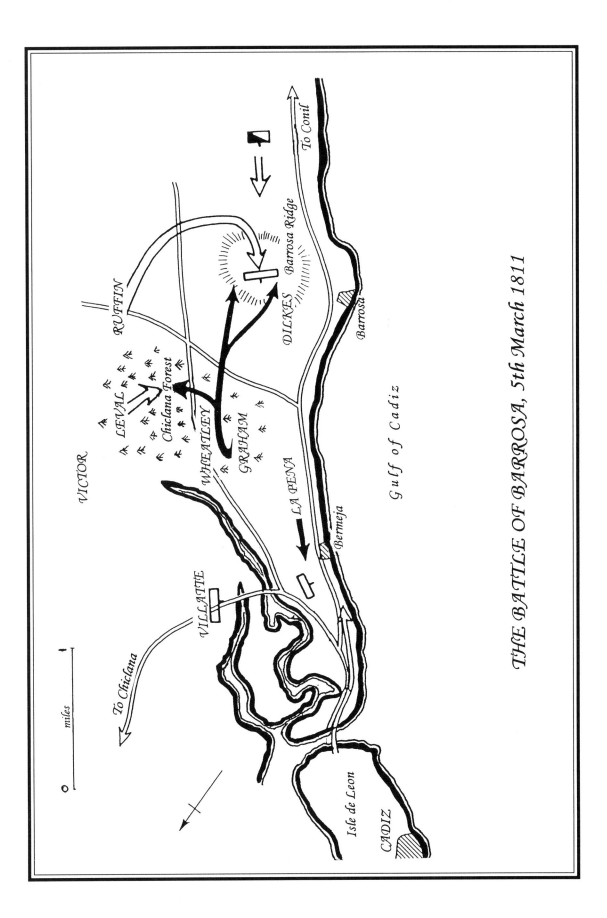

THE BATTLE OF BARROSA, 5th March 1811

single out any particular unit for special praise in a battle where, as he himself said, all had so distinguished themselves. But he did go on to say that,

Your Lordship will, however, observe how gloriously the brigade of Guards, under Brigadier-General Dilkes, with the commanders of battalions, Colonel Honourable C. Onslow and Lieutenant-Colonel Sebright, (wounded), as well as the three separated companies under Colonel Jackson, maintained the high character of His Majesty's household troops.[10]

The victory at Barrosa was all the remarkable for the fact that Graham's triumph was achieved without the assistance of a single Spaniard. While the battle had been raging La Pena's troops had done absolutely nothing to aid their British allies. The British themselves were too exhausted to pursue the French but the same could certainly not be said of the Spaniards. However, La Pena refused to follow up the British success leaving a infuriated Graham to withdraw from the ridge of Barrosa to the Isle de Leon whilst Victor's battered and bruised French returned to their lines and resumed the siege of Cadiz. To add insult to injury La Pena then accused Graham of losing the battle by withdrawing without his sanction. Naturally enough, it was the last time Graham agreed to serve under the command of the Spaniards.

Upon returning to the Isle de Leon the command of the 2nd Battalion First Guards devolved upon Colonel Wheatley. However, such were the losses sustained by the battalion during the battle that it was ordered home to be replaced by the 3rd Battalion of the regiment under Colonel G. Cooke. This was the battalion that had suffered during the retreat to Corunna two years earlier and also in Holland. It had now fully recovered and on April 2nd six companies sailed from Portsmouth to replace their comrades at Cadiz where they disembarked on April 27th.[11]

The remaining four companies of the battalion left London for Portsmouth on May 25th and sailed for Cadiz in mid-June, arriving at Cadiz on the 23rd of that month. However, before they left London they took part, along with the rest of the Brigade of Guards, in a grand parade held on May 11th to mark the reception and deposit in Whitehall Chapel of six colours and six standards taken by Graham's troops at Barrosa. The Guards turned out in full-dress at the Horse Guards as the captured trophies were displayed and carried in procession in front of the Brigade of Guards who marched with their Colours flying. The captured standards were then brought before the Colours and lowered before being laid up with great ceremony in the Chapel.[12]

In the summer of 1811 Graham left Cadiz in order to assume command of a division of Wellington's main field army. He was succeeded by Major General Disney, of the First Guards, but when he too left Cadiz, returning to England, Major General Cooke, also of the First Guards, took over command. There were no further significant actions around Cadiz during the war, save for the defence of Tarifa in December 1811, and the siege dragged on in a desultory manner with the odd bombardment until the siege was finally raised by Victor in January 1812.

NOTES

[1] Wellington, *Supplementary Despatches, Correspondence and Memoranda of Field Marshal Arthur Duke of Wellington*, (London, 1852), vii. 126.

[2] Anthony Brett-James, *General Graham, Lord Lynedoch*, (London, 1959), 207.

[3] Ibid. 210.

[4] Lieutenant General Sir F.W. Hamilton, *The Origin and History of the First or Grenadier Guards*, (London, 1874), 207.

[5] Brett-James, *General Graham*, 211.

[6] *Supplementary Despatches*, vii. 126.

[7] Hamilton, *Grenadier Guards*, ii. 417.

[8] Colonel Daniel Mackinnon, *Origin and Services of the Coldstream Guards*, (London, 1833), ii. 158.

[9] Major General Sir Frederick Maurice, *The History of the Scots Guards, from 1642 to 1914*, (London, 1934), ii. 338.

[10] Hamilton, *Grenadier Guards*, ii. 419. See also Mackinnon, *Coldstream Guards*, ii. 157-158.

[11] Hamilton, *Grenadier Guards*, ii. 423.

[12] Ibid. ii. 426.

ON THE PORTUGUESE FRONTIER

On the very day that Graham's force defeated the French at Barrosa their comrades to the north woke up to discover that Massena's army had pulled back completely from its position around Santarem. The French, sick and starving, had retreated thirty miles to a position between Leira and Thomar, having first employed their usual trick of leaving behind straw dummies in place of their sentries in an attempt to conceal their withdrawal as long as possible.

Leaving Beresford and his command south of the Tagus to watch Badajoz which, following the treachery of its governor, José Imaz, was delivered up to Soult on March 12th, Wellington gathered together his army to begin the pursuit of Massena. Before the army marched, however, Wellington issued an order summoning the regiments of the 1st Division to witness the execution of a private of the 24th Regiment who had been condemned to death for desertion and theft. The order said that the troops had been assembled to watch the execution as a deterrent to others. However, the Guards were excused this duty, as the second part of the order ran thus:

As, for the two years during which the Brigade of Guards have been under the command of the Commander of the Forces, not only no soldier has been brought to trial before a general court-martial, but no-one has been confined in a public guard, the Commander of the Forces desires that the attendance of this brigade at the execution tomorrow may be dispensed with.[1]

The Guards saw little action during Wellington's pursuit of the French as the 1st Division remained the whole time with the reserve. The Light Division on the other hand, temporarily under the bungling Sir William Erskine - Craufurd was home on leave - led the pursuit and clashed on many occasions with the French rearguard, notably at Pombal, Redinha, Cazal Nova, and Foz de Aronce.

As they followed in the wake of Massena's retreating army, the British were shocked by the harrowing scenes of death and devastation that greeted them. In order to facilitate their retreat the French abandoned most of their baggage, including ammunition supplies, wagons and carts and had slaughtered all useless animals. Most of these poor, dumb animals were hamstrung and simply left to die in misery by the roadside. Worst of all was the sickening and shocking state of the towns and villages along the route. As the French passed through they destroyed and burned houses, wrecked furniture and left it scattered around the streets, dead animals lay rotting everywhere and the nauseating stench of death filled their air. Wherever they went British troops saw the evidence of French atrocities - women brutally violated, women and children dangled from trees with fires smouldering beneath their feet and the corpses of murdered Portuguese peasants lay strewn about everywhere. As Daniel Mackinnon wrote:

The desolation in Portugal occasioned by Massena's invading army can scarcely be conceived: not an article of subsistence was to be found; every town and village was deserted; the wine that could not be consumed was left running in the gutters; the corn-stacks burnt; in the houses, which from want of means or time were not destroyed, all the furniture was broken; neither horse, mule, cow, nor ass, not even a goat could be seen. The women captured by the French in their marauding excursions were brought in as to a market and sold for the benefit of the captors; many of these unfortunate females were left to perish by famine and disease remote from their native villages.[2]

The direction of the French retreat could easily be traced by the pillars of smoke that drifted into the air marking the sight of another burning town or village as 'the habitation of the peasant and mansion of the noble were alike consumed,'[3] and by the wreckage and discarded debris that lay scattered everywhere along the wayside.

By early April Massena had been pursued as far as the Coa river and on April 3rd Wellington attacked him at Sabugal where, in a confused fight in thick fog and heavy rain, the Light Division took on an entire French corps and forced it to retire in what Wellington called, 'one of the most glorious actions British troops were ever engaged in.' The action at Sabugal precipitated a general retreat by Massena and soon the last starving French soldier had crossed the frontier into Spain. Portugal was at last free of French troops and with their expulsion so ended Napoleon's grand strategy for the domination of Portugal and the driving into the sea of the British army.

The size of the disaster that had befallen Massena can be measured by the fact that when he reached Salamanca, he surveyed the shattered remains of his army and saw that of the 50,000 men he had in November 1810 only 46,000 were able to march back into Spain in March 1811, and this included 11,000 reinforcements that had joined him during this period.

But although the French field army had been driven from Portugal the country could never be considered secure owing to the fact that the French still held the strong frontier fortresses of Badajoz and Ciudad Rodrigo, 'the Keys of Spain', and the fortress of Almeida that lay inside the Portuguese border opposite Ciudad Rodrigo. If Wellington was to tighten his grasp on Portugal then it was of paramount importance that he recover these three fortresses and in mid-April he set in motion his plan to do so. On April 16th Wellington rode south, covering seventy miles in a day and wearing out two horses in the process, in order to visit Beresford who was given orders to invest Badajoz. One wonders whether Wellington intended this to be a serious attempt as Beresford had just 20,000 troops and, more significantly, a woefully inadequate siege train. Wellington meanwhile, with around 38,000 men, moved towards Almeida to begin its blockade.

On May 2nd news was received at Wellington's headquarters at Freneida that Massena, his troops having rested and after having procured supplies, was advancing once again towards Ciudad Rodrigo with 48,000 men with the obvious intention of relieving Almeida. The French were advancing in two columns, one by way of Gallegos and the other through Espeja. Both columns seemed to be centring on the village of Fuentes de Oñoro, a jumbled maze of small houses that straddled the Dos Casas river. Wasting no time Wellington marched his army to Fuentes de Oñoro that same evening and during the night of May 2nd-3rd his men began to take up their positions there.

The position at Fuentes de Oñoro was not the strongest one but the geographical features of the surrounding area did afford Wellington the type of characteristics well-suited to his defensive tactics. The Dos Casas river that runs through the village is no more than a stream in places and in summer weather can often dry up completely. However, it is wide and deep enough in places to represent an obstacle for any army wishing to cross. The ground on the right bank of the river is wooded and slopes gently down to the river, the only cover being afforded by a series of stone walls that criss-cross the ground. On the left bank is situated the village itself, with its maze of single-storeyed dwellings that creep down to the river's edge. The village extends to the top of a ridge about 2500 feet high which ran north to south about ten miles in length and which was Wellington's main position, centring on the village itself.

Keeping his main force at Fuentes de Oñoro, Wellington

despatched the 5th and 6th Divisions to the north of the ridge towards Fort Conception, a strong fort used intermittently by the army throughout 1810 to 1812, in order to block any attempt by Reynier's corps to cross the frontier by way of Alameda towards Almeida. Behind the village were positioned the 1st, 3rd and 7th Divisions, as usual on the reverse slope of the ridge, whilst the village itself was held by a battalion of the 84th Regiment as well as the light companies of all the units of the 1st and 3rd Divisions, except the Guards. The Light Division was held in reserve on the right flank.

The Brigade of Guards had marched from Almadilla on the night of May 2nd and, guided by a full moon, took up positions amongst the trees and rocks on the reverse slope of the ridge behind the village:

As soon as we sniffed the morning breeze, and the early summer dawn broke, we began to examine our neighbourhood and reconnoitre our neighbours; we found, at no great distance, plenty of friends, which was pleasant, as we knew that we had a much greater number of enemies in our vicinity.[4]

But if the British army was outnumbered by about 10,000 men the Guards could console themselves with the fact that the 1st Battalion Third Guards was the strongest battalion in the army having a strength of 24 officers, 65 sergeants, 16 drummers and 854 rank and file fit and present for duty on May 1st.

Massena attacked on the afternoon of May 3rd, sending five divisions plunging across the Dos Casas to make a massive frontal attack on the village. There was a great deal of bitter and bloody hand-to-hand fighting during which the village changed hands several times. Colonel Williams, who commanded the light companies holding the village, was badly wounded and when the British troops were slowly forced from the confused and cluttered streets it was Wellington himself, as usual riding back and forth in the smoke of battle, who personally ordered the 71st and 79th Regiments to re-take the village which they did but only after more bloody fighting.

The Guards stood to arms throughout the night of May 3rd, fully expecting a French attack on the morning of the 4th. However, the day passed off peacefully enough as both sides took away their dead and wounded from the streets and ground around the village and there was some fraternisation between the two opposing armies as they stopped to either drink or wash at the Dos Casas. The highlight of the day was

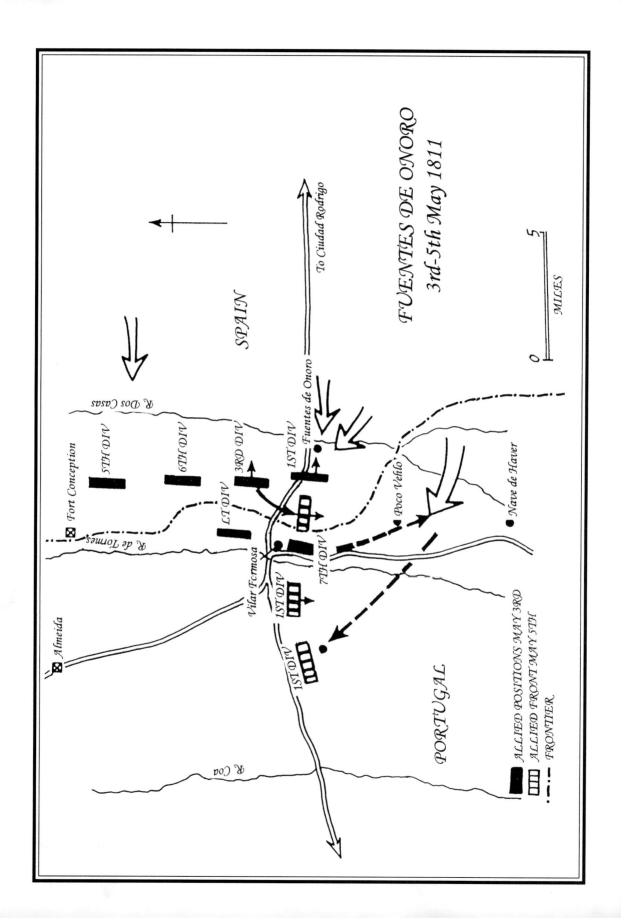

FUENTES DE ONORO
3rd-5th May 1811

0   5
MILES

SPAIN

PORTUGAL

R. Dos Casas

R. de Tormes

R. Coa

Fort Conception

Almeida

Vilar Formosa

Fuentes de Onoro

Poco Velho

Nave de Haver

To Ciudad Rodrigo

5TH DIV

6TH DIV

3RD DIV

1ST DIV

LT DIV

7TH DIV

1ST DIV

1ST DIV

1ST DIV

ALLIED POSITIONS MAY 3RD
ALLIED FRONT MAY 5TH
FRONTIER

a grand parade held by the French in the cool of the evening whilst the British sat peacefully watching. 'The moon rose, the bivouac fires were trimmed, the cigar smoked, and our soldiers sank to rest.'[5]

The Guards were stood at arms long before dawn on the 5th, shivering after a night of heavy dew and anxious for some heat and movement. As the first light of day streaked through the morning mist French columns were seen moving against Nave de Haver on the right of Wellington's line. Here were positioned Julian Sanchez's guerrillas and some British cavalry who, in the face of overwhelming French numbers, were driven steadily back on Poco Velho. This tiny hamlet was held by Houston's recently-formed 7th Division which quickly became sorely-pressed by the French who threatened to cut off their retreat to the main Allied position.

Massena appeared to be trying to put more pressure on the right of the Allied line with the object of forcing Wellington into bringing more of his troops south to meet the growing French threat. In theory, this would weaken the left of the Allied line and so allow Massena to feed his cavalry through to escort his convoy into the beleaguered garrison of Almeida. However, Wellington refused to be panicked into uncovering · Almeida and in response to the increasing enemy threat decided to replace the 7th Division with the Light Division whilst the 1st and 3rd Divisions were moved to their right. As the Light Division, under Craufurd, entered the fray, the 7th Division withdrew towards the Allied line to take up a position in rear of the 1st Division.

During the movement of the 1st Division to the south, earlier in the day, the 92nd Regiment - part of Howard's brigade of the 1st Division - had undergone a particularly difficult march through the marshy woods close to the ridge and when they arrived to take up a position behind the Guards they did so, according to Mackinnon, 'much exhausted and without food.' When the Guards heard of this they immediately took from their haversacks part of their own ration of biscuit and gave it to the Highlanders who responded with three loud cheers.[6]

At this point there occurred a strange incident involving the Coldstream Guards. A few days before the battle Julian Sanchez' men had captured a convoy of French clothing and immediately donned the tunics and turned out in a bewildering array of varying colours. As Sanchez' cavalry fell back upon the 1st Division following their withdrawal from Nave de

Haver, his chief lieutenant placed himself in front of the Coldstream Guards who unfortunately mistook him for a Frenchman. One of the Coldstreamers levelled his musket and opened fire on the Spaniard, killing him instantly. Sir Brent Spencer, commanding the 1st Division, rode up and appeared to be annoyed by the tragic mistake but when Wellington himself arrived on the scene he is reported to have said, 'Never mind, Spencer, it is only a Spaniard!'[7]

Meanwhile, the Light Division was in the process of regaining the Allied line after their magnificent achievement in withdrawing across a barren plain for a distance of about three miles, all the time surrounded by French cavalry. As one historian later put it, 'no more masterly manoeuvre is recorded of any general [Craufurd]; no grander example of triumphant discipline is recorded of any regiments in the history of the British army.'[8] It was indeed a glorious feat and when Craufurd's men reached the Allied line the Guards wheeled back to let them through amidst much cheering.

As the Guards reformed their line their picquets were charged by French cavalry. Commanding the picquets was Lieutenant Colonel Hill of the Third Guards and as the French cavalry bore down on him he formed his men into small clusters whose accurate fire drove off the first horsemen. As the French retreated, however, he formed his men into a line again at which point the 13th Chasseurs charged and rolled up the line, wounding Hill - who was also taken prisoner - and causing sixty other casualties amongst the two Guards battalions.

The Third Guards lost twelve men taken prisoner and the Coldstream one officer and seven men, the officer being Ensign William Stothert, who is not to be confused with the ensign of the Third Guards who bears the same name and from whose journal many quotations have taken for this book. The remainder of the picquet staggered back to the main line, bruised, battered and a little shaken, but still able to take part in the rest of the battle. Amongst the wounded was Captain Harvey, of the Coldstream, who was ridden over by French cavalry after being felled by an enemy sabre. As we shall see, Harvey was to have another narrow escape later in the day.[9]

During the mêlée Captain Home, of the Third Guards, was attacked by three of the Chasseurs who flayed away at him with their sabres. One of them grabbed the strap of a bottle that hung at his side, which snapped leaving the Frenchman to ride off with the bottle, whilst another tore an epaulette from Home's tunic but was driven off by the Guardsman's sword. The third trooper thrust at Home with his sabre and attempted to cut him down but Home put up a furious fight and in the ensuing struggle almost pulled his assailant from his horse. Home was a big man and the Frenchman soon realised he was likely to come off second best in the fight and so turned his horse around and rode off. As he did so, however, Home grabbed the prized Cross of the Legion of Honour that the Frenchman had worn and carried it back in triumph to his cheering comrades of the Third Guards.[10] The rest of the French cavalry were driven off by the light companies of the Third Guards, under Lieutenant Colonel Guise, and some artillery. Guise was later mentioned in despatches for his conduct.

Whilst the French cavalry charges had been in progress, the fighting in Fuentes de Oñoro itself had escalated to a new level of ferocity. Wave after wave of French infantry swept into the village but on each occasion were thrown back by Wellington's infantry who pressed home their counter-attacks with extreme violence. At one point, about a hundred Frenchmen became trapped in a cul-de-sac by an element of the 88th Regiment, the Connaught Rangers. The blood-curdling yells of these wild Irishmen were the last sounds the French were to hear as the 88th charged home with their bayonets to put each and every one of them to death in an appalling burst of ruthless, lethal savagery. Finally, at about two o'clock in the afternoon, the final French attack was beaten back and the village remained in Allied hands.

The Brigade of Guards took no further part in direct action on that day although they did remain under fire. They had taken up a relatively safe position on the ridge above the village but many a shell came bouncing in amongst them or exploded nearby. John Stepney Cowell relates that lying inactive amidst this shellfire, not being able to return it, was a most trying and worrying experience, which tried the patience of the men:

A man of our company fell asleep, and amused his comrades much by snoring loudly; poor fellow! a cannon-shot fell on his neck, just between his head and his knapsack; instant death ensued, without consciousness, and probably without pain. His own particular friend and comrade immediately requested to have his shoes!.....The whistling of a shell, and its striking amongst us, next occurred; the felt of a cap flew in the air. Thinking, of course, that the cap and head had gone together, I turned to see who it was, when I beheld amidst the titter and laughter of his comrades, the great, broad, good-humoured countenance of an Irishman named McCulloch: he was sitting upright, a queer figure, with half his cap cut off close to his head. I asked him if he was hurt; the fellow replied, with a grin, 'No, plase your honour, only a bit dizzy!'[11]

The dreadful effects these shells were capable of can be judged from another passage from Cowell who recalled that on another occasion a round shot came bouncing in *en ricochet*, missing the ranks of the Coldstreamers to fall amongst a group of staff officers who had gathered at the bottom of the ridge, taking off the head of General Howard's horse, killing that of his aide-de-camp Captain Battersby, taking off the leg of Major Stewart of the 92nd and knocking over two rank and file before 'hopping' on like a cricket ball. As Cowell said, 'this shot may be fairly said to have done its duty.'[12] Another shell narrowly missed Captain Harvey, who had already had a brief flirtation with death that morning, courtesy of the French cavalry. Harvey was riding in front of the Coldstream when the shell passed clean through his horse's body and hit Harvey below the knee, badly wounding him and throwing him from his horse. He was, of course, badly shaken and hurt but refused to leave the battlefield.

When the fighting finally died down on the evening of the 5th Massena had been forced to abandon his attack and gave up all hope of relieving Almeida. The day had ended in victory for Wellington but it had not been an entirely satisfactory one. Indeed, he himself later said that, 'if Boney had been there we should have been beaten.' Allied casualties were 1,545 killed and wounded whilst Massena's army suffered 2,192. The Coldstream Guards lost four rank and file killed, and one officer - Captain Harvey - two sergeants and 49 rank and file wounded. As we have already seen, Ensign Stothert and seven men were taken prisoner. The Third Guards lost five rank and file killed, one officer - Captain Clitheroe - and 52 rank and file wounded, whilst one officer - Lieutenant Colonel Hill - and twelve men were taken prisoner.

When night fell the Guards lit their bivouac fires and posted picquets and then, as the moon rose in the night sky, the officers wrapped themselves in their cloaks and lay down, their eyes being quickly sealed by the heat and exertions of the day. And as they fell to sleep they dreamt, as one of the put it, 'the happiest of all English soldiers' dreams - that of England, friends, and home.'[13]

On May 8th Massena withdrew his army towards Salamanca having failed in his object to relieve Almeida. It was to be the last time that the ageing, war-weary Massena commanded the army for soon afterwards he was recalled to Paris by Napoleon who replaced him with Marmont. Two days later, on the night of May 10th-11th General Brennier and the garrison of Almeida were allowed to escape after blowing up the works there. This happened because the bungling Sir William Erskine failed to place a guard at the bridge at Barba del Puerco, over which Brennier and his 1,400 men made good their escape. The order had been given to Erskine by Wellington but he put it in his pocket and forgot about it! Needless to say, Erskine was removed from Wellington's field army and later committed suicide in Lisbon.

There was little action during the remainder of the year although there was much manoeuvring by both armies. On May 11th the Guards were back in their old positions at Fuentes de Oñoro. Two weeks later the 1st Division marched through Soita to Penamacor but here the Guards were ordered to return and on the 29th had reached Puebla.

On May 12th meanwhile, Beresford, who had been laying siege to Badajoz, was forced to give it up when he learnt that Soult, with 25,000 men and fifty guns, was moving towards him from the south. Four days later Soult attacked Beresford at Albuera. As the Guards were not involved here it will not be necessary to go into too much detail about the battle. Suffice to say that it was one of the bloodiest contests of the war, fought by Beresford in a badly-chosen position. In fact, Beresford had little influence on the outcome of the fight - it turned into a 'soldiers' battle, much like Inkerman some fifty-odd years later. At the end of the day the British infantry stood victorious but paid an immense price for their triumph, suffering about fifty per cent casualties, much to Wellington's annoyance.

The siege of Badajoz was renewed a month after Albuera but with little success owing to an inadequate siege train and when Soult and Marmont joined forces, bringing their number to around 58,000 men, Wellington abandoned the siege altogether. On June 20th the two French marshals entered Badajoz to revictual the place and two days later departed, 'breathing blood and fire, eager to get to grips,'[14] However, news of an insurrection in Andalusia took Soult away whilst Marmont marched to the Tagus. With these two gone Wellington turned his attention yet again to Badajoz but the unhealthy climate of the valley of the Guadiana put several thousand British soldiers sick into the hospitals and towards the end of July he gave up the siege.

The Brigade of Guards had played no part in the actual siege operations at Badajoz. On June 5th the brigade left Puebla for Almadilla and a few days later had reached Castello Branco. After crossing the Tagus the brigade camped, on June 23rd, near St Oloia where the Guards took out their bill-hooks once again to build huts in order to protect them from the burning heat of the day. Indeed, as the army marched through deep valleys covered with gumcistus the heat of the day caused the shrub to emit a strong smelling and thick effluvium which, when combined with the clouds of dust kicked up by the men produced uncomfortable marching conditions. According to Cowell, it was not uncommon to see a man's haversack wet with sweat that seeped through the man's red coat, 'as if it had been dipped in water....It is no joke to be exposed to the sun in Spain or Portugal in the middle of a summer's day, when the thermometer stands between 80° and 90°of Fahrenheit.'[15] Ensign John Mills, of the Coldstream, was another to comment on the weather, when he compared it to the English climate:

The climate is by no means a delightful one - we are apt to complain of the fickleness of our own, but a fine day, doubly repays a bad one, and holds out the greater inducement to enjoy it. The laws of weather are here fixed. There is the wet, and the dry season. For more than two months I have seen but one shower of rain - three hours in the evening is all that can be enjoyed of this mass of sunshine, and this will be all repaid by several months of wet. Until you have left it, you know not the delights of England.[16]

Two days later the 1st Division, including the Brigade of Guards was inspected by Wellington who was accompanied by the Prince of Orange. The Guards left St Oloai on July 22nd and marched to Portalegre. On the last day of the month, however, the brigade received orders to return north in consequence of Wellington having recrossed the Tagus, his intention being to blockade Ciudad Rodrigo. It was during this march that General Graham, the hero of Barrosa, joined the army and assumed command of the 1st Division, Sir Brent Spencer going home. In spite of his age, his appointment was welcomed by the Guards:

Graham is the life of the army - all alacrity - he is on horseback from morning to night and that at sixty. He commands our division and is a good friend to every forlorn Guardsman.[17]

However, Wellington's attempts at blockading Ciudad Rodrigo fared little better than his siege of Badajoz. No sooner had he arrived before the town than he received news that the French were concentrating once more and were advancing against him. Wellington himself had scattered his divisions between Fuentes de Oñoro and Fuenteguinaldo, a move which was to place him in an extremely perilous situation, because Marmont advanced so rapidly that on September 25th Wellington found himself at

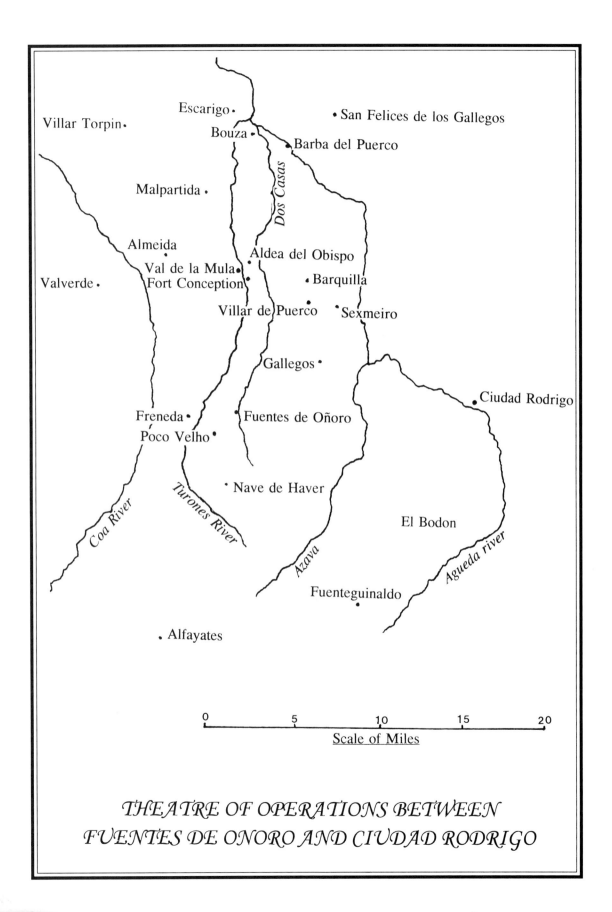

Villar Torpin .

Escarigo .

. San Felices de los Gallegos

Bouza .

. Barba del Puerco

Dos Casas

Malpartida .

Almeida .

Aldea del Obispo

Val de la Mula .

. Barquilla

Valverde .

Fort Conception

Villar de Puerco

. Sexmeiro

Gallegos .

Ciudad Rodrigo

Freneda .

Fuentes de Oñoro

Poco Velho .

Coa River

Turones River

. Nave de Haver

El Bodon

Azava

Agueda river

Fuenteguinaldo

. Alfayates

0   5   10   15   20

Scale of Miles

THEATRE OF OPERATIONS BETWEEN
FUENTES DE ONORO AND CIUDAD RODRIGO

Fuenteguinaldo with just 15,000 men against Marmont's 45,000. The 3rd Division was several miles away at El Bodon while the Light Division was also absent, a day's march away and Graham, with the 1st Division, was at Nave de Haver. Therefore, Marmont, throughout the whole of September 26th, was in a position to attack the British line with odds of three to one in his favour. Fortunately for Wellington, however, Marmont did not know this. He could not be sure just how many British troops were out of sight behind the ridge at Fuenteguinaldo and remembering the unpleasant French experience at Busaco he was unwilling to risk another frontal attack but merely probed away at Wellington's position. Thus, the opportunity went begging and the chance of a crushing blow for France was lost.

On October 1st, having taken a look at Wellington's position, and having decided not to risk an attack, Marmont retired once more to the Tagus having first thrown six months' food into Ciudad Rodrigo.

The campaign of 1811 was effectively over and the Guards went into winter quarters, appropriately enough, at Guarda and while the officers took the opportunity to indulge in some fox hunting with Wellington's hounds, and enjoy themselves shooting and riding, the rest of the army settled down to recover from the year's campaigning and to prepare for the crucial campaigns of the coming year.

We leave the year of 1811 with John Stepney Cowell who, along with his comrades of the Coldstream, was just coming to terms with their first really cold winter in the Peninsula, having spent the last couple of years further south around Lisbon where the climate was milder:

We sat, when indoors (for *in-windows* we could not call it, there being none beyond broken shutters), wrapped in our cloaks, on the family household chests of the poor inhabitants, round a *brazarico*, or pan of hot ashes, to warm the extremities of man; a joke or a cigar in the mouth, to console the stomach or brush up the intellect; our drink, when we could get it, some kind of wine or alcohol, to fill the internal portion of human nature's commissariat depot. These, together with a sincere good wish for a better abode, a battle, or anything, in short, that would circulate the blood or interest the mind, formed our desiderata; though we bore our hardships with the true spirit of well-tried, red-coated philosophers.[18]

NOTES

[1] General Order, March 4th 1811.

[2] Colonel Daniel Mackinnon, *Origins and Services of the Coldstream Guards*, (London, 1833), ii. 154.

[3] John Stepney Cowell, *Leaves from the Diary of an Officer of the Guards*, (London, 1854), 53.

[4] Ibid. 82.

[5] Ibid. 84.

[6] Mackinnon, *Coldstream Guards*, ii. 161.

[7] Stepney Cowell, *Leaves from the Diary*, 86. Cowell says the incident took place shortly after dawn whereas Mackinnon claims it took place much later, correctly so in the authors' opinion.

[8] J.W. Fortescue, *History of the British Army*, (London, 1910-1930), viii. 166.

[9] Harvey was later killed during the abortive siege of Burgos.

[10] Stepney Cowell, *Leaves from the Diary*, 90-91. See also Sir Frederick Maurice, *History of the Scots Guards, from 1642 to 1914*, (London, 1934), i. 346-347.

[11] Stepney Cowell, *Leaves from the Diary*, 93.

[12] Ibid. 95.

[13] Ibid. 97.

[14] Major H.L. Aubrey-Fletcher, *A History of the Foot Guards to 1856*, (London, 1927), 281.

[15] Stepney Cowell, *Leaves from the Diary*, 125.

[16] John Mills, Penamacor, August 20th 1811.

[17] John Mills, Val dos Ayres, near Celorico, October 2nd 1811.

[18] Stepney Cowell, *Leaves from the Diary*, 191.

TWO SIEGES

For Wellington, the year of 1812 was perhaps one of the most disappointing of the Peninsular War, beginning as it did with the glorious capture of Ciudad Rodrigo and Badajoz, continuing with his great victory at Salamanca in the summer, but culminating in the disastrous attack on Burgos and the subsequent terrible retreat back to Portugal.

As the year of 1811 faded Wellington set about a campaign of disinformation intended to deceive Marmont into believing that he did not intend carrying out any offensive operations until the spring at the earliest. His army was kept purposely scattered, exaggerated reports of the numbers of British sick in the hospitals were skilfully leaked, senior officers were allowed to go home on leave and Almeida was strengthened in order to encourage speculation that Wellington intended carrying out a defensive campaign. In all, everything that could be done to encourage Marmont's belief in his own security was carried out. However, while the French commander settled into his winter quarters at Toledo all was frenzied activity behind the Allied lines as preparations for offensive operations were got quietly underway, as John Stepney Cowell, of the Coldstream, wrote:

Our battering train had also arrived here, composed of seventy-eight heavy pieces of ordnance. A great number of cars were also in the course of construction, to facilitate the conveyance of ammunition; and we were occupied in making fascines and gabions, and rapidly preparing, in every way possible, for carrying into effect the immediate siege of Ciudad Rodrigo. The dilapidated state of Almeida, and the arrival of our heavy artillery, served as an excuse to the enemy for our operations, which they believed were confined merely to defensive measures for precautions, in preparing and arming this Portuguese frontier fortress.[1]

Wellington's siege train was landed at Oporto and brought up in secret to Almeida where large numbers of gabions and fascines were constructed, both measures apparently employed solely for the purpose of strengthening Almeida. Also, a trestle bridge was built in secret for the passage of the Azava and Agueda rivers and by January 3rd Wellington was sufficiently satisfied with the state of affairs to issue orders for an advance the next day.

On January 4th, therefore, amidst heavy snow and biting rain Wellington, at the head of the 1st, 3rd, 4th and Light Divisions, rode out of his headquarters, crossed the Azava by way of the trestle bridge and by the 8th had reached the fortress of Ciudad Rodrigo. The Brigade of Guards had crossed the Coa river at 7am on January 4th to begin what was an unpleasant march, as Surgeon Good, of the Third Guards, relates:

We started in a perfect hurricane, which continued all morning. The road was bad, the rain unpleasant, and the wind occasionally so strong as almost to take us off our legs. However, after passing the Coa at the bridge of Almeida, the weather moderated. We took the right-hand road and proceeded up the hill to the village of Junca, the Coldstream went to Las Navis.[2]

Good goes on to say that he thought it strange that Wellington should commence a siege at that time of year. This, of course, is proof that Wellington's sudden forward movement had the desired effect, ie. that if his own troops were surprised then the French would be even more so. In fact, Marmont thought his position suitably safe as to order a large part of his army to the east to reinforce Marshal Suchet at Valencia.

When the Guards marched through Fuentes de Oñoro on January 8th and then entered Spain, it was the first time they had been in that country since the battle of Talavera in the summer of 1809. By the evening of the 8th the Guards had reached Espeja where fires were quickly lit and as the officers of the Guards smoked their cigars and drank mulled wine the sound of distant gunfire came booming through the frosty night air, causing them to dash into the streets:

the cannonade continued and became heavy; distance, and the wind in an adverse quarter, prevented our hearing any sound of musketry, but we saw, by the flashes from the guns, the horizon lighted far above the woods and undulating ground which intervened between our village of espeja and the town of Ciudad. A large assembly of officers and men were collected, in order to try and make out results from sound, but to little purpose beyond ascertaining that, as the cannonade continued throughout the night, the siege had begun.[3]

The siege of Ciudad Rodrigo had indeed begun. That same day, January 8th, the French looked out from behind the ramparts of Ciudad Rodrigo and were startled to see Wellington's infantry before the walls of the place. The French apparently thought they were mad to begin siege operations in such appalling weather and did not take the threat seriously at first, many of their officers coming to the foot of the walls to make mocking gestures at their opponents. However, they laughed on the other side of their faces when the Light Division stormed the outwork upon the Great Teson, a hill overlooking the fortress, later that night, the sounds of which had carried to Cowell and his comrades as they sat around their fires at Espeja.

The importance of Ciudad Rodrigo lay in the fact that not only did it control the northerly route between Portugal and Spain - Badajoz commanded the southern route - but the bridge there over the Agueda river was the only one for many miles on either side. The place was well fortified but its weakness lay in the fact that it was overlooked by the Great Teson, a hill to the north-west of the town, at a distance of about 600 yards. Between here and the walls of the place lay another smaller hill, known as the Little Teson. As mentioned above, the Light Division stormed the outwork on the Great Teson on the night of the 8th, thus quickly establishing a commanding hold over Ciudad Rodrigo almost immediately. It was upon the Great and Little Tesons that Wellington would place his siege guns once trenches, or 'parallels' as they were called, had been dug.

Siege warfare was an unpleasant occupation for Wellington's infantry. His army possessed no miners or sappers and so the business of constructing trenches and parallels fell to the ordinary infantryman who naturally hated the work. The men would spend long hours digging, all the time under fire and whilst the danger of death from French fire was not as great as that experienced by their descendants one hundred years or so later in Flanders, the conditions in the trenches were very similar. At first it was difficult to break ground as the ground was frozen, but when it began to thaw, the earth refused to pile up as it was dug out but ran back in stream of mud. The trenches quickly filled with icy, muddy water and the dangers of exposure to the weather and enemy fire combined to make life very unpleasant indeed.

The sons of gentlemen they may have been, but the officers of the Guards were not spared this discomfort. The 1st Division, including the Brigade of Guards, endured its first spell of duty in the trenches on the 8th. From their assembly points the Guards had to ford the Agueda which was partially frozen and flowing with ice. So cold was it, in fact, that Ensign John Mills, of the Coldstream, wrote that the water froze in the men's canteens.[4] As they reached the water the Guards were ordered to stop and take off their shoes and stockings, an unusual order given the extreme cold of the water. However, as Cowell says in his diary, this was of no small comfort to them because as they were to be exposed to a hard frost for the next twenty-four hours, the men saved both their feet and their shoes.[5] The march into then trenches then continued, as Surgeon Good relates:

At daylight this morning we started, leaving our baggage behind. It was very cold but cold as it was, the men were obliged to ford the river Azava (a tributary of the Agueda)..... We descended to the river, which we forded, it was up to the men's middles and the stream very rapid..... It was now 11 o'clock am, the wind high and piercing cold with occasionally a fall of snow. The Light Division now marched off and our brigade remained under arms in rear of the hill, forming the right of the Germans... The enemy were amusing themselves by throwing shell and grape alternately, in consequence of which several wounded Germans were brought in. At six o'clock our people relieved the Germans in the trenches. 1,200 men of the brigade marched to the park of the artificers and each man taking with him his musket, carried a gabion, a fascine, a spade, and a pick-axe, and so entered the works. It was not long before wounded were brought to us, whom during the night we were employed in dressing, [Good had occupied a house near the trenches] having also two amputations by the light of a miserable candle, the flame of which was perpetually agitated by the wind. I was not sorry when morning came and our people relieved by the 3rd Division.[6]

It had indeed been a trying time for the Guards as the French poured in a great number of shells on them. The damage caused by the shells was increased by the amount of flint and stone that was thrown up as the shells hit the hard, frosty ground. However, things were not that bad that the Guards lost their sense of humour. 'On entering the trenches,' according to Cowell, 'they welcomed us with a pretty brisk cannonade and fire of shells, a species of cricket-ball that no-one seemed in a hurry to catch; indeed, as an old cricketer, I may presume to say, that, fortunately, the "fielding" was *most*, indifferent.'[7]

As the Guards worked on through the night heavy snow began to fall, adding to their miseries, although spirits were kept up by one particular Guardsman who sang beautifully to cheer his comrades, having first put on three shirts to help 'preserve his voice.' Every now and then a shout of "shot!" or "shell!" would be given by look-outs posted to watch for the incoming shells that smacked into the British trenches causing some material damage but little in the way of casualties owing to the gabions and fascines thrown up by the men as they worked. In the darkness the shells looked like rockets and the lookouts were able to follow them the whole way and judge where they would fall.[8] The enemy directed their fire during the hours of darkness by means of light-balls or the lighted carcasses of animals which illuminated the area for a distance around the town's walls. These light-balls were quickly followed by a salvo from the French guns as the trenches became visible and the Guards would hastily bury themselves in the earth as the shells came in, as John Mills, wrote:

no sooner did they hear our pick-axes at work than they threw a fire ball which fell about 20 yards in our front and threw out such a light that they could see every button upon our coats. The ball burnt for twenty minutes during which time we lay upon our faces to hide ourselves, and they fired most gloriously. When the light was burnt out we set to work, and before daylight completed our battery.[9]

All in all it was a testing time and the first grey, frosty streaks of dawn were greeted with some relief by the Guards as it meant that their particular turn of duty was about to come to an end.

By the time the Guards marched out of the trenches the Third Guards had lost 3 men killed and 9 wounded, two of whom later died, whilst the Coldstream suffered one man killed and 5 wounded. Colonel Fermor, of the Guards, the commanding officer in the trenches, had his hat ripped off by the splinter of a shell. On the way back to their camp the many of the men fell out from cold and fatigue. John Stepney Cowell relates that when he returned to Espeja, he found Sanguinetti the sutler, 'a man of elastic views in moral and monetary obligations,' waiting there with a cargo of hams, porter, brandy, champagne, tea, cheese, and other commodities, 'to warm the inward and strengthen the body.' After a spell in the trenches such luxuries were welcome indeed. For the ordinary private soldiers, however, there was little cheer and they were to be similarly employed in the trenches on January 13th and on the night of the 17th-18th. According to John Mills, the Guards distinguished themselves by digging a greater length of trench with fewer men than any other unit:

The Engineers said that they [the Guards] would do more in one night than any other two divisions - and it is natural they should, for they are all strong men, and accustomed to hard labour as a proof of it, though they had fresh ground to break for the three times that it came to their turn to work, they lost fewer men in the trenches than any other brigade, because they would cover themselves in, in one third of the time.....A portion only of officers went into the trenches, two to a hundred men - it came to my turn twice. The first time we had to break ground for a battery, for the first hour I hardly knew what to make of it, as we were on a rising ground, and they threw a blue light which burnt in our front, and discovered our sinister intentions.[10]

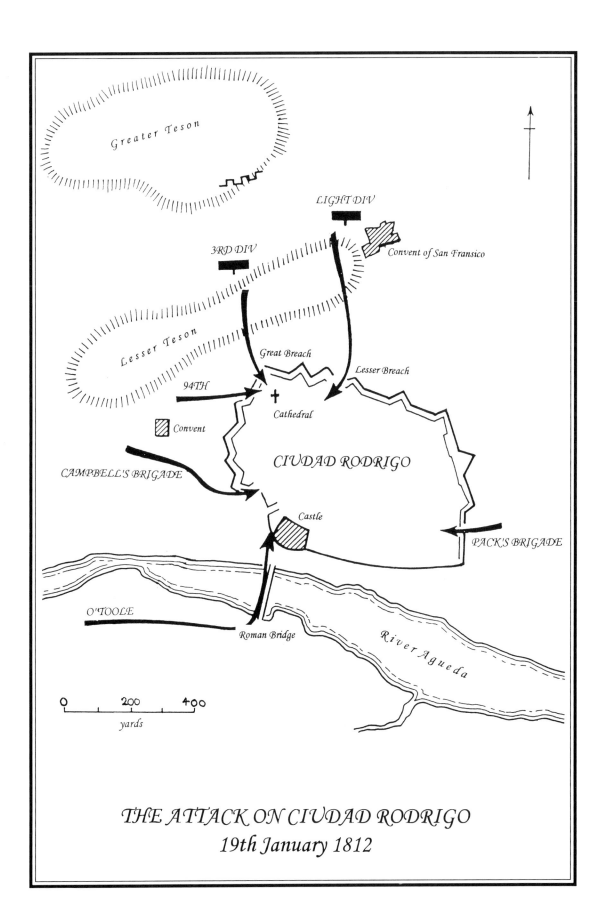

THE ATTACK ON CIUDAD RODRIGO
19th January 1812

On the night of January 19th Ciudad Rodrigo was successfully stormed. The place was not taken without great loss, however. As well as some 1,300 casualties, Robert 'Black Bob' Craufurd, commander of the Light Division, was mortally wounded whilst leading the attack on the Lesser Breach and General Henry Mackinnon, of the Coldstream - although commanding a brigade of the 3rd Division at the time - was killed whilst attacking the Great Breach. Mackinnon was buried on January 23rd in the market-place at Espeja, his funeral being attended by his brother officers of the Guards regiments. The Guards took no part in the storming, however, as the attack was entrusted to the 3rd and Light Divisions. Ciudad Rodrigo, therefore, was taken in just twelve days, a remarkable achievement, but as we shall see in this chapter the siege operations in the Peninsula were by far the unhappiest aspect of the war as far as Wellington was concerned. Nevertheless, one of the two 'Keys of Spain' was in his hands - as well as Marmont's siege train, captured inside the town - and he could now turn his attention to the much tougher fortress of Badajoz.

When the siege was over the 1st Division retraced its steps to Espeja where, as Good relates in his diary, he set about recovering from the vigours of the operation by sitting down to a hearty dinner with Lieutenant Colonel Guise, also of the Third Guards, who served up soup, boiled neck of mutton, pork cutlets, patties, roast goose, woodcocks, and pudding washed down with champagne and madeira![11]

With Ciudad Rodrigo now in his hands many thought Wellington would halt and consolidate his position, after all, it was still winter and the weather hardly suitable for campaigning. Wellington, however, was not prepared to simply sit back on his laurels. Indeed, he had already shown by his capture of Ciudad Rodrigo that the weather was not going to thwart his plans and as soon as the trenches there had been filled in and the breaches repaired, he began to put in motion his plans to move south in order to make his third attempt at taking Badajoz.

Preparations began immediately. Once again Wellington needed the French to believe that his main force was still on the frontier at Leon whereas in fact, his guns were making their way south. Wellington himself remained at his headquarters at Freneida until March 5th to keep up the deception but as early as February 19th his divisions had begun to slip away to the south towards Badajoz and when he finally left his headquarters only the 5th Division and some cavalry remained to act as a screen.

The Guards had begun their march south on February 8th,

marching first to Abrantes where new clothes were issued. These had been sent up from Lisbon and as Stepney Cowell remarks, they were issued not a moment too soon as, 'in the *haberdashery line* we were a little like those troops with which Falstaff, from a delicate sense of propriety, would *not* march through Coventry.'[12] After refitting the march continued and by March 10th the Guards had reached the vicinity of Elvas, a fortress town on the Portuguese border, opposite Badajoz, where Wellington concentrated his army. Once again the march was an unpleasant one as strong gales, cold, driving rain and a frosty ground underfoot made marching treacherous and demanding:

The rain which we have had since we began our march is become very serious indeed. We have as yet bivouacked, and last night the wind and rain were so tremendous that our tents were blown over, and I am still wet.[13]

This time the Guards were spared the rigours of siege warfare as they took no part in the operations, the 1st Division, along with the 6th and 7th, under Graham, was sent south to cover the siege and prevent any interference from Marshal Soult who was approaching from that direction. As the Guards were not involved we need not dwell too long on the siege of Badajoz, suffice to say that it was taken by storm on the night of April 6th after possibly the most savage and bloodiest fighting of the whole war. The British troops went berserk afterwards and sacked the town from top to bottom in an orgy of violence and destruction that lasted for a full 72 hours.

With both Badajoz and Ciudad Rodrigo in his hands Wellington now commanded the two major routes between Spain and Portugal and he could now look ahead to advancing deeper into Spain. However, before he could do so he had to return north to face the growing threat posed by Marshal Marmont around Ciudad Rodrigo. Therefore, on April 11th the Guards were back in Elvas and two days later had begun their march north to the area between the Agueda and Coa rivers where Wellington concentrated the bulk of his army in readiness for his advance into Spain.

Here we must leave the main operations of the British army to take a look at the conclusion of the siege of Cadiz. The city came under renewed attack on May 16th 1812 from several of Soult's gunboats in the Trocadero canal. This was repeated on July 16th but two weeks later, following news of Wellington's victory at Salamanca on July 22nd, King Joseph sent orders to Soult to withdraw and come to his assistance at Madrid. By coincidence, Major General George Cooke, of the First Guards, commanding at Cadiz, received orders from Wellington at about the same time, directing him to make an attack upon the French. Accordingly, Colonel Skerrett sailed from Cadiz on August 10th bound for Huebro with 4,000 men and marched to Seville from where it would be possible to threaten French communications with Cadiz. Amongst his force were six companies of the First Guards, under Colonel Peregrine Maitland. Skerrett's force arrived at Huebro, some seventy miles north-west of Cadiz the following night. On the morning of the 13th the Guards clambered unsteadily into boats and were finally put ashore after spending thirty-six hours cooped up aboard ship.

On the 16th Skerrett's men began their march towards Seville, sweating and labouring beneath the hot summer sun until on August 24th they located the enemy and during a night fight, launched at one hour before midnight, they put to flight the French outposts at St Lucar la Major.

With pressure increasing upon him, Soult was finally forced to abandon the siege of Cadiz altogether and on August 25th, after a siege of almost two and a half years, he abandoned the works in front of the place and began to retire. On August 26th Skerrett's force attacked Seville. During the fighting the grenadier companies of the First Guards and some Spanish troops stormed the gate of the suburb of Triana, driving the enemy before them. The French force consisted of some eight battalions of infantry and two regiments of cavalry but when the Guards burst in upon their positions they were soon retreating headlong down the road to Cordoba, leaving behind them their baggage, accumulated plunder and 200 prisoners. Peregrine Maitland, Lieutenant Colonel Colquitt and Captain Thomas, all of the First Guards, were mentioned in Skerrett's despatch.

On September 11th the four other companies of the 3rd Battalion First Guards, left behind in Cadiz, reached Seville after an exhausting march across flat, burnt country, all the time in the shimmering September sun, to rejoin their comrades of the battalion that had helped take Seville on August 26th. These companies were then ordered by Wellington to march north to join the main Allied army. The march undertaken by the First Guards is certainly worthy of note. Starting on September 30th at Seville they marched via Truxillo, Villafranca, Guarema and Medellin. The weather was still very hot and the roads long and dusty but the Guards, in spite of their heavy packs and thick uniforms, kept up a good pace and by October 18th they had reached Talavera, after a march of 404 miles, an incredible achievement. A week later, the 3rd Battalion First Guards was detached from Skerrett's command and attached to Cole's 4th Division which formed part of Hill's corps, then positioned near Madrid.

Thus, with the 3rd Battalion First Guards now returned from the defence of Cadiz, all three battalions of Foot Guards in the Peninsula were once again serving in the main theatre of war as Wellington prepared for the advance on Madrid.

NOTES

[1] John Stepney Cowell, *Leaves from the Diary of an Officer of the Guards*, (London, 1854), 199.

[2] Major General Sir Frederick Maurice, *The History of the Scots Guards, from 1642 to 1914*, (London, 1934), i. 356.

[3] Stepney Cowell, *Leaves from the Diary*, 206.

[4] John Mills, January 12th 1812.

[5] Stepney Cowell, *Leaves from the Diary*, 212. John Mills (January 12th 1812) also remarks that he got his feet wet when starting which made him uncomfortable for the remainder of his spell of duty in the trenches.

[6] Maurice, *Scots Guards*, i. 357-358.

[7] Stepney Cowell, *Leaves from the Diary*, 213-214.

[8] John Mills, January 12th 1812.

[9] Ibid. January 12th 1812.

[10] John Mills, Espeja, January 29th 1812. George Bowles, of the Coldstream, writes that on the night of the 18th he occupied 'a warm berth', all the time under fire during which time he was bruised on his shoulder by a splinter. The Earl of Malmesbury, *A Series of Letters of the First Earl of Malmesbury, his Family and Friends from 1745 to 1820.* (London, 1870) ii. p.257.

[11] Maurice, *Scots Guards*, i. 358.

[12] Stepney Cowell, *Leaves from the Diary*, 253.

[13] John Mills, La Para, 18th March 1812.

SALAMANCA TO BURGOS

On June 13th Wellington, having concentrated the main body of his army around Ciudad Rodrigo, began his advance on Madrid. His force, totalling around 43,000 men, moving forward in three columns and four days later entered Salamanca. The Guards crossed the River Tormes on the 17th and along with the rest of the army took up a position to the east of the city on the San Christobal ridge, forcing Marmont to withdraw his forces - consisting of two divisions - from the city after leaving behind garrisons in the three forts that commanded the bridge over the River Tormes. These forts were situated virtually inside the city and as John Mills, of the Coldstream, wrote:

It was somewhat curious to see the French in possession of one part of the town, whilst we were walking about the other as if nothing had happened....the Forts are too strong to take by storm; we threw up some works last night, and I suppose shall get them tomorrow. They fire at anything they see, and shot Lord Wellington's orderly's horse.[1]

Mills' optimism as to the taking of the forts was somewhat misplaced, however. Wellington himself had hoped to take them within four days of his arrival in the city but they did not capitulate until June 27th after a prolonged period of resistance, Soon after the fall of the forts, Sir Thomas Graham's health broke down and command of the 1st Division passed to General H. Campbell. Command of the Brigade of Guards fell to Colonel The Hon. T. Fermor, of the Third Guards whilst command of the 3rd Battalion of that regiment fell once again to Lieutenant Colonel Guise.

On the day after the fall of the forts a large celebration was held in the cathedral at Salamanca which was attended by Wellington and his general officers. There followed in the evening a firework display whilst in the streets women lit bonfires made from chairs and baskets whilst children danced the Bolero in groups. A Ball was also given by Wellington to which all the officers of the Guards were invited and by all accounts a splendid time was had by all as British, Portuguese and Spanish officers danced the night away.

During the next few days there followed a series of marches, counter-marches and manoeuvres as Marmont sought to sever Wellington's line of communications. In fact, on July 16th at

Castrejon there ensued some confused skirmishing during which both Wellington and Beresford were almost captured by the French, both being forced to draw their swords before galloping away to make good their escape. These marches certainly proved exhausting for all concerned as the hot weather and vast, dusty openness of the campaigning country made life hard, as John Mills wrote:

The whole of the country between this [Medina Del Campo] and Salamanca is a vast plain, covered as far as the horizon with corn; the crops as fine as ever I saw. There is hardly a tree, and the inhabitants make use of straw instead. It is a shocking bad campaigning country at this time of year. For there being no trees there can be no shade and I assure you I am quite burnt up. I have been but one night in a house since the 1st of June. We are marching in such heavy columns that it is impossible to find houses for us. But at this present moment I envy not any Prince in Christendom for the sun is intense, and I have discovered two very nice rooms in a ruined convent into which I have stowed myself. It is very near the camp but the exterior appearance promised so little that no one thought it worthwhile to go in; how completely all luxury is comparative.[2]

By this time both armies were marching parallel and in full view of each other as they tried to outmarch one another, as Surgeon Good, of the Third Guards, relates:

At daylight we expected to be wakened by the rude sound of warlike implements but all was quiet. We were forming lines and otherwise getting ready, when we saw the black columns of the approaching enemy, they came on by beat of drum like locusts, covering the surface of the earth. They did not march direct to us but moved over some rising ground to our right for the purpose of turning it. To accommodate them we turned too and thus the two armies marched parallel with each other for many leagues, a thing seldom seen.[3]

John Aitchison, of the Third Guards, also mentioned this remarkable spectacle in his diary:

As the enemy continued to advance on the high ground the British army moved forward by the road in a parallel direction, and for the space of three hours there was the most beautiful movements perhaps ever witnessed of two armies of 40,000 men each trying to arrive at a certain point first. The skirmishers close on the flank of the column engaged - on reaching the village Babila Fuente the advance of the enemy halted and began to cannonade from the hill above it - they threw a great number of shot and shells at the column in passing but with almost no effect.[4]

On July 21st the Guards bivouacked by the side of the River Tormes before resuming their march at dusk that evening. Shortly afterwards they forded the river at Santa Marta and camped for the night a short distance from it. As fires were lit and meals cooked dark clouds began to gather overhead and as the moon began to disappear the rumbles of distant thunder was heard as flashes of lightning lit up the sky as if mother nature was laying down a barrage of her own. As the troops donned greatcoats and oilskin covers for their shakos the clouds opened, a gentle trickle at first and then an almighty downpour which lasted throughout the night. Flashes of lightning illuminated the camp and at one point a bolt of lightning struck the earth in the middle of the horses of a squadron of the 5th Dragoon Guards, scattering them and causing them to charge over their riders as they galloped around in a panic. Some twenty men were wounded in this way and fifty horses were missing at roll call the following morning. John Aitchison, of the Third Guards, left a graphic account of the storm on the eve of the battle of Salamanca:

As we crossed the river the sky became very dark. There was every appearance of a great storm. The lightning began as we ascended the heights. The flashes, which were very frequent, served to guide us to our proper position and it seemed as if the fire was sent by heaven to assist our righteous cause - here was a grand and imposing spectacle that ever was witnessed - upwards of 20,000 men formed in line and in close columns of brigades within musket shot, only seen by the flashes of lightning, and nothing heard but the occasional report of a gun at a distance fired upon the enemy from our advance.[5]

At length, however, dawn broke, the sun came up and the troops were warmed by its rays, cheering them up as they cooked breakfast. The storm would later be held up as a good omen, particularly on the eve of Waterloo when a similar storm raged.

The battlefield of Salamanca is dominated by two very distinctive-shaped hills, the first, a rounded ridge to the north-east of the village of Los Arapiles called the Lesser Arapil, and the second, called the Greater Arapil, a box-shaped hill some 100 feet high about half a mile to the south of the Lesser Arapil. These two hills lay in the middle of a plain about nine miles long, stretching from the small village of Calvarasa de Arriba in the east, to Miranda de Azan in the west. The village of Los Arapiles lay just to the left of centre of the plain.

Soon after dawn on the 22nd Marmont looked towards the Ciudad Rodrigo road and saw a long column of British troops marching along it. He assumed that this was the British rearguard and immediately gave orders for an advance in order to cut off these troops. What he saw, in fact, was Wellington's advanced guard. As Marmont's men hurried to their left Wellington, upon seeing the manoeuvre, quickly ordered a Portuguese brigade forward and soon a race developed between them and the French, the result ending with the French occupation of the Greater Arapil and the Portuguese the Lesser Arapil.

The Guards, along with the rest of the 1st Division and the Light Division, occupied the extreme left of Wellington's line directly opposite the small village of Calvarassa de Arriba, where they kept a watchful eye on the French divisions of Foy and Ferrey, Meanwhile, Marmont, now atop the Greater Arapil, spotted a cloud of dust rising from behind the Lesser Arapil moving in the direction of Ciudad Rodrigo. This movement seemed to confirm his suspicions that Wellington intended to retreat along the Rodrigo road but he was to be proved fatally incorrect. The troops moving out of sight of his position were, in fact, those of Edward Pakenham's 3rd Division which Wellington had brought forward to Aldea Tejada to protect his right flank against any French attack. However, Marmont had already given orders for the divisions of Thomieres, Maucune and Clausel to march west to cut off the Ciudad Rodrigo road.

As morning turned into afternoon the long, dusty-blue columns of French infantry lumbered into life and were soon trekking west in a line spanning almost four miles from the head of the leading column right back to Calvarassa de Arriba. As they continued their movement it soon became apparent that Thomieres column, in the lead, had opened up quite an distance between itself and the next column, that of Maucune's, a fatal gap that did not go unnoticed by a group of British officers, busy eating their lunch atop the Lesser Arapil. Among them was Wellington and as he peered through his telescope he suddenly exclaimed, "By God! That will do," and throwing away the leg of chicken he was munching upon he mounted his horse and galloped away to Aldea Tejada to order forward Pakenham's 3rd Division with instructions to `drive them to the devil.' What followed was one of the most devastating attacks of the Peninsular War as waves of red-jacketed infantry tore into Thomieres' division, killing him and either killing or wounding over 2,000 of his 4,500-strong division, as well as taking every single one of their guns. As is often said Wellington defeated 40,000 Frenchmen in just forty minutes.

The Guards played no part in the main fighting but the light companies of the Guards were thrown into the village of

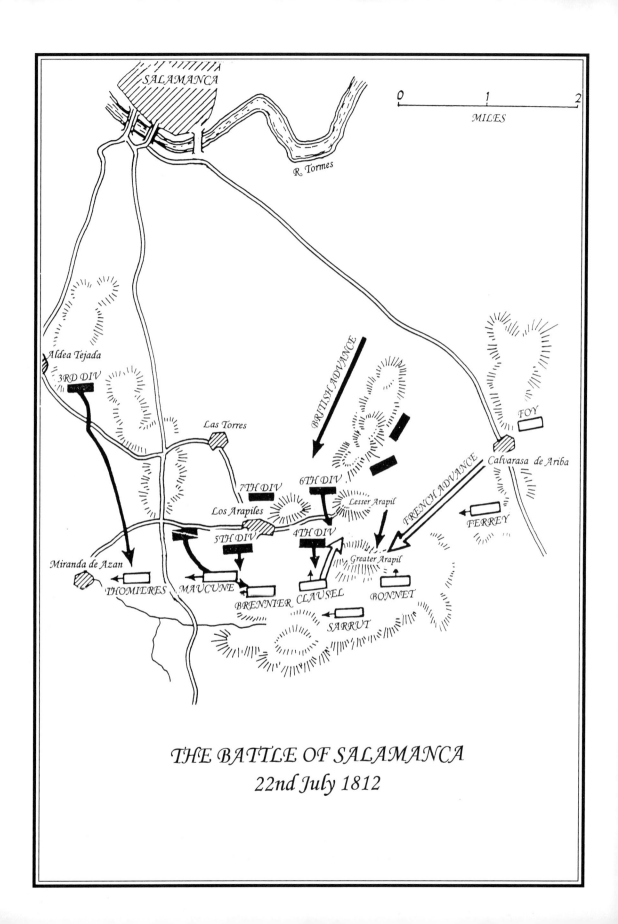

SALAMANCA

R. Tormes

0   1   2
MILES

Aldea Tejada

3RD DIV

BRITISH ADVANCE

FOY

Las Torres

7TH DIV

6TH DIV

Lesser Arapil

FRENCH ADVANCE

Calvarasa de Ariba

FERREY

Los Arapiles

5TH DIV

4TH DIV

Greater Arapil

Miranda de Azan

THOMIERES

MAUCUNE

BRENNIER CLAUSEL

BONNET

SARRUT

THE BATTLE OF SALAMANCA
22nd July 1812

Los Arapiles which acted as a pivot for Wellington's attack. The Guards there came under the command of Lieutenant Colonel Woodford of the Coldstream Guards and in spite of repeated French attacks they held the village for the remainder of the day. The fighting here was not dissimilar from that at Fuentes de Oñoro as the streets of Los Arapiles were and still are very narrow and there was a good deal of hand-to-hand fighting as the French tried in vain to snatch the village from the Guards.

As the fighting involving the Guards revolved only around the village we need not dwell too long on the great battle itself, suffice to say that there was a great deal of bitter fighting later in the day, particularly following Clausel's counter-attack. This attack, in fact, almost turned the battle but Wellington, as ever, was on the spot and he deployed the 6th Division and a Portuguese brigade to meet the threat and restore the balance of the fighting in his favour. Following the failure of this attack the French, having seen five of their eight divisions smashed by Wellington's men, began to slowly break and then begin to retreat towards the east, Ferrey's division acting as a rearguard as the battered remnants of the French army made good their retreat. However, they only escaped owing to a blunder on the part of a Spanish commander, Carlos de Espana who, despite being ordered to hold the bridge over the Tormes at Alba de Tormes, failed to do so, thus enabling the French to escape.

It had been a hard fight. Of a total of 47,000 men the French had suffered 15,000 casualties, including 7,000 prisoners. The French also lost three generals killed and four wounded as well as a further 136 officer casualties. Marmont himself was seriously wounded by a cannonball early in the battle and Bonnet and Clausel were wounded also. As well as Thomieres, Ferrey was killed. British casualties numbered about 5,000 of which a third were Portuguese. The Third Guards suffered one man killed and Captain White and twenty rank and file wounded. Two men were missing. The Coldstream lost seven men killed and Ensign Howard and twenty-two men wounded. Eighteen were listed as missing. The Guards' casualties came from the light companies only, who were engaged in the fighting in the village of Los Arapiles. The conduct of the Guards during the battle was praised by Wellington who said in his despatch:

I must also mention Lieutenant Colonel Woodford, commanding the light battalion of the brigade of Guards, who, supported by two companies of the Fusiliers, under the command of Captain Crowder, maintained the village of Arapiles against all the efforts of the enemy.[6]

News of Wellington's victory at Salamanca spread quickly throughout Europe raising his reputation as a military commander to that of Marlborough and nailing the widely-held French belief that he was simply an over-cautious, defensive general. From now on French commanders would never again risk any speculative offensive actions against him. It also sent alarm bells ringing in Paris and amongst the French field armies in the Peninsula who could no longer consider themselves unbeatable, a fact that was to be all too painfully reinforced when Napoleon began his fateful invasion of Russia the same year.

Following the disaster at Salamanca Clausel took his shattered army away to the east towards Arevalo and then, despite Joseph's orders to join him for the defence of Madrid, he turned north for Valladolid. Wellington followed him, although he was somewhat hindered by the fact that he had sent his baggage down along the road to Ciudad Rodrigo prior to the battle and was forced to halt before Valladolid in order to wait for them to come up again, provisions being in short supply.

Once resupplied, Wellington now had to decide whether to continue his pursuit of Clausel or turn south to confront Joseph's Army of the Centre, now positioned at Madrid. As Clausel's army was in no condition to fight again Wellington chose the second course, after all, not only was Joseph's army still a threat, but the Allied occupation of Madrid would have enormous moral and political consequences for the Allies. Therefore, whilst Clinton's 6th Division remained to keep an eye on Clausel Wellington turned south towards Madrid which he entered on August 12th after meeting no opposition whatsoever. Joseph, in fact, had retreated towards Valencia leaving behind 2,500 men and 180 guns to be taken by Wellington in Madrid.

The people of Madrid, of course, were overjoyed to see Wellington enter their city and afforded him and his men a tumultuous welcome. The city was illuminated every night and during the army's stay it became one long gala, the houses hung with silk and gold curtains. On the 16th a magnificent ball was held which was attended by so many people that George Bowles says he was almost 'squeezed to death.'[7]

Joseph's army, meanwhile, short of food and other supplies, headed east and suffered not only from these shortages but also from the constant harassing raids of the Spanish guerillas. With Joseph now at Valencia and having secured Madrid Wellington decided it was time to turn his attention once again to Clausel whose army had recovered slightly from its defeat at Salamanca and now numbered 24,000 men. In spite of this, however, he had not recovered sufficient confidence to make a stand and upon being informed of Wellington's approach he ordered a withdrawal towards Burgos which he garrisoned with 2,000 men under General Dubreton whilst he himself pulled the bulk of his force back across the Ebro river.

The siege of Burgos was destined to become probably the most unhappiest of Wellington's operations in the Peninsula. In fact, all of the major sieges carried out by his army were distinctly wretched affairs but at least those at Ciudad Rodrigo and Badajoz were successful. Burgos was not to go the way of those particular places, however, although the Guards were to gain great credit during the operations. The Coldstream Guards suffered a great loss even before they arrived at Burgos, however, with the death of Colonel Richard Hulse, who was commanding a brigade. He died of low fever at Arevalo at the beginning of September.

The city of Burgos was not fortified in the same way as Ciudad Rodrigo and Badajoz. There were no walls around the place but it was dominated by a castle perched on a hill overlooking the city and commanding all approaches. This was the object of Wellington's attention. Protected by two lines of defences, the castle was a difficult although not exactly formidable proposition but it did have one major weakness, namely a hornwork situated upon a hill called the heights of San Miguel which overlooked the castle and its defences.

Wellington obviously considered Burgos a not too formidable proposition as he began the siege without the 3rd and Light Divisions, veterans of the two previous sieges and both tried and proven units. Instead, for the siege of Burgos Wellington decided to use the 1st, 5th, 6th and 7th Divisions, a decision based partly on the fact that the 1st Division had complained to Wellington that it had been 'ill-used' at Salamanca - only the light companies of the Guards had really been involved in the fighting during the battle - and had missed out on the greater share of glory there. Following this complaint he agreed to put it right at the first opportunity and therefore the 1st Division was given the honour of leading the assault on Burgos. The decision to use these four divisions ultimately backfired as only the Guards were to come out of the episode with any credit while the more experienced stormers of the 3rd and Light Divisions were left kicking their heels in frustration.

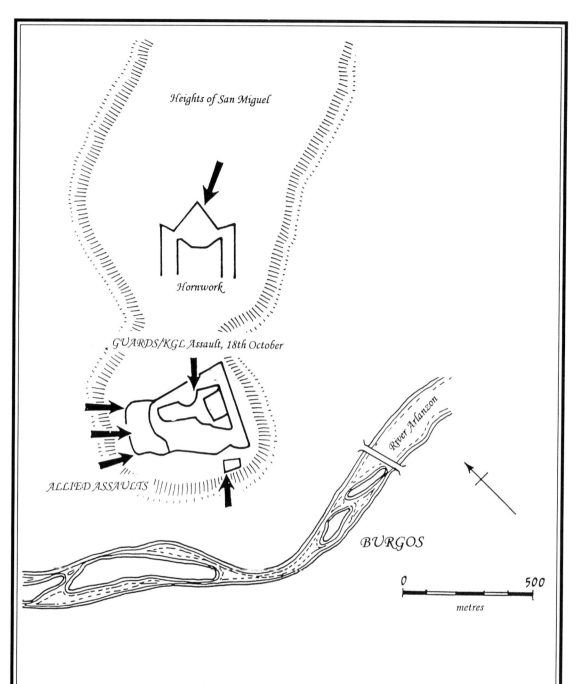

Heights of San Miguel

Hornwork

GUARDS/KGL Assault, 18th October

River Arlanzon

ALLIED ASSAULTS

BURGOS

0   500
metres

THE SIEGE OF BURGOS
September-October 1812
Showing the various Allied assaults

Also, the siege was handicapped from the outset owing to a lack of guns and ammunition. He had with him only three heavy guns and as the supply of ammunition dwindled his gunners were forced to resort to collecting and re-using cannonballs fired by the French. And matters were not helped by the usual woefully insufficient number of engineers and adequate siege tools.

Nevertheless, the siege got off to a promising start when, on the night of September 19th, the hornwork on the heights of San Miguel was successfully - if not satisfactorily - stormed by the flank companies 1/42nd, 1/24th and 1/79th regiments. Whilst other Allied infantry gave covering fire Pack's Portuguese brigade was to attack the angles of the hornwork, the light companies were ordered to try and gain entry through the gorge. The stormers crept forward in silence but surprise was virtually impossible to achieve owing to the moon which shone brightly above, revealing the attackers to the alert French defenders. There was to be no artillery support either, which would probably have given the game away completely anyway. The Portuguese were flung back in disarray by the concentrated French musketry but the light companies, although suffering from the guns inside the fortress, stormed through the palisades and forced their way into the hornwork, chasing out the defenders at bayonet point. The 1st Division had shown Wellington that like the 3rd and Light Divisions it too was capable of storming a fort, although the whole business cost the Allies dear. The French suffered 198 casualties compared to the Allies 421.

With the hornwork now in his hands the reduction of the castle should have been a formality. However, as we have seen, Wellington possessed no heavy guns and so it was to be the sheer blood and guts of the infantry upon which the attack was to depend.

On September 23rd the first assault on the castle was made at its north-western wall. Once again, no attempt at breaching the defences had been made but instead the infantry were simply flung forward and the result was as disastrous as it was predictable with almost half the 400 men involved in the attack becoming casualties. Six days later a huge mine was exploded beneath the first line of the French defences, heralding yet another attack by the Allies. Once again, however, the assault failed.

By now shot, shell and powder had begun to run short and fresh supplies were slow to come up. On October 1st

Wellington suffered another setback when two of his three heavy guns were put out of action and as if things were not already bad enough the weather turned, the skies opening up to turn the Allied trenches into boggy, water-filled ditches. The conditions in the trenches were all too reminiscent of those at Badajoz where the earth refused to pile up but instead ran away in streams of mud. Life in the trenches was unpleasant enough at the best of times but when the rain became heavy and constant discipline began to deteriorate. There was a great deal of moaning and grumbling amongst Wellington's infantry and on at least one occasion the men refused to carry out their duties. Indeed, only the Guards came through the ordeal with any credit. 'The Guards,' one historian wrote, 'because of their internal discipline and *esprit de corps* could be relied to carry out the work regardless of circumstances, but others considered the work beneath them.'[8] However, even for them the siege of Burgos was a miserable time, and when Ensign John Rous, of the Coldstream, wrote to his father on November 1st he said that he had never passed a more unpleasant month in his life, being in the trenches twelve hours at a time where he had the pleasure of being shot at without being able to return the compliment.[9]

On October 4th a second mine was exploded and an attack was carried out against the second line of defences. The attack was successful, although some 190 men were either killed or wounded in the attempt. Captain Clitheroe, of the Third Guards, was severely wounded whilst the light company of the regiment suffered a further three men killed or wounded. Later that night, however, Dubreton ordered a sortie against the besiegers' works during which much damage was done, trenches filled in and valuable entrenching tools carried off.[10] Having carried out their 'mischief' they retired having lost 17 killed and 21 wounded, whilst the Allies suffered 142 casualties.

The siege was making painfully slow progress to the extent that Wellington, on October 7th, issued an order severely criticising the troops in the trenches, although he did point out that he was, 'happy to make an exception in favour of the Guards, who, he is informed, have invariably performed their duty, as they have every other in the army, in the most exemplary manner.'[11]

The day after Wellington issued his order he suffered yet another blow following a second French sortie on the Allied trenches. The sortie was driven back but with great loss of life and amongst those killed was Major Somers-Cocks, one of Wellington's bright lights and a soldier of whom he said had the potential to become one of the greatest generals in the British army. The

Commander-in-Chief took Cocks' death rather badly and is said to have wept at his funeral.

With the death of Cocks, and with conditions seemingly stacked against him, Wellington's heart seemed to go out of the siege. Even his own officers began to doubt the wisdom of his attacking Burgos. 'This is one of the longest jobs the noble Marquis has had in hand some time,' wrote George Bowles, 'and, much as I *revere* him, I must say that in this case he has shown rather more of a quality nearly allied to obstinacy than is to be wished.'[12]

On October 18th, one final effort was made to carry the castle of Burgos. Whilst a detachment of the King's German Legion attacked the northern breach a detachment of 200 Guards attacked the western breach. The signal for the attack to begin was the exploding of a mine beneath a church at the opposite end of the castle and as the explosion sent earth and rubble whirling into the air the Guards scrambled over through the breach in the first line of defences and over the unbreached second line. The French defenders were hustled out at bayonet point but as the Guards stormed onwards their numbers were quickly reduced as the enemy rushed reinforcements forward who poured out a galling fire of grape shot and musketry at their assailants.

However, with no support forthcoming from the Allied trenches the Guards were forced to withdraw to the outer line of defences, fighting furiously all the way. To the north the King's German Legion met with a similar result and so the day ended with the Coldstream losing 4 officers and 60 men dead and wounded[13] and the Third Guards 2 officers and 25 men dead and wounded[14] on the bloodstained ground they had fought so hard to hold. The dead Coldstream officers were Captain Edward Harvey and Ensign Wentworth Noel Burgess. The attack had failed, but as Wellington pointed out in his despatch a week later:

It is impossible to represent in adequate terms the conduct of the Guards and the King's German Legion upon this occasion. And I am quite satisfied that if it had been possible to maintain the posts which they had gained with so much gallantry these troops would have maintained them.[15]

Nevertheless, the attack had failed and with it ended the siege of Burgos for on October 21st Wellington decided to abandon the siege and depart what he called, 'this damn place', his army withdrawing in silence with straw wrapped around the wheels of their wagons, guns and gun carriages. The retreat had not come a moment too soon, for even as the dejected Allied soldiers peered over their shoulders to curse the miserable place for a last time French forces were stirring elsewhere in the country as they began their march towards Burgos.

Indeed, the French force under Souham - he had succeeded Clausel - was advancing from the north-east whilst Joseph, having been joined by Soult, was marching towards Madrid from the east, thus leaving Wellington with little option but to fall back upon Salamanca. Wellington's retreat was not without danger either, for having got his force across the River Arlanzon on October 22nd his rearguard was pressed so hard that it was forced to turn and fight at Venta del Pozo on the 23rd.

The one piece of good news came on October 24th with the arrival at Torquemada of a reinforcement which included the 1st Battalion First Guards which had landed at Corunna. The march from Corunna must have been rather melancholy for them as the Guards retraced the steps taken during the retreat to Corunna in the terrible winter of 1809. Indeed, the signs of destruction, particularly at Astorga, Lugo and Benavente, were much in evidence even after three and a half years. On October 23rd the battalion reached Ampadia where it was received by seven men dressed in colourful jackets and silk brocade and with ribbons in their hair. Music was played and as the Guards entered the town the men danced before them, the mayor, priests and alcaldes turning out also to greet them.[16]

But even as the 1st Battalion First Guards arrived at Torquemada the event was soured somewhat by the disgraceful behaviour of some elements of the army that broke into and looted the wine cellars in the town and proceeded to get blind drunk with the result that throughout the night of the 24th a large part of the army was staggering around the streets of the town in a stupor and was totally unfit to defend itself against any enemy attack. It was just as well, therefore, that the French, having hotly pursued Wellington since Burgos, stopped to do likewise a few miles away and were also too drunk to continue the chase.

On October 25th Wellington's rearguard clashed once again with the pursuing French on the Carrion river but as soon as he crossed the Pisguera river his engineers blew up the bridges over the river at Valladolid and Tordesillas and his much-harassed army was able to grab two days respite from their pursuing enemy. However, the Allied army was not safe yet, for on October 29th a group of about 50 enterprising and extremely brave French soldiers swam naked across the river Douro at Tordesillas, all the time under fire, and after having driven back a picquet of Germans proceeded to build a pontoon bridge forcing Wellington to resume his retreat.

By now Souham's pursuit had lost some of it's momentum and the Allied army was able to continue its march at a more leisurely pace. However, when Wellington received news that Joseph and Soult were advancing in force upon Madrid he made the painful decision to abandon the Spanish capital and fall back towards Salamanca. Accordingly, Hill left Madrid on October 31st and on November 8th Wellington joined him at his old position around Salamanca. Hill, of course, had with him the 3rd Battalion First Guards which had joined him on October 18th having marched under Skerrett from Cadiz. Here the battalion was temporarily attached to the 4th Division. As we have already seen, this battalion had marched some 400 miles in nineteen days but the retreat from Madrid meant there was to be little respite for them. In fact, by the time Hill's force had reached Salamanca the 3rd Battalion First Guards had marched an astonishing 640 long, hot and dusty miles from Seville, to Talavera, to Madrid and eventually back to Salamanca.[17]

Having arrived at Salamanca the battalion was joined with the 1st Battalion First Guards to form the 1st Guards Brigade under General Howard of the Coldstream. The 1st Battalions of the Coldstream and Third Guards were reconstituted as the 2nd Guards Brigade under Major General the Hon. E. Stopford and the two were immediately formed into the 1st Division which was placed under the command of Lieutenant General the Hon. Sir William Stewart. The following day, November 9th, an order was issued commending the behaviour of the 3rd Battalion First Guards for its conduct during the march to Salamanca:

Lieutenant General Cole requests Colonel Lambert will express his sincere thanks to the Battalion of Guards under his command for their exemplary conduct during the short time they have been attached to the Fourth Division. When straggling and every species of irregularity was committed by the troops, they alone remained uncontaminated, and he trusts that their example may recall the Fourth Division to its former good conduct.[18]

With Wellington now having linked up with Hill, the Allies numbered 52,000 British and Portuguese, 18,000 Spaniards and 100 guns. Meanwhile, Souham had joined forces with

Joseph and Soult, giving the French a combined total of 90,000 men with 120 guns, and when Soult crossed the Tormes on November 13th about three miles above Alba, completely turning Wellington's right flank in the process, Wellington was once again forced to move on. It was just as well that Soult, despite his numerical superiority, did not choose this moment to attack, having acquired a healthy respect for Wellington's men ever since the battle of Albuera the year before, a reputation they had more than enhanced at Salamanca. Instead, Wellington was able to withdraw his army towards Portugal by way of the Ciudad Rodrigo road.

However, if Wellington thought he would be able to make the retreat to Portugal as easy as he had his withdrawal from Salamanca he was very much mistaken. Indeed, the retreat was all too familiar to those who had trudged along the terrible road to Corunna three and a half years earlier. If the cold, biting snows of 1809 were missing on this occasion the torrential rain more than made up for them. The men were thoroughly soaked by the seemingly endless downpours that turned the roads into boggy quagmires. The Commissariat broke down and supplies hard to come by and some 2,000 men were left floundering in the mud to die whilst a further 1,000 were taken prisoner by the French, including General Sir Edward Paget who had only recently arrived in the Peninsula to assume the position of second-in-command of the army. Surgeon Good, of the Third Guards, wrote in his diary:

We marched again at the head of the centre column without breakfast and with little hope of dinner. It had rained all night and our people were wet through and I have never seen them so dispirited. The road was in many places deep in mud, and the wind was perishing cold. The men fell out in numbers, in part from exhaustion having had nothing to eat and in part because they lost their shoes in the mud and broke their feet upon the stones of the road.[19]

John Mills, of the Coldstream, was another who recorded the dreadful conditions during the retreat. Mills' account is also of interest as he is very critical of the Spanish peasantry, so-called allies, but who proved to be as much an enemy as the terrible weather along the way:

The scenes I have witnessed during my journey are all beyond belief. All the sick and wounded were ordered off to make the best of their way here [Salamanca]. I saw a great many who had literally had nothing to eat for three days. Many died and some I saw unable to move, their wounds not dressed for four days, and nothing in the world to eat. You would suppose that the Spaniards would assist them - quite the contrary. They find that there is in fact but little difference between the depredations of a French and an English army; and they are quite tired of us. I never saw anything more different than the reception we meet with now and what it was three months ago. I really have now no hopes, and it is really difficult to say whether they are culpable for not making exertions. They are plundered by both parties and a change is not worth the exertion.[20]

By the time Wellington's army concentrated around Ciudad Rodrigo on November 18th it had suffered as many losses during the retreat as it had done at the battle of Salamanca and it is little wonder that Wellington called it the most agonizing retreat of his career. When the army reached Ciudad Rodrigo Wellington issued an order severely criticising his officers and men for their conduct during the retreat although as at Burgos the Guards were exempt owing to their good behaviour and discipline. As Napier said, when comparing the retreat from Burgos with that to Corunna, 'the reserve and Foot Guards in Moore's campaign, the Light Division and Foot Guards in Wellington's, gave signal proof that it was negligence of discipline, not hardships, that caused the losses in the other regiments.'[21]

The failure of the attempt on Burgos, combined with the miseries of the retreat to Portugal, had taken the gloss off the 1812 campaign which had opened with the taking of the fortresses and had been followed up, of course, with the victory at Salamanca. However, if the year had turned somewhat sour for Wellington he could take much comfort from the fact that even as his men began to drag themselves wearily away from the trenches in front of Burgos, Napoleon's army began its own terrible retreat from Moscow, a retreat which would not end until the shattered remnants of his army had been prodded and pushed at sword point from Russian soil.

After lingering in the vicinity of Ciudad Rodrigo for eight days Wellington's army continued its retreat to Portugal which was reached at the end of November. For the Guards the year ended in winter quarters at Vizeu, which they reached on December 8th, where both the newly formed 1st Guards Brigade and the 2nd Guards Brigade were left to reflect on the coming year when, in spite of the disappointing end to 1812, they could look forward to fighting a French army which had been greatly reduced by the disasters in Russia and would be further reduced as troops were withdrawn from Spain in order to face the growing threat from the Russian, Prussians and Austrians in the north as they advanced through Germany towards France.

As far as the Guards were concerned, the campaign of 1812 was summed up by George Bowles, of the Coldstream, writing home to Lord Fitzharris on December 10th:

We have this year marched upwards of 1,700 miles; and you may form some idea of the severity of our services when I tell you that during that time I have lost *six mules*, who have all but one dropped dead from absolute fatigue (a tolerable expense for a poor man); and my case is by no means singular - the road from Salamanca to Rodrigo is literally strewed. We are allowed 100 dollars per annum to carry the camp kettles, &c., and no tolerable animal can be purchased under that sum, so that it is rather a losing concern. You will hardly believe that in the Coldstream there are only *four* officers who had stood the *whole* campaign, one of whom is your humble servant.[22]

NOTES

[1] John Mills, camp near Salamanca, 18th June 1812.
[2] John Mills, Medina Del Campo, July 5th 1812.
[3] Major General Sir Frederick Maurice, *The History of the Scots Guards, from 1642 to 1914*, (London, 1934), i. 362.
[4] W.F.K. Thompson, (Ed), *An Ensign in the Peninsular War; the Letters of John Aitchison*, (London, 1981), 173. George Bowles also mentions the extraordinary spectacle of English and French armies quietly camped on a plain near each other on two occassions, once before July 6th and again on July 20th. The Earl of Malmesbury, *A Series of Letters of the First Earl of Malmesbury, His Family and Friends, from 1745 to 1820*, (London, 1870), ii. 293 & 297.
[5] Thompson, *An Ensign in the Peninsular War*, 175.
[6] Colonel Daniel Mackinnon, *Origins and Services of the Coldstream Guards*, (London, 1833), ii. 176.
[7] Malmesbury, *A Series of Letters*, ii. 306-307.
[8] Jac Weller, *Wellington in the Peninsula*, (London, 1962), 236n.
[9] Ian Fletcher, (Ed), *A Guards Officer in the Peninsula; The Peninsular War letters of John Rous, Coldstream Guards, 1812-1814*, (Tunbridge Wells, 1992), 37.
[10] Entrenching tools in the Peninsula were in such short supply that defending commanders, Barrie at Ciudad Rodrigo, Phillipon at Badajoz, and Rey at San Sebastian, offered bounties for them.
[11] General Order, October 7th 1812.
[12] Malmesbury, *A Series of Letters*, ii.316-317.
[13] Mackinnon, *Coldstream Guards*, ii. 179.
[14] Maurice, *Scots Guards*, i. 378.

[15] Wellington, *The Despatches of Field Marshal the Duke of Wellington*, (London, 1837-39), vi. 134.

[16] Lieutenant General Sir F.W. Hamilton, *The Origin and History of the First or Grenadier Guards*, (London, 1874) ii. 438.

[17] The full march of the 3rd Battalion First Guards is recorded in detail in Hamilton, *Grenadier Guards*, ii. 434 and 440-441.

[18] Ibid. ii. 442.

[19] Maurice, *Scots Guards*, i. 369-370.

[20] John Mills, Salamanca, November 3rd 1812.

[21] Sir W.F.P. Napier, *History of the War in the Peninsula and in the South of France, from the year 1807 to 1814*, (London, 1876).

[22] Malmesbury, *A Series of Letters,* ii. 332. There were indeed only four captains who served the whole year, the others being George Croften, Thomas Sowerby and Thomas Steele. There were, however, five ensigns who served throughout the whole year, George Percival, George baynes, John Stepney Cowell, John Mills and Frederick Vachell.

TO THE PYRENEES

With the Allied army in winter quarters, and with the arrival in the main theatre of war of the 1st and 3rd Battalions First Guards, it will be useful to take a look at their organisation. The four battalions of Foot Guards were organised into two brigades: the 1st Brigade of Guards consisted of the 1st and 3rd Battalions of the First Guards, under the command of Major General Howard, the 2nd Brigade of Guards consisted of the 1st Battalion Coldstream and the 1st Battalion Third Guards, under the command of Major General the Hon. E. Stopford. The other brigades of the 1st Division consisted of the 1st, 2nd and 5th Battalions of the King's German Legion, under Major General Lowe, and the 1st and 2nd Battalions of the King's Light German Legion, under Colonel Halkett. The 1st Division itself was placed under the command of Lieutenant General the Hon. Sir William Stewart.

Unfortunately, the Guards had not long been in their winter quarters at Vizeu when they were hit by a severe outbreak of low fever. The outbreak was particularly rampant amongst the 1st Brigade of Guards, so much so in fact, that by in the first seven months of 1813 the brigade had lost no less than 800 men dead.[1] Although the light company of the 3rd Battalion First Guards had only eight men on the sick list at the beginning of February 1813 the rest of the two battalions were being decimated, and not even a change of billets to some neighbouring villages helped matters. Captain George Bowles, of the Coldstream Guards, wrote on February 14th 1813:

The mortality in our army is beyond anything ever known in this or any other country. The deaths for the last six weeks have averaged more than 800 per week, and are rather increasing than otherwise...The most extraordinary part of this lamentable state is, that those troops which have lately joined and gone through no hardships of any kind are even more sickly than those who have served the whole campaign. The first brigade of Guards is nearly non-effective, and will not, I fear, be able to take the field this year. What this is owing to, God only knows; our cantonments are very tolerably good, rations excellent, and clothing new from head to foot. The prevailing disorder is a kind of low fever, which usually proves fatal in a few weeks.[2]

Eventually, Wellington ordered the 1st Brigade of Guards to march to Oporto in the hope that a change of air might do them good. This meant, of course, that the First Guards had still to see much serious fighting in the Peninsula - Corunna and Barrosa excepted - but instead had seen two retreats, to Corunna in 1808-09 and to Portugal from Salamanca following the Burgos debacle. The tally might be put at three if one includes the march to Oporto. Little wonder that the other Guards battalions began to consider their presence with the army as a bad omen![3]

The 1st Brigade of Guards began its march to Oporto on March 26th and 27th and arrived at its destination on April 1st. The Guards were housed in the St Ovadio Barracks whose large spacious surroundings had an immediate beneficial effect on the men. There was little rise in the number of men in the hospital and soon the numbers began to fall, although towards the end of March there were still only 355 and 430 men fit for duty in the 1st and 3rd Battalions First Guards respectively and it would not be until June 24th that the 1st Brigade of Guards left Oporto to rejoin the main body of Wellington's army.[4]

Wellington, meanwhile, had been contemplating his strategy for the campaign of 1813. He had received reinforcements from England which brought his army up to a total of 80,000 men of whom 52,000 were British. His plan involved another advance on Burgos, by-passing central Spain and then moving on towards the Pyrenees and, finally, France. Deception and speed of movement and concentration were the key elements of Wellington's plan. He needed the French to believe that his main thrust would come through central Spain via Salamanca which was achieved when he himself moved on the place with Hill who commanded 30,000 men and six brigades of cavalry. Wellington, however, stayed with Hill only a short time in order to deceive the French into believing that this was his main attack whereas, in fact, Graham's corps, some 66,000 strong, would represent his main thrust, crossing the Douro, and marching through northern Portugal and the Tras-os-Montes before swinging down behind the French defences. Wellington would soon leave Hill to join him. Another part of Wellington's plan involved shifting his supply bases as he advanced from Lisbon to northern Spain so as not to over-extend his lines of communication.

The advance was planned for May 22nd and it must have been quite a poignant moment as Wellington, upon crossing the Portuguese border, turned and raising himself in his saddle, he waved his hat in the air and exclaimed, 'Farewell, Portugal, for I shall never see you again.'[5]

To the north, meanwhile, the 2nd Brigade of Guards had begun its march with Graham's corps, tramping through the

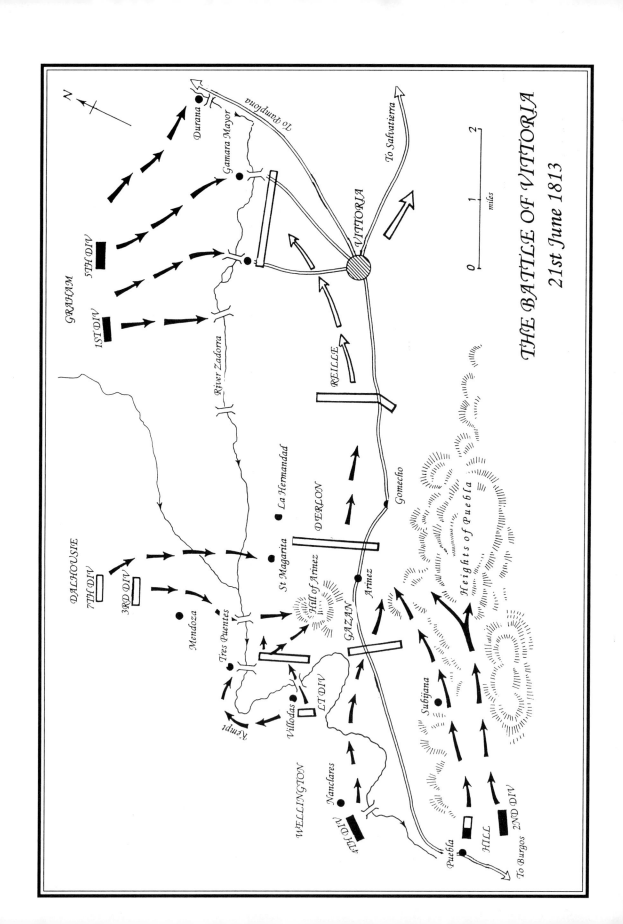

THE BATTLE OF VITTORIA
21st June 1813

N

miles
0 1 2

To Salvatierra

Durana
Gamara Mayor
To Pamplona
VITTORIA

GRAHAM
5TH DIV
1ST DIV

River Zadorra

REILLE

DALHOUSIE
7TH DIV
3RD DIV

Mendoza
Tres Puentes

St Magarita
La Hermandad
D'ERLON

Gomecho

Heights of Puebla

Hill of Arinez
GAZAN
Arinez

Kempt
Villodas
LT DIV

WELLINGTON
Nanclares

Subijana

4TH DIV
Puebla
To Burgos
HILL
2ND DIV

harsh mountainous country of the Tras-os-Montes. The morale of the army was high, however, and as the men had enjoyed a prolonged period of recuperation following the retreat of the previous winter they were in good health.[6] It was just as well that they were as the rugged mountainous country through which they soon found themselves marching tested all their powers of endurance. Indeed, the route they took was considered impassable by the French. Heavy rain made the march worse, particularly when Graham's corps had to cross the River Esla which flowed south into the Douro. The river was quickly swollen by the rains and when the infantry crossed each man was forced to grip the stirrups of the cavalry in order assist in crossing. In fact, so much equipment was lost that for weeks afterwards whenever an item was found to be missing when checked the men simply put it down to the crossing of the Esla! Eventually, a pontoon bridge was built and the corps able to continue its advance.

By June 3rd Wellington had his entire force, by now numbering about 100,000 men, on the northern side of the Douro, completely surprising the French who, realising too late that Salamanca was not to be the object of his advance, retreated hastily to the north and began to try and concentrate their own forces. Wellington, however, was in no mood to allow this to happen and as a result the French were forced to abandon Burgos which they blew up on June 13th. As Joseph fell back he drew up his army on the line of the Ebro river but once again was forced to retreat as Graham hustled him from his position.[7] Finally, on June 19th, the French reached the town of Vittoria, the centre of Joseph's communications, and it was here that he decided to stand and confront the advancing Allies.

Joseph had with him some 66,000 men against Wellington's force of 79,000, although messengers had been despatched to Clausel telling him to move on Vittoria with the utmost haste. Clausel, however, would not be able to reach Vittoria until June 22nd by which time it would be too late.

When Wellington attacked on the morning on June 21st, moving forward from the west along the valley of the Zadorra, the Brigade of Guards was still marching forward as part of Graham's corps which was hurrying forward to cut off Joseph's escape route to France. The Guards remained throughout the day as spectators, for after toiling through the mountains north of Vittoria as the battle unfolded and raged in the valley below them they, along with the rest of Graham's corps, were only participants in the battle insofar as their advance threatened Joseph's rear who, upon realising just what was happening, ordered an immediate retreat. This is not to say, of course, that Graham's emergence from the hills to the rear of the French army was the deciding factor in the battle of Vittoria. No, the French army had already begun to crumble at around 5pm, but his arrival on the battlefield did help precipitate the total collapse and rout of the French who fled through Vittoria in sheer panic, abandoning the whole of their baggage train as well as 415 caissons, 151 of their 153 guns and 100 waggons. 2,000 prisoners were taken also.

More incredible, however, was the vast amount of treasure abandoned by Joseph as he fled - he himself was almost taken by the 14th Light Dragoons. The accumulated plunder acquired by him was simply abandoned to the clutches of the astonished Allied soldiers, to which George Bowles testified in a letter written on June 25th:

So complete a *smash* of artillery, stores, baggage, &c. has rarely been witnessed. The booty taken is immense. The military chest, which was full of the late contributions, consisted of nearly 23,000,000 of livres, mostly in specie; some of this was saved, but a good deal found its way into the pockets of the cavalry who took it, and the hussars in particular made large sums. Horses, mules, carriages, barouches, waggons, tumbrils, &c., in a most glorious and absurd state of confusion covered the face of the country around Vittoria, and afforded a scene which completely baffles all my powers of description. The pillage which took place you may easily imagine, and books, papers, linen, clothes, and furniture of every description and sort were seen strewed in all directions. Poor Madame Gazan [wife of the French General Gazan], who had jumped out of her barouche and stuck fast in a field about a hundred yards on one side, had the mortification of seeing the whole of her wardrobe ransacked and dispersed in about ten minutes.[8]

Never before nor since in the history of warfare has such an immense amount of booty been captured by an opposing force. Ironically, this treasure probably saved the French army from total destruction for as Wellington's soldiers filled their pockets with gold, silver, jewels and valuable coins, the defeated French soldiers were busy making good their escape along the road to Pamplona, much to Wellington's dismay and annoyance.

Wellington's annoyance at not being able to pursue the French with any great effect is reflected in a letter written to Earl Bathurst two weeks after the battle. It was destined to become one of the most famous of his phrases relating to his army:

We have in the service the scum of the earth as common soldiers; and of late years we have been doing everything in our power, both by law and by publications, to relax the discipline by which alone such men can be kept in order....It is really a disgrace to have anything to say to such men as some of our soldiers are.[9]

When the army had recovered from its orgy of plunder it resumed its march towards the Pyrenees. The Guards were already on their way, however, having had little to do with the chaos in Vittoria following the rout of Joseph's army. Indeed, Graham had already began to march through the western foothills of the Pyrenees with the 1st and 5th Divisions, Longa's Spaniards and two Portuguese brigades. By the end of June his corps had reached Irun on the Bidassoa river where the Guards were to remain for the next two months as Graham undertook the siege of San Sebastian. Their camp was situated in a wood at Oyarzun, about two miles from Irun on the banks of the Bidassoa. After the disastrous siege of Burgos the previous winter there was much optimism amongst the Guards as to the outcome of this siege. In fact, when John Rous wrote to his father on July 18th he may well have been a little too optimistic:

since there appears little probability of the French returning into Spain for the present we are in the meantime to have the benefit of another siege, but I trust very different from the last one we were engaged in. I was on duty from 11 o'clock last night till 7 this morning being unluckily the first for duty on our arriving here, as I was also at Burgos last year. The Engineers always boast at first sight that they will take a place in six or seven days; they have just found out that this place is very strong, but we have a magnificent Train and I hope we shall accomplish our undertaking in five or six days more.[10]

The siege was to be the third of the trio of successful sieges carried out by Wellington's army in the Peninsula but like the other two, at Ciudad Rodrigo and Badajoz, it still proved to be an unsatisfactory affair - proper siege guns were once again in short supply as were tools and engineers[11] - and when the town fell at the end of August it was accompanied once again by appalling and harrowing scenes of destruction as the troops sacked the place and set it on fire.

The siege began on June 28th when San Sebastian was blockaded by Graham but it was not until July 25th that the first assault was carried out after two breaches had been made in the walls of the town by the Allied batteries which had been constructed upon the Chofre sand-hills to the east of the place.

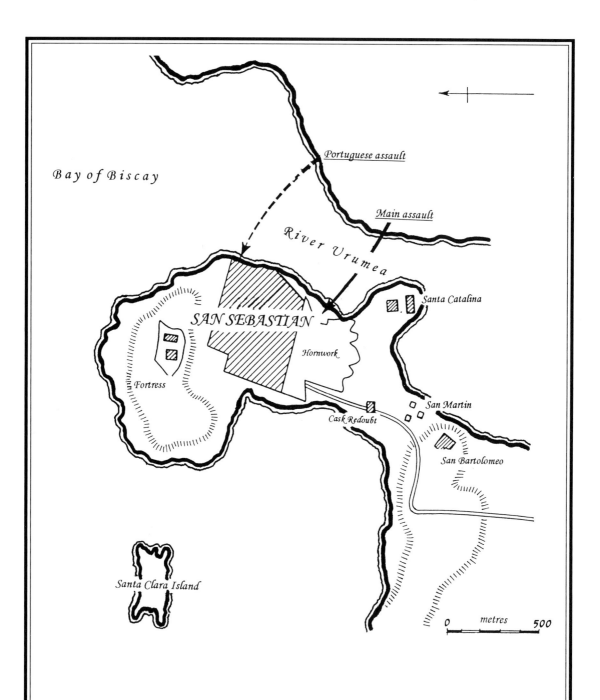

Bay of Biscay

Portuguese assault

Main assault

River Urumea

SAN SEBASTIAN

Santa Catalina

Fortress

Hornwork

Cask Redoubt

San Martin

San Bartolomeo

Santa Clara Island

0   metres   500

THE STORMING OF SAN SEBASTIAN
31st August 1813

The assault, however, did not succeed, despite the bravery of Oswald's 5th Division and Bradford's Portuguese brigade, who were unable to get into the town which was defended by an equally brave and tenacious French garrison of 3,000 troops who were commanded by General Rey.

Upon hearing of the failure of the assault Wellington rode over from his headquarters at Lesaca to see what was going on. He could not risk any further advance towards France with San Sebastian still in enemy hands as it would remain a threat to his left flank and as such he was growing impatient to see the place fall. He blamed the 5th Division - somewhat unfairly - for the failure of the assault and when further practicable breaches had been made in the town's eastern defences he snubbed the 5th Division by calling for volunteers from the 1st, 7th and Light Divisions to lead the assault. Some 750 volunteers came forward including one hundred each from the two Guards Brigades, the 1st Brigade of Guards having finally joined the 1st Division from Oporto on August 18th[12].

The storming party of the Guards was led by Lieutenant Colonel Cooke, of the First Guards, and included 53 men of the Coldstream, led by Captain Barrow and Ensign Chaplin, 50 men from the Third Guards and a further 100 men from the two battalions of the First Guards. They marched out of their camp at 6pm and camped about two miles from the walls of San Sebastian before marching again, at about 2am on the morning of the 31st, to the ruined convent of St Bartolomeo, in readiness for the attack.

The morning of August 31st dawned bright and fresh after a night of heavy rain and thunderstorms and as the columns of British and Portuguese stormers formed up ready to begin the assault crowds of local people wearing their holiday clothes began to congregate in order to watch the spectacle. When the signal for the assault began the Allied soldiers began to pick their way across the beach through shallow rocky pools and on towards the breaches which yawned silent and intimidating. As the 'forlorn hope' approached the walls the French gunners, waiting and watching in silence, opened up with grape shot, blowing away half of the 'hope' in an instant but the rest of the stormers followed with the 200 volunteers from the Guards among them. During the next sixty minutes or so Graham watched helplessly from his position on the sand-hills as his best men were smashed on the defences whilst the spectators looked on in awe and in silence as fiery explosion after explosion erupted amidst the despairing redcoated infantry.

At this point Graham, out of desperation, asked Colonel Dickson, commanding the artillery, to open fire over the heads of the stormers onto the French guns in the town. The move was an unprecedented but inspired one as Dickson's gunners opened fire on the French causing them severe casualties. The astonished British stormers pushed their faces to the ground as shot and shell screamed just a few feet overhead to cause death and destruction behind the ramparts which began to be torn apart by the accuracy of the Allied guns. The stormers lay listening to this cacophony of sound for some twenty minutes and when the guns lifted they surged forward to storm the defences which had by now been all but abandoned by the enemy and when a magazine exploded killing a large number of Frenchmen defending the breaches the town was as good as taken. Bugles sounded, shouts and cheers went up and as Graham watched from his position he could see his men disappear into the dust and smoke as they drove the French from the breaches. John Aitchison, of the Third Guards, arrived just as the stormers were carrying the breaches:

when I arrived they had already gained the breach, but were halted on the top of it by the obstacles which had been erected in the night behind it, and they were suffering severely from a destructive fire of musketry from the houses and of cannon from the castle and other parts of the works; in this situation they were detained at least half an hour; all the while however they were being reinforced, and at length the bugles sounding 'the advance' and a hearty 'hurrah' announced to the spectators that we had gained an advantage.....From this time our men gained ground gradually but the enemy fought desperately in the town and there was still a tremendous fire of musketry at three o'clock when I left it - the whole town, however, was taken and I hope we shall be able to keep it.[13]

San Sebastian was taken, although the castle itself, high upon Mount Urgull, continued to hold out until September 8th when General Rey finally surrendered. Describing the assault on the breaches, John Rous wrote:

we had detachments from the 1st, 4th and Light Divisions to assist the 5th Division in storming the town of San Sebastian, which was carried after a most severe loss on our side. 400 of the 1st Division were engaged of which number 200 were Germans, 95 of the 1st Brigade [Guards] and 105 of our Brigade, 50 of which were of the Coldstream. We had two officers, two sergeants and fifty men who attacked the town; one of the officers, Mr Chaplin, had his thigh broken and was shot through the body; the ball has been extracted, he also had severe contusions on his head. Both the sergeants were wounded, - you may imagine it was pretty sharp work.[14]

Allied casualties were 856 killed and 1,520 wounded, which bears testimony to the intensity of the struggle. The 1st Battalion First Guards suffered one officer - Ensign Burrard - and 9 men killed, eleven men wounded and 3 men missing. The 3rd Battalion First Guards lost ten men killed, one officer - Ensign the Hon. Orlando Bridgeman - and 22 men wounded, and 3 men missing.[15] The 1st Battalion Coldstream Guards lost 5 men killed, one officer - Ensign Thomas Chaplin - and 27 men wounded, and 1 men missing.[16] The 1st Battalion Third Guards lost 1 man killed, 20 men wounded and 12 men missing.[17]

The aftermath of the storming of San Sebastian was much the same as at Ciudad Rodrigo and Badajoz as the victorious troops embarked on an orgy of debauchery and destruction. On this occasion, things were made worse by a fire that completely engulfed the town and led to fierce accusations from the Spanish government that Wellington himself had ordered the town to be burnt as it had been carrying on trading with France. The accusations were, of course, denied by Wellington although he certainly might have felt justified in this course of action.

Whilst the siege of San Sebastian was in progress Soult made three attempts to relieve the French garrison at Pamplona but failed to do so despite making strong attacks at the passes of Maya and Roncesvalles, and at Sorauren, between July 25th and 28th. The two Brigades of Guards were engaged at San Sebastian and so were not involved during these battles which have become known as the Battle of the Pyrenees.[18]

Following the storming of San Sebastian there would be a period of one month's recuperation for the two Brigades of Guards and the rest of Wellington's army before they would be ready to move forward once again, this time to cross the Bidassoa river after which, following five years of hard fighting, the army would at last be fighting on the 'sacred soil' of Napoleon's France.

NOTES

[1] The First Guards' returns for November 25th 1812 show 696 men sick out of a total of 2541 men, the ratio being about one in every four. Lieutenant General Sir F.W. Hamilton, *The Origin and History of the*

First or Grenadier Guards, (London, 1874) ii. p.448.

[2] The Earl of Malmesbury, *A Series of Letters of the First Earl of Malmesbury, His Family and Friends, from 1745 to 1820,* (London, 1870), ii. 336.

[3] John Rous wrote on June 20th 1813, 'The 1st Guards are still at Oporto, where I hope they will remain the whole year; they have seen three retreats and have never seen an advance; we fancy that their appearing is the omen of bad luck.' Ian Fletcher, *A Guards Officer in the Peninsula; the Peninsular War letters of John Rous, Coldstream Guards, 1812-1814,* (Tunbridge Wells, 1992) p.64)

[4] Hamilton, *Grenadier Guards,* ii. 450.

[5] Elizabeth Longford, *Wellington: The Years of the Sword,* (London, 1969),

[6] George Bowles, of the Coldstream, attributed the army's good health to the carrying of tents instead of camp kettles which, as he said, 'preserved our men from the cold and unwholesome dews they formerly suffered so much from.' Malmesbury, *A Series of Letters,* ii. p.351.

[7] Unlike the crossing of the Esla the river Ebro was forded with hardly any difficulty. In fact, so low was the river that George Bowles was able to cross it on a 'middle-sized' mule. Malmesbury, *A Series of Letters,* ii. p.357.

[8] George Bowles, in Malmesbury's *A Series of Letters,* ii. 352-353. Bowles compares the French army's disaster at Vittoria with that suffered by them at the crossing of the Berezina during the retreat from Moscow.

[9] Wellington to Earl Bathurst, Huarte, July 3rd 1813.

[10] Fletcher, *A Guards Officer in the Peninsula,* 69. When George Bowles wrote to Lord Fitzharris on July 28th, he also expressed his dissappointment at not being able to describe the fall of San Sebastian, which he had hoped would have fallen by then. Malmesbury, *A Series of Letters,* ii. 364.

[11] The Royal Corps of Sappers and Miners had been created the previous year but by the time of the siege of San Sebastian their numbers were still woefully short.

[12] Hamilton, *Grenadier Guards,* ii. 454.

[13] W.F.K. Thompson, (Ed), *An Ensign in the Peninsular War; the Letters of John Aitchison,* (London, 1981), 264.

[14] Fletcher, *A Guards Officer in the Peninsula,* 72.

[15] Hamilton, *Grenadier Guards,* ii. 457.

[16] Colonel Daniel Mackinnon, *Origins and Services of the Coldstream Guards,* (London, 1833), ii. 190.

[17] Major General Sir Frederick Maurice, *A History of the Scots Guards, from 1642 to 1914,* (London, 1934), i. 407.

[18] Pamplona, in fact, did not surrender to Wellington until October 25th.

General Sir Thomas Graham, Lord Lynedoch, 1748-1863. Graham was the victor of Barrosa in 1811 and subsequently commanded the 1st Division of the army until the late summer of 1813.

Sir John Hope, later Earl of Hopetoun. Hope assumed command of the 1st Division following Graham's return to England. His courage was such that Wellington feared he should lose him. Sure enough, Hope was taken during the sortie from Bayonne in April 1814 whilst riding into the thick of things.

(Right); The Third Guards Cemetery, Bayonne, last resting place of three of their officers who were killed during the sortie.

(Below); The Coldstream Guards Cemetery at Bayonne. Herein lie those officers of the Guards, and a few others besides, who were killed during the sortie from Bayonne on April 14th 1814.

(Above); The Waterloo Ball. Officers leave the ball in order to join their regiments, and (Below); the interior of Hougoumont, on June 18th 1815. Both paintings by Hillingford.

Alexander, Lord Saltoun, First Guards, in the uniform of a lieutenant, light infantry company 1810. Saltoun commanded the light companies at Waterloo and took part in the repulse of the Imperial Guard.

(Above); The light companies of the Guards open fire on the French outside the south gate of Hougoumont, early in the day. (Below); A mid-nineteenth century photograph of the scene as it looked then, prior to the building of the extension which now stands inside the wall at right.

(Above); The Chateau of Hougoumont as it appeared before the Battle of Waterloo. (Below); The north gate of Hougoumont. This remarkable photograph, taken around the mid-nineteenth century, shows the gate as it looked before the present much lower gates were installed. Compare this photograph with the painting by Ernest Crofts, featured on the cover of this book.

The Defence of Hougoumont, by Richard Caton Woodville.

French troops launch their attack on the south gate at Hougoumont. Painting by Ernest Crofts.

(Right); The shako of a Coldstream Guardsman, light infantry company. This was probably picked up off of the field of Waterloo as
it remained in the collection of Sgt-Major
Cotton for many years.

(Left); The Chapel at Hougoumont,
as photographed in the mid-nineteenth century.

(Above); The well inside Hougoumont, lost until recently when it was excavated. In the background the old gates are visible. Mid-nineteenth century photograph. (Left); Colonel Edward Stables, First Guards, who was mortally wounded at Waterloo.

(Above); The garden wall at Hougoumont, showing just how high it was in places. Mid-nineteenth century photograph. (Right); Lieutenant George Mure, First Guards, wearing his Waterloo Medal.

(Above); The Guards defend the garden wall at Hougoumont. Painting by Woollen. (Below); Squares of the Coldstream Guards under attack on the ridge of Mont St Jean, on June 18th 1815. Painting by Dighton.

The north gate of Hougmont showing the original height of the walls. From an mid-nineteenth century photograph.

(Above); The First Guards repulse the Imperial Guard at Waterloo, by Richard Simkin. (Below); How the film makers saw things - the Coldstream Guards at Waterloo, as depicted in the 1970 film, *Waterloo*.

SOUTHERN FRANCE

As Wellington's army rested after the storming of San Sebastian the French were busily digging in along the right bank of the Bidassoa river, the crossing of which would be Wellington's next objective. Once across he could at last establish himself on French territory. The force opposing him consisted of 47,000 French troops but as Soult had yet to ascertain the exact whereabouts of Wellington's line of advance these troops were over-extended and scattered along the right bank of the river. This shortage of troops was also due to the fact that by this stage of the war the French were short of supplies and although they were fighting on their own soil it was becoming increasingly difficult to feed even this relatively small number.

The line of the Bidassoa was about thirty miles in length and herein lay Soult's main weakness, namely, that there were just too few troops at his disposal with which to defend such an extensive position. Soult had divided his front-line force into three; the right, under Reille, holding the river from its mouth as far as the town of Vera; the centre, under Clausel, holding the heights of La Bayonette and the Great Rhune, a 2,800 foot high mountain; and the left, under D'Erlon, the approaches from the valley of Batzan. Throughout September thousands of Soult's men had been busy, frantically constructing redoubts and retrenchments on the summits of the hills and mountains and along the banks of the Bidassoa. Soult decided to make the Great Rhune the centre of his line believing the estuary of the Bidassoa to be impassable. He was to be proved spectacularly wrong.

Wellington's plan was as daring as it was simple. While Hill, with the 2nd and 6th Divisions, kept D'Erlon occupied at the passes of Maya and Roncesvalles, Alten's Light Division would assault the French position on the Great Rhune, supported by Longa's and Giron's Spaniards. The crossing of the Bidassoa at the river's estuary would be carried out by the 1st and 5th Divisions. The 5th Division would cross at Fuenterrabia, crossing to Hendaye, whilst the 1st Division, including the 1st and 2nd Brigade of Guards, would cross from Irun to Behobie. The whole operation was hazardous to say the least, the more so since the Bidassoa was a tidal river and within an hour or so of the crossing it would be in full flow. This meant, of course, that should Wellington's men fail to achieve a hold on the right bank of the river they would be cut off and the consequences disastrous. It was Wellington's 'who dares wins' approach that would win him the day at the crossing of the Bidassoa and throughout the forthcoming operations north of the Pyrenees, thus maintaining his reputation as an offensive general, gained by him during the glorious Salamanca summer of the previous year.

The attack was planned for October 7th and throughout the previous night the troops moved forward in silence to take up their positions for the crossing the next morning, not that they need have worried too much about the noise, for a heavy thunderstorm accompanied by much lightning erupted which not only drowned all sounds of their advance but which also compelled the French sentries to seek shelter from the rain. By now a thunderstorm on the eve of a battle, such as that before Salamanca, was beginning to be seen by Wellington's men as a good omen, one that would continue at Waterloo.

At first light at dawn on October 7th the men of Hay's 5th Division, after waiting for the local shrimpers who were to act as guides, plunged into the shallow waters of the Bidassoa to spearhead the crossing of Wellington's army. It was low tide but the water still came up to the men's waists and in some cases, their armpits, forcing them to hold their trusty brown bess muskets above their heads. The river was about half a mile wide at Fuenterrabia although at low tide part of this distance was a muddy flat and when the troops had got halfway across a rocket was fired high into the air from the steeple of the church in Fuenterrabia as the signal for the rest of the army to advance.

To the right of the 5th Division the 2nd Guards Brigade, along with the King's German Legion troops of the 1st Division, waited anxiously for the signal to advance. Opposite the French sentries suspected nothing, partly because the British continued sending out working parties which they had been doing for the last few days.[1] Suddenly, the bright red trail of a rocket was seen to arc in the sky, clear and vivid against the grey early morning, and all at once the Guards began their bold venture, crossing the river by a ford near a ruined bridge whilst to their right the 1st Brigade of Guards, along with Wilson's Portuguese, began their crossing at two other fords. The level of the water at these fords was not too deep and hardly got above the men's knees.[2] The Guards felt naked and exposed as they crossed the half-mile of mud and water, completely devoid of any cover, but if they crossed with some trepidation they must surely have felt excited also, as once across they would be doing something which some of them had waited almost five years to do - and which some must have felt they would never do - namely, they would be fighting the French on their own soil, and if they did feel any apprehension they drew much comfort from the sound of the Allied guns in Irun that boomed overhead as they shelled the French positions. For Ensign Rees Gronow, of the First Guards - the celebrated diarist - the crossing of the Bidassoa was his baptism of fire having not long arrived in the Peninsula:

We commenced the passage of the Bidassoa about five in the morning and in a short time infantry, cavalry and artillery found themselves upon French ground. The stream at the point we forded was nearly four feet deep, and had Soult been aware of what we were about, we should have found the passage of the river a very arduous undertaking. Three miles above, we discovered the French army and ere long found ourselves under fire. The sensation of being made a target to a large body of men is at first not particularly pleasant, but, 'in a trice, the ear becomes more Irish, and less nice'. The first man I ever saw killed was a Spanish soldier, who was cut in two by a cannon ball.[3]

The audacious crossing had caught the french completely by surprise and by the time they realised - with some shock - the full extent of the Allied operation, Wellington's men were scrambling up the slopes on the right bank of the river, driving the already retreating French from their positions.

They [the French] were regularly surprised, and we gained the first heights with scarcely any opposition. They attempted, however, to make a stand on the second range, but were instantly driven from it by the 5th Division, which had crossed the river near Fuenterrabia. One shell struck the Coldstream when in close column, and did some mischief. The light infantry were smartly engaged, and drove the enemy beyond the town of Urrugne.[4]

Once established on the opposite bank the Third and Coldstream Guards of the 2nd Brigade of Guards rushed forward and carried the Cafè Republican and drove the enemy from the Louis XIVth mountain. Meanwhile, on their right, the two battalions of the 1st Brigade of Guards - the 1st and 3rd Battalions First Guards - stormed the village of Hendaye and advanced towards the Croix de Bouguet, the key to the French position in this sector. The enemy were driven from the heights at no cost to either battalion of the First Guards and they camped that night atop the heights on the road to Urrugne. Here, the Guards found the French soldiers' huts very

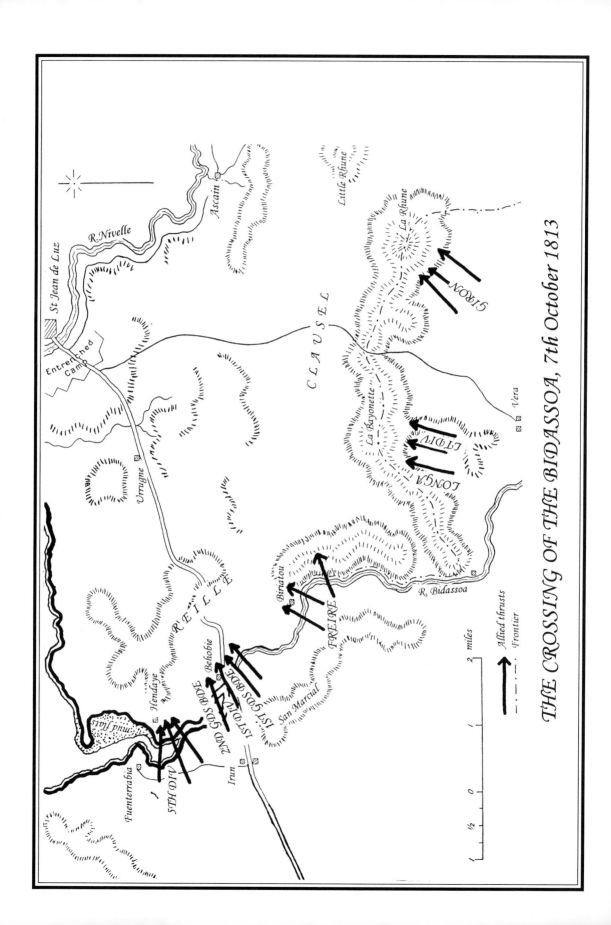

THE CROSSING OF THE BIDASSOA, 7th October 1813

comfortable, most unlike their own. They were built of branches and formed streets and squares and placards were stuck in the ground with 'street' names on them, such as Rue de Paris and Rue de Versailles.[5]

During the advance of the light companies of the First Guards, Lord Saltoun, commanding, saw one of his men go up to a wounded Frenchman lying by the side of the road with a number of others. Saltoun then watched in horror as the Guardsman proceeded to run the man through with his bayonet. Rushing forward, he shouted at the man and asked what on earth he was doing, at which the Guardsman told him that the man was no Frenchman but was, in fact, an Englishman named Evans, and worse still was a former soldier in the First Guards, who had run away on the eve of the battle of Corunna in 1809. As he lay wounded Evans recognised the uniform of his old regiment and called out for a drink of water. Unfortunately, Evans got more than he bargained for and although he was sent to the field hospital he died the next day of the bayonet wound given to him by his former comrade.[6]

The assault by the Guards and the 5th Division upon the right of the French position was a complete success and by 9am Reille's troops had been forced from all of their positions and had withdrawn as far as Urrugne. Losses were 400 on the Allied side against 450 French casualties. Casualties amongst the Guards were 9 men wounded and 2 missing amongst the Coldstream, and 2 men killed and 10 wounded amongst the Third Guards. The First Guards came through the crossing unscathed.

The fighting elsewhere along the Bidassoa was heavier but La Bayonette was carried as was the Great Rhune and by midday on October 7th the Light Division stood atop the Pyrenees having driven the french from all of their positions. he fighting in this sector cost the Allies 800 casualties against 1,250 French. Soult, meanwhile, withdrew to a much stronger position along the line of the Nivelle river whilst Wellington ordered a halt for the time being while his men got themselves under canvas as heavy rain set in. 'No part of the army has moved since we crossed the Bidassoa,' wrote John Rous of the Coldstream,

It has rained almost incessantly for the last five days; the inside of my tent is nearly as wet as the outside, and my horse and mules look terribly rough, but are not fallen away much in flesh, which I must expect should we remain here much longer.[7]

With Pamplona still holding out Wellington was in no hurry to push forward but with its fall on October 30th he could feel more secure about advancing deeper into enemy territory. Moreover, at this time he received news of the Allied powers' victory over Napoleon at Leipzig and of his subsequent retreat across the Rhine. This had far reaching effects throughout Europe, as well as in the south of France, sapping further the morale of the French armies but boosting that of the Allies. With this in mind, therefore, Wellington decided to advance against Soult's position on the Nivelle river.

Soult's position on the Nivelle was similar to that on the Bidassoa only in the way in which his troops were distributed. The position rested on the mouth of the river at St Jean de Luz, where an entrenched camp had been constructed on the left bank. Once again Reille took the right of the line, holding the area between the sea and the village of Ascain; Clausel took the centre of the line, between Ascain and Amotz, with picquets placed in advance on the Little Rhune and in redoubts on the hills south of Sare; and D'Erlon held the left of the line amongst the heights of Mounts Atchulegui, Chapora and Mondarrin. Foy, meanwhile, was still in a position away to the east of the line watching the exit of the pass at Roncesvalles. Soult's position was far more compact than that on the Bidassoa but it was still rather too extended given the number of troops with which he had to defend it, something which he again tried to compensate for with heavy use of pick and shovel as his men dug in along the line of the river.

Wellington divided his army into three; Hope commanding the left - which included the two Brigades of Guards, Beresford the centre, and Hill the right. His army totalled 82,000 men, of whom 22,000 were untried Spaniards, against Soult's 70,000, of whom nearly 7,000 were cavalry and could be virtually ruled out of the contest, the country being unsuitable for them. Wellington's plan involved a grand attack along the whole of the 20-mile, thinly-defended front, with the main assault taking place in the centre between Sare and Amotz where Soult's line was at its weakness. A breakthrough at this sector would mean that the French forces on the right of their line, hugging the coast, would be in danger of being cut off.

The 1st Division, still under the command of General Howard, included the 1st Brigade of Guards under Maitland, and the 2nd Brigade of Guards under Stopford, as well as Halkett's King's German Legion brigade. Just prior to the attack the 1st Battalion Third Guards received two drafts from England and now numbered 34 officers and 1,093 men, making it the strongest battalion in Wellington's army.[8] Once again the 1st Division would be attacking alongside the 5th Division, assaulting Reille's troops holding the entrenched camp in front of St Jean de Luz on the right of the French line. Both the 1st and 5th Divisions, as well as Freire's Spaniards, formed part of Sir John Hope's command and it was his attack that would be launched first with the intention of deceiving Soult into believing that this would be the main point of Wellington's thrust.

The attack was timed to begin at 6am on November 10th and at 3am that morning the Brigades of Guards began to move down from their camp upon the heights where they had been since the crossing of the Bidassoa and advanced slowly to the Allied outposts where they halted. The weather had been wet and windy of late but the morning of the 10th dawned dry and clear and by the time the Guards attacked the sun would be beginning to break through. The Brigades of Guards waited in silence along with the rest of the 1st Division, checking their weapons and equipment as the tension increased, and then, at the appointed hour, the booming of three guns fired from the top of the Alchabia mountain echoed along the river and all at once lines of red and brown coated infantry surged forward supported by 100 guns that roared like thunder overhead.

First into action were the picquets of the 1st Division, under Lieutenant Colonel West of the First Guards, who let loose a volley before driving the French troops from their advanced posts at bayonet point, pursuing them down the hill almost to their retrenchments. Away to their left the crackling of musketry announced the attack by Maitland's 1st brigade of Guards who advanced resolutely against the French on the heights behind the village of Urrugne. A heavy fire of musketry ensued along the whole of the front being attacked by the 1st and 5th Divisions, the light companies of the First Guards being particularly busy, but as Hope had not been issued with any orders to take the entrenched positions in front of St Jean de Luz his men remained where they were, keeping the French occupied at this sector of the line. However, the men of the 1st and 5th Divisions kept up such a hot fire that Hope was able to take the heights in front of the village of Siboure which meant that he was in a position to thwart any movement east by Reille's troops in order to assist their comrades elsewhere. This allowed the main attacks by both Beresford and Hill to proceed successfully and without interference. Hill duly pushed D'Erlon's troops back and when Beresford took the bridge at

Amotz, cutting the French army in two, Soult gave orders for a general retirement, pulling his force back beyond the river Nive.

Wellington's objective had been to break through the French line and cut off those still in position along the coast. A variety of reasons prevented this, however, but he could take comfort from another success which cost the French some 4,321 casualties against 2,526 Allied. The Guards part in the battle had been 'useful rather than glorious'[9] and it had cost the two Brigades just one officer - Ensign Anstruther of the Coldstream - and 9 men wounded. Captain Charles Allix, of the First Guards although serving as a staff officer, was also severely wounded whilst acting as temporary brigade major of the 1st Brigade of Guards.

Following the battle Soult's troops retreated to the heights of Bidart, on the road to Bayonne, from where they would defend the passage of the river Adour, the next obstacle in the path of Wellington's army. The day after the battle the Guards advanced over the former entrenched camp of the French, passed through the suburbs of Siboure and entered St Jean de Luz where they went in billets as the rain once again began to pour in torrents, frustrating any chances of a possible pursuit.

As the Allied army began to push into French territory Wellington took the decision to send all but Morillo's Spaniards back to Spain. He had been received numerous reports of Spanish troops murdering and plundering the local people and having seen the damage caused to the French army by the *guerrillos* in Spain the last thing he wanted was for a similar movement to raise its head amongst the French people. Wellington had written to General Freire explaining his decision:

Indiscipline is general in your corps.....Now I do not enter France in order to plunder: I have not had so many thousands of officers and men killed and wounded merely in order that the survivors should be able to rob the French. On the contrary, it is my duty, and the duty of all of us, to stop pillage, especially if we intend to make our army live off the resources of the country.[10]

Soult, meanwhile had been busy deploying his troops at Bayonne. The city itself was strongly fortified with defences based on those laid down by Vauban. To the west lay the Atlantic and the east the river Adour. On the northern bank of the Adour lay a citadel which commanded the place. Wellington decided to approach the city from both the east and the south but an approach from the south would involve an advance along the coast on the left bank of the river Nive which flowed south-east from Bayonne. This operation was potentially dangerous, of course, as Wellington's

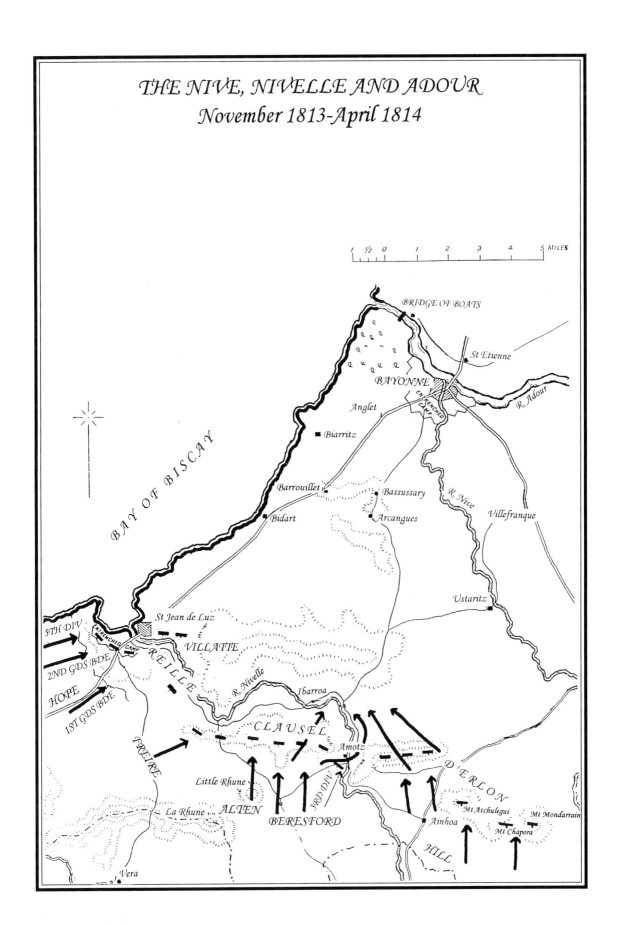

THE NIVE, NIVELLE AND ADOUR
November 1813-April 1814

army would be divided and the force on the left bank exposed to a possible attack by Soult who would be able to deploy the greater part of his force to attack them.

Soult's line ran south-east from Bayonne, along the right bank of the Nive as far as Cambo. The Allied right rested upon Cambo and ran north-west to Arrauntz and from there west to Bidart, on the coast. Wellington, however, decided to establish himself on the right bank of the Nive and on December 9th Hill crossed the river at Cambo and Beresford did the same at Ustaritz. Whilst these operations were in progress diversions were taking place elsewhere and for the two Brigades of Guards this meant taking part in an attack on the entrenched position in front of Bayonne which would be carried out by the left wing of the army, under Hope, who was also to reconnoitre the mouth of the river Adour as it was Wellington's intention, once established on both sides of the Nive, to make a crossing there.

At 2am on the 9th the Guards duly paraded before beginning their march along the coast towards Bayonne. Once again the weather was wet, windy and cold and the march at such an early hour was a miserable one. However, the Guards had soon reached Barouillet, close to Bidart whilst on their left the 5th Division dragged itself through the muddy valley between Biarritz and Bidart. At about 8am the 1st Battalion First Guards advanced, covered by the fire of the light companies and some artillery. The firing on both sides was heavy for a while as the French disputed every yard of ground. They fell back firing from behind trees, bushes and hedges, and from ditches and streams, but the Guards soon gained the upper hand and drove the French defenders from their positions until by 1pm they had reached the village of Anglet, the French having retreated down the slopes in the rear of the place to the entrenched camp in front of Bayonne. The rest of the 1st Division then came forward and camped that night in and around Anglet. Whilst this diversionary attack was going on both Beresford and Hill had been able to cross to the right bank of the Nive at Cambo and the operation having been completed the Brigades of Guards were ordered to return to their quarters at St Jean de Luz, the 5th Division remaining at Anglet, an operation not without complication, however, due to the muddy condition of the roads. Indeed, the mud was knee deep in some places and at one point a drummer boy, belonging to the First Guards, became so completely stuck that he had to be freed by his comrades who then carried him for the next few miles.[11]

Of course with Beresford and Hill having crossed the Nive it meant that Wellington's army was separated by the river with under 30,000 troops on the left bank. Shrewd as ever, Soult was quick to seize the opportunity. On the night on December 9th, amidst more heavy rain, some 50,000 French troops under D'Erlon began to slip silently forward from Bayonne, keeping their camp fires burning, and proceeded to move against Hope's scattered force of 30,000. At first light on the 10th the French attacked and drove the Allies from Anglet before advancing resolutely upon Barouillet. On the right of the 5th Division, meanwhile, the Light Division was attacked and driven back some two miles to the village of Arcangues, where it held on throughout the rest of the day, clinging to a position on a ridge, dominated by a dark and dingy Basque church. In all, the Allied line was forced back three miles.

The Guards, meanwhile, had stirred into action as soon as they began to hear reports of firing in their front, and when a breathless aide-de-camp arrived in their camp to warn them of the attack they were soon back on the muddy road to Barouillet. Fortunately, the bad weather that had dogged the Allied advance now came to their assistance and when Soult's forces found it impossible to deploy effectively, the attack floundered and came to a halt. As a precaution the Brigades of Guards camped that night at Bidart.

This was just as well for on the morning of the 11th Soult resumed his attack, pushing back the outposts of the 5th Division at Barouillet. That division was then pulled back and relieved by the two Brigades of Guards who came rushing forward to plug the gap, the 1st Brigade, under Maitland, taking up a position near a farmhouse on some heights in front of Barouillet, whilst the 2nd Brigade took up posts in and around the Mayor of Bayonne's house. The whole position was covered by picquets of the 3rd battalion First Guards who threw his men into a thick wood on the slopes in front, whilst those of the 1st battalion First Guards, under Captain West, covered the position from an orchard on their right. Another picquet of the First Guards, under Lord Saltoun, covered the road which led to the enemy's position and kept open the communication between the two brigades. The Guards remained in these positions throughout the wet, blustery and tense night of the 11th.

The following morning a large concentration of French troops were seen approaching the Guards' position and soon a heavy skirmishing developed between the Guards' outposts and the enemy, with artillery on both sides joining in the fighting also. This firing continued throughout the day but there seems to have been little danger on a French breakthrough and the line was never pierced. During the fighting Lieutenant Colonel Coote Martin was shot whilst giving orders to his men in the orchard. However, the two Brigades of Guards incurred some 219 casualties owing to their exposed position on the slopes in front of Barouillet, as George Bowles stated:

A severe *tiraillade* was kept up by the enemy during the greater part of the day, from which the first brigade of Guards suffered severely, owing principally to the unmilitary way in which the ground was taken up, the advanced line being much overcrowded with troops, who being without any cover afforded every opportunity to the enemy's skirmishers to annoy them.[12]

The First Guards lost two officers - Lieutenant Colonel Coote Martin and Captain Charles Thompson - and 21 men killed, and two officers - Captain Streathfield and Ensign Latour - and 126 men wounded. The Coldstream Guards suffered just three men wounded, whilst the Third Guards had one officer - Captain Watson - and 7 men killed, and 3 officers - Captains Seymour and Holbourne and Ensign Montgomery - and 54 men wounded.

Soult still refused to give up and on the morning of December 13th attacked once more, this time on the right bank of the Nive where Hill held the line with 14,000 men. The attack by 35,000 Frenchmen came within a whisker of succeeding but when Wellington brought forward three of Beresford's divisions Soult was finally forced to abandon the offensive. During the fierce fighting the colonel of an infantry regiment ordered his men to retire upon which the eighteen year-old Lord Charles Churchill, of the First Guards, although serving on the staff at the time, dashed forward and grabbed the regimental colour, shouting, 'if your colonel will not lead you, follow me, my boys!' at which the regiment rallied and rejoined the fight.[13] During the day the 1st Brigade of Guards and the Coldstream came under fire which lasted for most of the day although no serious attack was made on their line. The four days of fighting had cost the French 5,947 casualties against 4,662.[14]

The two Brigades of Guards returned to quarters at St Jean de Luz whilst Soult withdrew to Bayonne, reflecting no doubt on the failure of his assault along the Nive. He had attacked half of Wellington's force with the whole of his own on two occasions but had still failed to achieve a positive breakthrough and the morale of his troops thus sank further. His men withdrew to the entrenched camp at Bayonne where 11,000 men were left under the command of General Thouvenot whilst his main force was extended east along the line of the Adour as far as Port de Lanne. From there the line ran south along the small river Bidouse as far as St Palais.

There was to be no more fighting throughout the cold, wet winter of 1813 as the bad weather brought all operations to a halt. However, with his army firmly established along the south bank of the river Adour Wellington was perfectly placed to resume his inexorable march as soon as the weather improved and it was the crossing of the Adour that would be his next operation, one in which his two Brigades of Guards would play a prominent part.

It had been a hard and exhausting year for Wellington and his army during which there had been much hard fighting and many fatiguing marches. But now they were well established on French territory and were on the verge of victory. As George Bowles of the Coldstream wrote, 'thus ended the campaign of 1813, commenced on the Douro and concluded on the Adour!'[15]

NOTES

[1] The Earl of Malmesbury, *A Series of Letters of the First Earl of Malmesbury, His Family and Friends, from 1745 to 1820,* (London, 1870), ii. 392.

[2] Ibid. ii. 385. Bowles called the crossing `a mere joke,' and added that `though rather terrific in appearance, was very easy in reality, and was in fact merely an affair of outposts.' Gronow, of the First Guards, estimated the depth of the water as being four feet. Nicholas Bentley, (Ed), *Selections from the Reminiscences of Captain Gronow,* (London, 1977), 13.

[3] Bentley, *Gronow,* 13.

[4] Malmesbury, *A Series of Letters,* ii. 392.

[5] Bentley, *Gronow,* 13.

[6] Lieutenant General Sir F.W. Hamilton, *The Origin and History of the First or Grenadier Guards,* (London, 1874), ii. 461.

[7] Ian Fletcher, (Ed), *A Guards Officer in the Peninsula: The Peninsular War letters of John Rous, Coldstream Guards, 1812-1814,* (Tunbridge Wells, 1992), 81.

[8] Major General Sir Frederick Maurice, *The History of the Scots Guards, from 1642 to 1914,* (London, 1934), i. 390.

[9] Major H.L. Aubrey-Fletcher, *A History of the Foot Guards, to 1856,* (London, 1927), 335.

[10] Wellington, *The Despatches of Field Marshal the Duke of Wellington,* (London, 1837-39), xi. 288-289.

[11] Captain Robert Batty, *The Campaign in the of the Left Wing of the Allied Army in the Western Pyrenees and South of France, in the Years 1813-14,* (London, 1823), 86.

[12] Malmesbury, *A Series of Letters*, ii. 395.

[13] Bentley, *Gronow,* 21-22.

[14] Sir Charles Oman, *A History of the Peninsular War,* (Oxford, 1902-30), vii. 547.

[15] Malmesbury, *A Series of Letters*, ii. 396.

ON TO BAYONNE

On the grey, damp and windy morning of February 20th 1814, Wellington stood on the sea wall at St Jean de Luz, gazing out to sea as the Atlantic waves came crashing and rolling in from the Bay of Biscay. Moored in the harbour were line after line of *chasse-marées*, small boats which, when roped together, would form the pontoon bridge over which Wellington's men would cross the river Adour and begin the drive deeper into Napoleon's France, an advance which he was almost certain would bring about the final and apparently inevitable victory. The city of Bayonne lay on the south bank of the Adour but was commanded by a citadel situated on the north bank and it was this that would be the object of the whole operation. Once the citadel was in Allied hands then the fall of Bayonne would be a formality.

The two Brigades of Guards were still encamped in and around St Jean de Luz but the camps were soon buzzing and alive with activity as the prospect of imminent action increased daily. Wellington had been waiting for the weather to ease since the beginning of February but as he stood on the sea wall as the wind threatened to snatch him into the water he reflected on the fact that as all arrangements for the crossing had been made he could wait no longer, and decided to rejoin Hill's corps away to the south-east at Garris, leaving the crossing of the Adour in the hands of Sir John Hope.

The following day the two Brigades of Guards, along with the rest of the 1st Division began to march north from St Jean de Luz towards the Adour. When they reached the village of Anglet they halted and then headed west towards the coast, marching in silence so as not to disturb the French picquets in the village. Here they were joined by a brigade of 18-pounder guns and a brigade of the Rocket Troop.[1] Whilst Stopford's brigade continued on to the mouth of the river Maitland's brigade advanced into Anglet itself, driving the French from it whilst other units were thrown into the villages of Biarritz and Bidart, and in the thick pine forest that reached down to the river's edge. The crossing would take place across the mouth of the Adour by means of the *chasse-marées* which would form the bridge and the crossing would be covered by some small warships.

On the afternoon of February 22nd, the winds that had been howling constantly for the last few weeks suddenly dropped and Hope decided that the moment had come to cross. Accordingly, orders were issued and the *chasse-marées* put to sea, along with their escorts. At midnight, the 1st Brigade of Guards was put in motion and the troops headed off for the designated point of crossing, a march that was not without its problems, for not only had the rain turned the roads into muddy tracks but as they neared the river the roads and paths were very sandy and several guns became stuck and had to be hauled out by cursing, sweating infantrymen. The First Guards eventually debouched from the wood at the water's edge at dawn on the 23rd and formed under cover of a sand-hill and set up their guns in order to be able to prevent any interference from the French when the crossing of the river began. On the river itself, the French had placed some gunboats which opened fire on Maitland's brigade as soon as they debouched. In order to combat the fire from these boats part of the Rocket brigade was despatched to the water to open fire. At this the gunboats immediately retired, but not, however, as Captain Robert Batty, of the First Guards, wrote:

before the soldiers had the satisfaction of seeing the rockets strike some of the gunboats, and sink them. The effect of the rockets was very remarkable, darting through the water like fiery serpents, and piercing the sides of the boats, burning, apparently, even under the water with undiminished force.[2]

At dawn the 2nd Brigade of Guards, under Stopford, which was to spearhead crossing, had reached its starting point. Unfortunately, as the Guards waited at the river there was no sign of either the *chasse-marées* or their escorts which had all been blown out to sea during the night. This left Hope with something of a dilemma. He could either wait for the reappearance of the flotilla which might not appear for some time yet, or he could cross the Adour using the pontoons and five small boats he had with him. Every moment that passed threatened his chances of success as it would only be a matter of time before the French spotted the mass of red and grey hiding in the woods opposite them. Hope paced up and down for a few hours during the morning, waiting in vain for a glimpse of the boats until he finally decided to risk making the crossing without them.

The troops destined to make the crossing would have little protection as they crossed, should the French discover them, and therefore Hope ordered diversionary attacks to be made on the French camps on the southern bank of the river to the east of the estuary in order to lead Soult into believing that an attack was being made on the French lines to the east of Bayonne. This deception was increased with the appearance of Hill and Beresford away to the east which further distracted Soult and convinced him that Wellington's line of advance lay along the main road through the town of Pau.

At 11am Hope launched the five small boats that had been brought up with the pontoons. Each of these small craft was capable of carrying just ten men each, which meant, of course, that the vanguard of Hope's force would be just fifty strong. It was just as well that there was no opposition. The small boats were pushed out into the river with groups of men from the Coldstream Guards and the Third Guards squeezed tightly into them and as the rest of the 1st Division watched anxiously from the shore they began to glide slowly across to the opposite bank. As soon as the boats hit the shore the Guardsmen scrambled out and whilst some took cover amongst the sand-hills others secured a hawser to which the pontoon would be attached.

As soon as the signal was given other groups of Guards - along with some of the 5/60th Regiment - began to cross on rafts made from pontoons lashed together with ropes, each of which could hold fifty men. Once again the tense business of crossing the river began, an operation which was painfully slow owing to the tide which had begun to run again. Indeed, by 5pm only five companies of the Guards and two companies of the 5/60th had got across.[3] As each man clambered from his raft on the opposite bank he was thrown into a defensive position by Stopford who stood, sword in hand, hurriedly but calmly deploying his men to meet any possible attack which the French might make. In fact, at this stage if Thouvenot, commanding the garrison at Bayonne, had attacked Stopford and his small party of 500 the small force would almost certainly have been annihilated.

Eventually, Thouvenot realised that the action away to the east was just a diversion and that an attempt was being made to cross the Adour at its estuary. But instead of ordering an attack in force Thouvenot despatched two incomplete battalions of infantry, estimated by eye-witnesses at between 600-700, under General Maucomble, to 'reconnoitre the troops which had got across.'[4] When Maucomble's infantry approached Stopford's men they were hit by a galling fire of musketry from an enemy hidden behind the sand-hills. The French were unaware of the strength of the British force but must have imagined it to be much stronger than it actually was. The musketry checked the nervous French but the issue was settled by a group of the rocketeers who had crossed with the Guards. The rocketeers hastily set up a flight of the new-fangled Congreve rockets, a weapon seldom encountered by the French and when a few of them came fizzing in to explode amongst them the French scattered in blind panic. Maucomble had only lost forty men but he withdrew his men in haste to the citadel of Bayonne. John Rous, of the Coldstream, on the northern bank of the river, attributed the poor performance of the French to their inexperience:

The French attacked with 1200 men about five o'clock on the evening of the 23rd, at which time we had only 500 men of our Brigade on this side of the river, and a few men with rockets. They drove in our advanced posts and were moving rapidly upon the main body. When they were within 200 yards we fired a few rockets at them which frightened them so much that they immediately retired in confusion. Our light companies pursued them, and killed some; we took four prisoners, none of whom had been soldiers more than two months. had they advanced 100 yards nearer, very few would have returned to Bayonne; the French officers were seen beating their men to get them on, but the unsteady behaviour of the conscripts was worse than anything I ever saw, excepting the usual behaviour of the Spaniards, and they could not have done worse; 1200 British under the same circumstances would have cut to pieces every man; we had no retreat, the sea on our left and our rear and the Adour on our right, everything depended on the steady conduct of our men, which could not be exceeded.[5]

A short while afterwards darkness fell and whilst a bright moon shone in the sky the Guards worked feverishly to get more of their men across, toiling by the light of bonfires lighted upon the shore. Trees were cut down also, not only to provide light but also warmth as it was a very cold and clear night. The tide had slackened by now, making the operation much easier, and when the first rays of dawn revealed the flotilla lying in the mouth of the river the safe crossing of the river was assured, although it was not completed without further incident. Indeed, one of the large boats, the *Lyra*, was overturned by some swell at high tide and although the Guards managed to pull out most of the captain and crew, some sailors were drowned.

As the day wore on the number of troops on the northern bank of the Adour began to steadily increase. Some of Vandeleur's cavalry had even got across, the horses swimming behind the boats as the light dragoons held their reins. By evening the remainder of the 2nd Brigade of Guards had got across as well as the 1st Brigade and a brigade of the King's German Legion.

The construction of the bridge was begun on the 25th and completed on the afternoon of the following day. Some twenty-six boats were moored forty feet apart and connected by strong cables. Planks were laid over these to form a secure roadway which rose and fell with the tide. A boom was constructed above the bridge and further protection was provided by shore batteries.

Even as the bridge neared completion Hope had begun the investment of Bayonne when, on the morning of February 25th the 1st Division and Bradford's Portuguese advanced to the citadel which was situated on the northern bank of the Adour. The 1st Brigade of Guards advanced with the Adour on their right whilst the 2nd Brigade and the King's German Legion brigade wheeled around behind them to take up positions in the centre and left respectively, and with the 5th Division still on the south bank a circle was formed around Bayonne, severing all communications with the rest of France. The French, meanwhile, had troops entrenched in the fortified town of St Etienne which commanded the ridge along which ran the road to Bordeaux. Further protection was provided by the guns in the citadel.

On February 26th the Guards advanced to within cannon shot of the French advanced positions in a display of marching calculated to depress the already sagging morale of the French troops even further. The First Guards advanced in echelon of battalions on the left with the 3rd Battalion in front. When the battalion reached some high ground in front of the French it halted and unfurled the battalion's colours at which the 1st battalion advanced also. When the battalions had crossed the marshy plain which had been flooded by the enemy on the left of the citadel the French guns opened fire but covered by the light companies the Guards were able to drive the French from their entrenchments and halted when they were just 900 yards from the citadel with their right resting on the Convent of St Bernard on the banks of the Adour. The 2nd Brigade of Guards, meanwhile, had made a similar advance to the village of St Etienne where, in spite of fierce resistance put up by the French, they swept the enemy out and forced them to flee to the citadel, leaving behind one gun. Both brigades now began to set about strengthening the positions in preparation for the investment of Bayonne.

Sir John Hope made his preparations for the attack on Bayonne throughout March of 1814 but he had no heavy artillery, without which he could not hope to take the city by storm, the more so since Thouvenot had turned the place into a strongly fortified place with every house being converted into an armed position. The accuracy of the French gunners also proved a major hindrance.

Whilst Bayonne was being besieged events elsewhere in the Peninsula - and in Europe - were moving quickly. On February 27th Wellington defeated Soult at Orthes, forcing the French commander to retreat to Toulouse which he entered on March 24th. Six days later the Russians and Prussians entered Paris and on April 4th Napoleon was forced to abdicate. News was slow to travel, however, and neither Soult nor Wellington received news of the abdication until April 12th, by which time the Allies had stormed Toulouse in a major battle which cost Wellington 4,568 unnecessary casualties. Wellington duly entered Toulouse on April 12th which all but brought the Peninsular War to a close. However, there was still one bloody postscript to come, one in which the Guards would find themselves deeply involved.

The two Brigades of Guards in front of Bayonne were having a miserable time of it, kicking their heels in frustration in the Allied lines whilst the rest of Wellington's army pushed on towards Bordeaux and Toulouse. John Rous, with the Coldstream, bemoaned the lack of activity and the missed opportunities to socialise with the locals, particularly at Toulouse:

The inhabitants are civil, and they are glad to have the English in their houses; there are Balls &c. in all the large towns the army passes through, and since the Guards are supposed to carry with them all the gold of the army, we should be more happy even than we should be in England. Here we see nobody, nothing going on, not even a library within reach; when we are not on duty the only amusement is to see the trees and grass grow.....William [Rous, his brother] is posted to the light infantry [company] which I tell him is a great honour. The first picquet he was on, he was struck in the face by a piece of mortar, owing to a round shot striking a house close to him, the wound was not sever enough to leave any mark on the following day....We are not allowed to ride two miles from camp, lest the French should attack us which is improbable; we know they are afraid to trust the garrison beyond their outworks.[6]

The last two lines of John Rous' letter, written to his mother on April 9th, are most ironic given the events that were to happen five days later.

On April 12th news of Napoleon's abdication finally reached Wellington at Toulouse whereupon he quickly informed Soult. The French commander then despatched a messenger to Bayonne in order to inform Governor Thouvenot. By now rumours were flying thick and fast in both French and British camps - Hope had received news of the fall of Paris on April 7th -and when word arrived on the 13th of the abdication the British commanders appear to have relaxed somewhat, one officer even going so far as to tell his men that they would soon be home in England with their wives and families.[7] The French, however, had different ideas and Thouvenot, still refusing to believe the news of his emperor's abdication, decided to make one final sortie.

Shortly before dawn on April 14th almost 6,000 French troops began to assemble in the citadel of Bayonne ready to attack the Allied line which was held that morning by Bradford's Portuguese on the extreme left, the King's German Legion on their right, Stopford's Brigade of Guards in the centre and Maitland's Brigade of Guards on the right. The line had been strengthened by Hay's brigade of the 5th Division that had been brought across from the south bank of the Adour. Hay was the officer of the day, in fact, and he had already been warned of the impending sortie by two French deserters who had come across to the Allied line at 2am. However, as Hay did not speak French the deserters were passed on to General Hinuber who got the information from them. Their story was not believed by Hay but at least Hinuber took the precaution of getting his men under arms and passing the information on to Hope.

At 3am the French began to move out from the citadel in three columns under cover of a very dark night, crawling up the side of the hill on which the Allied picquets were stationed, taking them by surprise.[8] Some of the sentries were killed almost immediately. Amidst loud cheers of 'En Avant! En Avant!' the French stormed forward, the flashes of musketry and glare of exploding shells lighting up their movements. The right hand column stormed the village of St Etienne, driving out all the Allied troops except for a group of the 38th Regiment who held on grimly to a single house there, and to make matters worse Hay was killed almost at once at the village church as he tried frantically to organise his men. His last order was for the church to be defended to the last man. It was impossible to distinguish friend from foe in the darkness and as the fighting escalated so did the chaos and confusion. On the left picquets of the 3rd Guards and Coldstream Guards were positioned in a sunken road, with its sides so steep as to make it difficult to get out of in a hurry except at intervals every

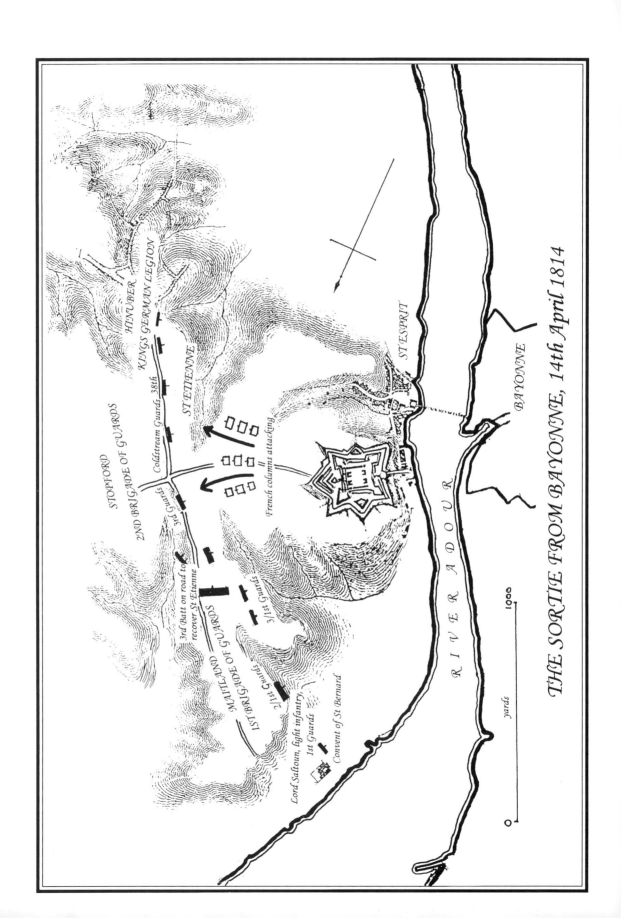

THE SORTIE FROM BAYONNE, 14th April 1814

HINUBER

KINGS GERMAN LEGION

ST.ETIENNE

STOPFORD

2ND BRIGADE OF GUARDS

Coldstream Guards 38th

3rd Guards

French columns attacking

ST.ESPRIT

BAYONNE

RIVER ADOUR

3rd Batt on road to
recover St Etienne

3/1st Guards

MAITLAND OF GUARDS

1ST BRIGADE OF GUARDS

2/1st Guards

Lord Saltoun, light infantry

1st Guards

Convent of St Bernard

yards

1000

0

few yards where gaps were broken in the hedges. When the French came on them the Guards here were completely overrun and the rest of their battalions forced from the sunken road in which they had been positioned:

When the French columns broke through the line in different places, parts of the picquets were completely cut off from all communication with their supports, and retreat was impossible; in these places the soldiers fought with desperation, and heaps of the slain, both French and English, were afterwards found on the points of attack; most of them had been killed with the bayonet.[9]

The 2nd Brigade of Guards suffered many casualties here and no less than 142 of Stopford's brigade were taken prisoner - Stopford himself was wounded, command of the brigade passing to Colonel James Guise - whilst the rest of his brigade was driven back. George Bowles, of the Coldstream wrote:

It was a sharp business for some minutes. My company on moving up to support the picquets consisted of seventy rank and file, of which number forty-eight were killed or wounded in about a quarter of an hour....I got off with a slight contusion on the leg, not so bad as *a good shiner*.[10]

At this point the guns inside the citadel opened up whilst the French gunboats on the Adour joined in, adding to the noise and the turmoil, and as the French advanced their sappers set about filling in trenches and destroying siege works.

With the 2nd Brigade of Guards having been driven back Maitland's 1st Brigade of Guards, which was already being attacked by Thouvenot's centre column, found their left flank exposed and for a time the situation was serious. Fortunately, Lord Saltoun had already seen to it that the Convent of St Bernard was barricaded and at the time of the French attack it was quite 'a respectable little fortress.'[11] The attack here was not push with the same vigour as elsewhere and the picquets of the First Guards were able to pull back in an orderly manner, although Lieutenant Colonel Townshend was badly wounded and taken prisoner. Worse was to come, for as Sir John Hope - always one to lead from the front - came galloping forward with his staff he ran straight into a group of enemy picquets, lining the sunken road from which Stopford's brigade had been driven. Hope was shot in the arm and as his horse was shot under him, he was trapped beneath it. His staff escaped although two of them tried to help him but were likewise wounded. Hope was then taken prisoner by some soldiers of the French 82nd Regiment.[12]

Command of the fighting on the Allied side now devolved upon individual unit commanders, none of whom had any idea what was happening around them. As the French attack continued nearly seventy guns were brought into action to support them, and as Robert Batty, of the First Guards, later wrote:

shells were continually flying through the air, describing beautiful curves of light as they fell; and the flashes from the cannon were almost incessant, rendering darkness doubly obscure at any momentary pause.[13]

Fortunately, General Hinuber, having already been warned of the sortie by the two deserters, had brought forward his Germans, some five battalions in all, on the left flank and the French attack here was stemmed. The French, meanwhile, still uncertain as to the extent of their attack, had also become disorganised and in the darkness the sortie ground to a halt which gave General Howard time to organise a counter-attack.

Howard ordered Maitland to bring forward his 1st Brigade of Guards in order to attack the left column of enemy, still occupying the sunken road on their left. Maitland ordered both 1st and 3rd battalions of the First Guards to lie down and wait whilst Colonel Woodford gathered together as many of the Coldstream as he could. In front were the French who could only be distinguished by the flashes of musketry from behind the hedges and walls but when the order was given, all three battalions sprang to their feet and after giving a huge cheer charged the French, driving them from their positions at bayonet point 'in great style.'[14] At this point the French, fearing that they might be cut off from the citadel, withdrew to Bayonne as grey streaks of dawn broke through the sky, exposing not only the retreating French but also heaps of dead and wounded soldiers from both sides, intermingled, and bearing testimony to the savagery of the fight. Robert Batty later wrote a graphic account of the sortie:

It would be almost impossible to convey an idea of the effect produced by the numerous flashes from the cannon and the sparkling light from the musketry, or of the confused noise from the roar of cannon, the bursting of shells, and the cheers of the soldiers, intermingled with the piercing shrieks and groans of the dying and wounded. At times the darkness was in part dispelled by the bright blue light of fire-balls thrown from the citadel, to show the assailants where to direct their guns; which they effectually did, by the great brilliancy with which they burned. Some of these fire-balls and shells fell in the midst of the depot of fascines, which instantly caught fire and burnt with great fierceness; so as to require constant exertions before they could be extinguished. Several houses caught fire, and two in particular burnt for a time with great violence, casting a lurid light under the vaulted clouds of smoke which rose to the skies. It seemed as though the elements of destruction had all burst forth together over this deep ensanguined scene of two contending armies.[15]

The sortie from Bayonne was a needless and futile postscript to the Peninsular War - it was also a bloody one. During the few hours of fighting the Allies suffered 1,544 casualties. The French lost 905 men. Casualties amongst the Guards were heavy. The First Guards got off lightly, the 1st Battalion suffering just one man killed and 6 wounded, whilst the 3rd Battalion suffered 2 men killed, and 2 officers, and 31 men wounded. one officer and 15 men were taken prisoner. The wounded officers were Captain Percival and Captain Vane. Lieutenant Colonel the Hon. H. Townshend was the officer taken prisoner after being wounded. The Coldstream Guards suffered 2 officers and 32 men killed and 6 officers and 122 men wounded. 84 men were taken prisoner. The two officers that were killed were Sir Henry Sullivan and Captain Crofton and of the wounded, Lieutenant Colonel Collier, Captain Burroughs and Ensigns Vachell and Pitt all later died of their wounds. The 3rd Guards lost 35 men killed and 5 officers and 106 men wounded. The wounded officers were Captains White, West, Shiffner, Mahon and Holbourne. Of these all but Captain West later died of their wounds. One officer, Ensign Northmore, and 57 men were taken prisoner. The casualties amongst the two Brigades of Guards during this short and unnecessary action represented as serious a loss as had been sustained at any time during the war.

When the fighting was over a truce was declared at the outposts and officers from both sides came forward to talk to each other. The British officers expressed much regret at the loss of so many good men in an action which should never have taken place. The French, however, showed little remorse:

It was quite disgusting to observe the *nonchalance* affected by these gentlemen, and the light manner in which they pretended to treat it, remarking that, after all, it was nothing more than a *petite promenade militaire*. But it would be difficult to convey an idea of their astonishment, when we informed them of the events which had recently occurred in Paris, and they would not believe it possible that their idol Napoleon had abdicated the throne.[16]

William Rous, of the Coldstream Guards, brother of John Rous of the same regiment, echoed these sentiments and added that, 'Thouvenot declares he is very sorry that he ordered the sortie the other day; it was extremely unlucky....'[17]

Nevertheless, Napoleon had abdicated although news did not reach the Allies before Bayonne until April 18th, one day after Soult had surrendered to Wellington. The news was immediately communicated to Thouvenot but he still refused to surrender. On April 20th the Bourbon standard was raised by the Allies in front of the city and a twenty-one gun salute was fired to which the French replied by raising the tricolour and firing two guns towards the Allied lines. However, it was to be a further seven days before one of Soult's aides-de-camp rode into Bayonne on April 27th with official news of the suspension of hostilities, dated April 17th the date that in spite of the prolonged siege of Bayonne can really be said to mark the end of the Peninsular War. Peace was officially signed at Paris on May 30th.

The war was over but the Brigades of Guards remained in and around Bayonne until June 16th when they were ordered to march to Bordeaux. The 1st Brigade of Guards remained in the town until July 23rd when the troops began to be transported in boats up the river Gironde where the ships *Tigre, Belle Poule* and *Freya* lay at anchor in the river's mouth. The troops being embarked the ships eventually sailed on July 26th and 27th, reaching Portsmouth at the beginning of August. Once ashore the two battalions of the First Guards marched to London where they arrived on August 10th.[18] The Coldstream Guards left Bayonne on May 2nd and arrived in Bordeaux on June 23rd. The battalion remained there for a month before it too was conveyed up river in boats before being embarked aboard the 74-gun ship *Stirling Castle*. The ship arrived at Spithead on July 28th and after a march from Portsmouth the battalion arrived at its barracks in Portman Street, London, on August 4th.[19] The Third Guards departed from Bordeaux at the same time and like the Coldstream Guards arrived in London in early August after being in the Peninsula for the previous four and a half years.[20]

NOTES

[1] Captain Robert Batty, *Campaign of the Left Wing of the Allied Army, in the Western Pyrenees and South of France, in the years 1813-14,* (London, 1823), 115.
[2] Ibid. 119.

[3] Sir Charles Oman, *A History of the Peninsular War*, (Oxford, 1902-30), vii. 334. Hamilton, Aubrey-Fletcher and Maurice all state that ten companies of the Coldstream and six companies of the Third Guards made the first crossing, but we believe these had not all got across until late in the evening.

[4] Ibid. vii. p.335.

[5] Ian Fletcher, (Ed), *A Guards Officer in the Peninsula; The Peninsular War letters of John Rous, Coldstream Guards, 1812-1814*, (Tunbridge Wells, 1992), 96.

[6] Ibid. 109-110.

[7] Julian Paget, *Wellington's Peninsular War*, (London, 1990), 241.

[8] Batty, *Campaign in the Pyrenees*, 159.

[9] Ibid. 160.

[10] The Earl of Malmesbury, *A Series of Letters of the First Earl of Malmesbury, His Family and Friends, from 1745 to 1820*, (London, 1870), ii. 412.

[11] Batty, *Campaign in the Pyrenees,* 160.

[12] Five months earlier, Wellington had predicted such an event. 'We shall lose him [Hope] if he continues to expose himself to fire.....indeed his escape has been wonderful. He places himself among the sharpshooters, without (as they do) sheltering himself from the enemy's fire.' *Wellington's Despatches*, xi. 371-372. To add insult to injury, Hope was wounded in the foot by an English bullet whilst he was being taken into Bayonne.

[13] Batty, *Campaign in the Pyrenees,* 161.

[14] Fletcher, *A Guards Officer*, 111.

[15] Batty, *Campaign in the Pyrenees*, 164.

[16] Ibid.165.

[17] Fletcher, *A Guards Officer*, 119.

[18] Lieutenant General Sir F.W. Hamilton, *The Origin and History of the First or Grenadier Guards*, (London, 1874), ii.483.

[19] Colonel Daniel Mackinnon, *Origins and Services of the Coldstream Guards*, (London, 1833), ii. 447.

[20] Major General Sir Frederick Maurice, *The History of the Scots Guards, from 1642 to 1914*, (London, 1934), i. 400.

QUATRE BRAS

Throughout the summer and late into the autumn of 1814 celebrations were held the length and breadth of Britain to mark the end of the Peninsular War and the defeat of Napoleon. In Europe, too, his abdication was welcomed and celebrated with joy and relief but even as the Congress of Vienna was meeting to redraw the map of Europe in the wake of his downfall the 'thief of Europe' as Napoleon had become known, was making plans to escape from his enforced exile on the tiny island of Elba.

On February 26th 1815, barely ten months after he had begun his period of exile, Napoleon set sail from Elba accompanied by just a few hundred soldiers and on March 1st he landed on the French mainland at Cannes from where he would begin his march on Paris. By March 10th he had reached Lyons by which time all of the troops sent to oppose him, including a large number under Marshal Ney, had fallen once again beneath his spell and deserted the royalist cause to follow their old master. Amidst great alarm, consternation and chaos King Louis XVIII fled his capital on March 19th and the following day Napoleon entered Paris in triumph, cheered by his men but greeted frostily by the population who seemed resigned to see their country torn apart by war once again. Once back in power Napoleon immediately set about recruiting large numbers for his army and within just two months he had gathered together a force of 250,000 regulars and an equal number of the National Guard and as each day passed so the numbers swelled further.

In Vienna, meanwhile, the news of his escape from Elba and his subsequent march on Paris stunned the Allied powers who were busy quarrelling over the future shape of the Continent. The news from France, however, came like a bombshell and shook the protagonists from their squabbles, galvanising them into action and sending the various leaders, Wellington included, hurrying off to assume command of their respective forces. There could be only one course of action open to the Allies, namely, an invasion of France and the extinguishing of the Napoleonic flame for ever. The resulting plan involved each of the four major powers, Britain, Austria, Prussia and Russia, fielding 150,000 men who would invade France from the north and east. The operation would, of course, take some months to prepare, especially for Austria and Russia, situated hundreds of miles away, and it became clear, therefore, that to the armies of Britain and Prussia would fall the initial thrust. Napoleon, however, had other ideas.

Wellington, meanwhile, had set about gathering his troops together, a task made appreciably more harder by the fact that many of his veteran Peninsular battalions had been sent overseas, to America, for instance, from where they were hastily recalled, sadly, for the most part, in vain. However, Sir Thomas Graham's force, which had taken part in the attack on Bergen-op-Zoom the previous year, was still in Belgium, where Wellington planned to concentrate his army. The 1st battalions of the Coldstream and Third Guards had long since arrived home safely from the Peninsula but Graham's force did include the 2nd battalions of the First, Coldstream and Third Guards and during the summer and autumn of 1814 they were joined by virtually all the King's German Legion as well as 15,000 Hanoverian Militia.

On the resumption of hostilities between Napoleon and the Allies other units were despatched to Belgium and by the time Wellington arrived in Brussels on April 4th 1815 his force numbered around 100,000 men although the British contingent numbered just 30,000. Of these, the majority were raw recruits, 'half-trained youths, hurriedly drafted in from the militia, and it is probable that not more than 6000 of them had ever heard a shot fired in anger.'[1] There were some seasoned units present, such as the Rifle Corps, the King's German Legion and those belonging to Sir Thomas Picton's 5th Division but on the whole Wellington would begin the campaign with an army he considered to be 'the worst...with the worst equipment and the worst staffs that he had ever commanded.'[2] In fact, the composition of his army provoked from Wellington one of his most famous pronouncements, when he wrote on May 15th:

I have got an infamous army, very weak and ill equipped, and a very inexperienced Staff. In my opinion they are doing nothing in England. They have not raised a man; they have not called out the militia either in England or Ireland.[3]

The two Brigades of Guards, under the command of General Sir George Cooke, were amongst his best troops. The 2nd Battalion First Guards, the 2nd Battalion Coldstream Guards and the 2nd Battalion Third Guards had all been in Holland with Sir Thomas Graham and these were joined in April by the 3rd Battalion First Guards, a veteran Peninsular battalion.

The three battalions of Guards already in Belgium at the outset of the campaign mustered in the Grand Place, Brussels, early on the morning of March 25th and immediately set off marching towards the village of Hal. From there they continued on to Ath with the intention of laying siege to Lille but as this project was abandoned the Guards returned to Enghien where, on April 4th, they went into cantonments and remained thus until the outbreak of fighting in June.[4]

Whilst the three battalions of Guards settled down to a routine of field sports, parties, sightseeing and regular army work, the 3rd Battalion First Guards was busy hurrying to join them having been ordered to join the Allied army at the beginning of April. The battalion marched from its barracks at Birdcage Walk, London, early on the morning of April 5th, accompanied by the Duke of York who turned out in his uniform as colonel of the regiment. After a march of four days along Kentish roads the battalion reached Ramsgate on April 9th where the Duke of York bade farewell and following an uneventful crossing of the Channel disembarked at Ostend on the 10th. The following day the Guardsmen clambered into barges and soon were gliding gently up river to Bruges which they reached the same day and Ghent which they reached on the 12th. Finally, the battalion marched to Enghien which they reached on April 14th to join their comrades of the other three battalions of Guards already waiting there.

At Enghien the Guards were formed into two brigades, the 2nd and 3rd Battalions First Guards, under Peregrine Maitland formed the 1st Brigade, and the 2nd Battalion Coldstream Guards and the 2nd Battalion Third Guards, under General Sir John Byng, formed the 2nd Brigade. The whole formed the 1st Division of the army, commanded by General Cooke. The four battalions of Guards numbered about 1,000 men each, making them by far the strongest battalions in Wellington's army. On May 1st the Guards Division was reviewed by Wellington who was most pleased with the appearance of his troops, the more so since he would need all the experienced soldiers he could muster to face the might of Napoleon. After the review General Maitland issued the following complimentary order:

Soldiers, I am desired by the Duke of Wellington to express his entire approbation of your appearance, and emphatically to communicate to you the satisfaction he was pleased to express at having once more under his command two such Brigades of Guards. I congratulate you on the good opinion he entertains of us; and I say, let us not only maintain it, but let us add to it by our good conduct. Let it increase with the growth of his longer acquaintance with us.[5]

Between now and the opening shots of the campaign, the Guards amused themselves with many pastimes. They played cricket matches, visited friends in other regiments and went sightseeing, balls were held at Brussels and countless reviews took place. On May 31st the Guards Division marched from its cantonments around Enghien to Bruyere de Corteau in order to be reviewed by the Prince of Orange, commanding the First Corps of the army of which the Guards Division was part. The division marched at 2am in the morning, beginning in darkness as rain began to fall. By the time the Guards returned to their camp, grumbling and questioning the necessity of undergoing such a task, they had marched a very fatiguing forty miles. Nevertheless, the Guards turned out in their customary fine style and earned yet another complimentary order, this time from General Cooke:

Major General Cooke has great pleasure in communicating to the division the entire satisfaction of HRH the Prince of Orange at their appearance yesterday morning, and the warm approbation that he expressed at the steadiness and discipline with which the several corps performed their movements. The Prince of Orange was pleased to remark also to other officers, that, although he had been many years with the British army, he never before had seen so perfect a body of men.[6]

The beginning of June still found Wellington's army scattered throughout the villages south of Brussels but whereas his own men occupied themselves in various ways Napoleon's army was on the march and beginning to concentrate on the French-Belgian border. The Emperor knew he could not hope to defeat the combined armies of the Allied powers but a victory against at least one of them may lead the others to sue for peace.

The obvious target for such an attack was north where the Wellington's Anglo-Dutch army and Blucher's Prussians were concentrated. These two armies had yet to present a united front and more significantly, their respective lines of communication - Antwerp and the Lower Rhine - were dissimilar to say the least. Should either Wellington or Blucher suffer a defeat at the hands of Napoleon they would inevitably, for safety's sake, have to retreat in the opposite direction, away from the other. This strategy of course depended on Napoleon's ability to defeat either Wellington or Blucher before the one could assist the other. It was a simple variant on the Roman strategy *divide et impera* - 'Divide and Rule.'[7] Such a victory, with its consequential advance on Brussels, would not only leave one army defeated and one dangerously isolated, it would also almost certainly dissuade the Russians and Austrians from any further military action for the time being and so gain Napoleon further time to strengthen his position.

On the morning of June 15th Napoleon struck. Having left Paris on the 12th he travelled quickly to join his army and on June 14th was addressing his soldiers, having concentrated his forces within just a few miles of the Allied outposts with such remarkable speed and secrecy that they had no knowledge of his whereabouts. His plan was to drive a wedge between the Anglo-Dutch and Prussian armies and whilst Marshal Ney held Wellington in check Napoleon himself would crush Blucher before his allies could come to his aid. This would then leave Wellington to be dealt with which meant the prospect of a bloody battle but by dealing with the Allied armies separately Napoleon's chances of overall success would be greatly improved. It all depended upon him being able to prevent Wellington and Blucher from joining forces and in order to try and achieve this he detached Marshal Ney, with 20,000 men to take the vital crossroads at Quatre Bras, commanding the road to Brussels, whilst he himself commanded 78,000 troops whom he would lead against Blucher's Prussians at Ligny, to the south-east of Quatre Bras.

With this plan planted firmly in his mind Napoleon gave the order to cross the Belgian border and soon his cavalry were plunging and splashing through the dark waters of the River Sambre. It was the morning of June 15th 1815 and some twenty-two years of Napoleonic warfare were about to come to an awesome and gigantic, bloody climax.

The campaign got off to a somewhat inauspicious start as delays as bad staff work prevented the bulk of the French army from crossing the Sambre until late in the afternoon. However, there were enough of them to force the Prussian outposts to retire through Charleroi and Fleurus to Ligny. With the main road to Brussels now open Napoleon began to feed his cavalry along it until they came up against a battalion of Nassauers at Frasnes, three miles south of Quatre Bras on the left flank of Wellington's army. Faced with large enemy numbers this battalion was forced back as far as the Bois de Bossu to the south west of the crossroads at Quatre Bras.

In Brussels, meanwhile, rumours and counter-rumours flew thick and fast about the capital but it was not until about 2 o'clock on the afternoon of the 15th that Wellington received confirmation of the French attack on the Prussians, following which he issued orders for the concentration at their assembly

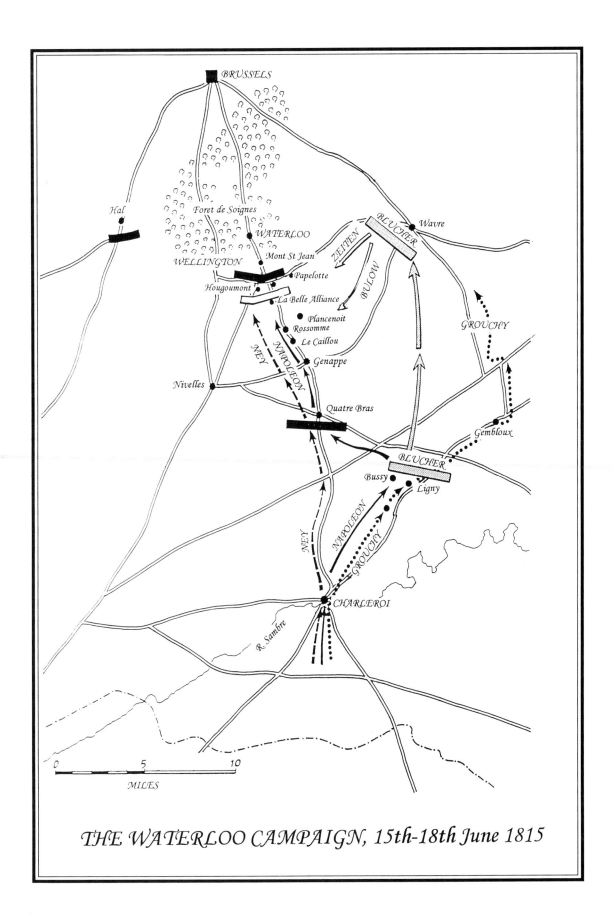

THE WATERLOO CAMPAIGN, 15th-18th June 1815

points of the divisions of his army, which he did at 5pm, Nivelles being the assembly point for the bulk of his troops.

The situation does not appear to have worried Wellington too much for on the evening of June 15th, whilst Napoleon advanced from the south, he donned his finest clothes and took himself off to a Ball given by the Duchess of Richmond in Brussels, held in the empty workshops of a coach builder in the Rue de la Blanchisserie.[8] Indeed, the majority of his officers likewise attended the Ball. The officers of the Guards, never ones to pass up such an opportunity of attending such an affair, were well represented and the Ball gave them the chance to don their full dress uniforms and take to the floor in the presence not only of the Commander-in-Chief but also a host of ladies who were residing in Brussels at the time. Indeed, it was a far cry from many of the Balls they had attended in the Peninsula where female company was at a premium.

Wellington has often been criticised for attending the Ball at such a moment but he was evidently satisfied with his arrangements and his presence had a tremendous morale-boosting effect on the civilian population as any sudden and hasty departure for the front might have precipitated panic amongst them. However, at around midnight, shortly after Wellington had sat down to supper, the Prince of Orange appeared at his side and whispered something in his ear for several minutes. The news obviously startled him but he composed himself and ordered the Prince back to his quarters at Braine-le-Comte. Wellington, meanwhile, continued eating and talking with the guests for about another twenty minutes until he turned to the Duke of Richmond and said, 'it is time for me to go to bed.' The Duke of Richmond's aide-de-camp, George Bowles, of the Coldstream Guards, takes up the story:

Wishing him goodnight, [Wellington] whispered to ask him if he had a good map in the house. The Duke of Richmond said he had, and took him into his dressing room, which opened into the supper room. The Duke of Wellington shut the door and said, 'Napoleon has *humbugged* me (by God), he has gained twenty-four hours' march on me.' The Duke of Richmond said, 'What do you intend doing?' The Duke of Wellington replied, 'I have ordered the army to concentrate at Quatre Bras: but we shall not stop him there, and if so I must fight him *here*' (at the same time passing his thumb-nail over the position of Waterloo.)[9]

Wellington then ordered all officers to leave the Ball quietly and return to their units although by now rumours were spreading and a mild calm turned into a minor panic. Many of the officers returned to find their baggage already packed and were unable to get to their campaign uniforms. 'Poor fellows, they found their baggage packed and gone, and many of them died next day in silk stockings and dancing pumps.'[10]

Soon, the streets of Brussels echoed to the blaring of bugles and the beating of drums as Wellington's troops began to pour out of the city to begin their march south towards Nivelles and Quatre Bras. The Guards Division, meanwhile, had been ordered to move from their camp at Enghien to Braine-le-Compte. The order was issued late on the night of June 15th and did not reach the General Cooke until 1am the next morning. Drums immediately called the men to arms and by 4am the Guards Division was ready to march, the light companies, commanded by Lord Saltoun, in the lead. The Guards reached Braine-le-Compte at 9am whereupon they halted four three hours, due partly to the difficulty in getting through the extremely crowded streets of the place, but also because of the excessive heat of the day, the men taking the opportunity to take off their packs and grab some rest after the rigours of the march. Whilst the Guards rested General Cooke took himself off on a reconnaissance mission towards Quatre Bras but when he returned at midday the march towards Nivelles was resumed. Another hard, sweaty march along dusty roads brought them to within half a mile of Nivelles at 3pm where the Guards halted and lit fires in order to cook their rations but if the they thought they were to savour the joys of another period of rest they were much mistaken for they had not long piled arms before an aide-de-camp came galloping breathlessly along the road with orders for Cooke's division to resume their march immediately, as Ensign Robert Batty, of the 3rd Battalion, First Guards later wrote:

The order was, of course, instantly obeyed; the meat which was cooking was thrown away, the kettles, &c. packed up, and we proceeded, as fast as our tired legs would carry us, towards a scene of slaughter, which was a prelude well calculated to usher in the bloody tragedy of the 18th.[11]

Any grumbling amidst the ranks of sore-footed Guardsmen was soon replaced by an anxiety to get forward as the sound of gunfire became clearer in the distance in front of them. In fact, in spite of the heat, the Guards marched at the double in their efforts to get forward an meet the enemy, the excitement and tension increasing further as they began to encounter a stream of wounded men passing to the rear. Batty again:

We marched up towards the enemy, at each step hearing more clearly the fire of musketry; and as we approached the field of action we met constantly waggons full of men, of all the various nations under the Duke's command, wounded in the most dreadful manner. The sides of the road had a heap of dying and dead, very many of whom were British: such a scene did, indeed, demand every better feeling of the mind to cope with its horrors; and too much cannot be said in praise of the division of Guards, the very largest part of whom were young soldiers, and volunteers from the militia, who had never been exposed to the fire of the enemy, or witnessed its effects.[12]

Ensign Edward Macready, of the 30th Regiment, later recalled that there was a good deal of good-humoured banter, much of it at the Guards' expense when his regiment came up with the Guards just after passing through Nivelles:

After passing Nivelles, we started double quick, for the firing increased, and we soon came up with the division of Guards. They jeered us about 'our hurry', and our fellows taunted them in return. 'Shall I carry your honour on my pack?' said one of ours to a Guardsman as he was falling out. 'Haven't you some gruel for that gentleman?' shouted another. 'It's a cruel shame to send gentlemen's sons on such business,' continued a third.[13]

Finally, at about 5pm and after a exhausting march of some twenty-six miles, the 1st Brigade of Guards arrived at the north-western edge of a wood called the Bois de Bossu which was situated on the right of the crossroads at Quatre Bras, the 2nd Brigade of Guards arriving shortly afterwards.

The Guards Division had arrived at Quatre Bras at a critical moment, just when the Belgian troops in the wood were giving way.[14] Picton's 5th Division was for some time the only British unit at Quatre Bras, assisting the left of the Dutch-Belgian army under the Prince of Orange, and several hours of hard fighting passed as other Allied units began to arrive piecemeal at the crossroads.

The Guards entered the fight just as Picton's right flank, which hinged upon the crossroads, was about to be swallowed up by Jerome's men who were debouching from the Bois de Bossu. The Prince of Orange, upon seeing the arrival of the Guards, came galloping up 'in a state of excusable excitement'[15] and ordered Saltoun to send his light companies of the First Guards into the wood to drive the French from it. Saltoun, however, could see no enemy and asked the Prince where they were, to which the latter replied, 'Sir, if you do not like to undertake it, I'll find someone.'[16] The Prince of Orange, a young man who was to be the centre of several controversial decisions during the campaign, thought Saltoun was hesitating but the commander of the Guards repeated the question and this time, on the enemy being pointed out to him, he formed his men into a line of skirmishers, drew his sword and led his men into the wood, followed by the battalion companies of the 2nd Battalion First Guards, under Colonel Askew, who had likewise been ordered into the woods by the Prince of Orange. Indeed, the Guards suffered through having to enter the wood company by company as soon as each of them arrived, instead of being allowed to form up and advance in a proper formation. The men were tired, weary and hungry after being on the march for fifteen hours but they fixed bayonets, gave three cheers and then entered the wood. Private William Blake, of the First Guards, wrote:

our regiment marched into the wood without the slightest suspicion, when we were attacked on all sides by the enemy who had lain in the ditches on each side of the wood where hundreds of brave fellows fell without an opportunity of defending themselves as they [the French] opened a heavy fire from their guns which were posted on a hill about half a mile distant, which threw the whole of our men into confusion, some running one way and some another.[17]

The ensuing fighting was confused and severe as the Guardsmen got to grips with the French amidst the thick undergrowth of the wood in which it was often difficult for the Guards to see the enemy until they were right on top of them. Many of the Guards, overcome with fatigue, sank to their knees but 'lent their voice to cheer their comrades.'[18] The Guards disappeared into the wood and did not emerge until about an hour later. During that time all those outside, unable to see what was going on inside, listened tensely as the sound of musketry from inside told of the Guards' steady advance.

Jerome's men, flushed with victory and expecting nothing more serious than the rounding up of a few scores or hundreds of Netherlanders, finding themselves suddenly faced by formed bodies of great red-coated men, their clothing and faces whitened with dust and streaked with sweat, their eyes deep-sunk with exhaustion but shining with eager fury, their muskets belching flame reflected from their gleaming bayonets. One can imagine the check of astonishment, the stagger of dismay, and then back through the wood, dodging through the undergrowth, stopping to fire from behind a tree.....small bodies of Frenchmen hastily rallying under some determined leader, forming across a ride, trying their utmost to stay the lumbering onrush of those great red devils.[19]

A small stream ran through the centre of the wood and French skirmishers lined this in an attempt to stem the red tide but the Guards came on, cheering and charging, driving the French from it until at last they reached the far side of the wood.

During their relentless advance through the wood the light companies of the Guards suffered heavy casualties following an unfortunate incident which was almost entirely due to the way in which the reckless and almost hysterical Prince of Orange threw the battalion companies of the First Guards into the wood. Upon hearing the firing coming from the wood as Saltoun's light companies advanced, the Prince, assuming it to be the enemy, hastily ordered the battalion companies forward, firing as they went. The 'enemy', however, turned out to be Saltoun and as he realised just who was firing on his men he sent his subaltern, Charlie Ellis, back to tell them to stop firing. In the smoky confusion that prevailed in the thick undergrowth, however, it was impossible to stop the firing and it was not until all of the Guards had reached the far side of the wood that the error was realised.[20]

As soon as they debouched, however, the First Guards came under fire from the French artillery and reserve infantry. Shot and shell began to rain in on them, forcing them to retreat into the wood where they took shelter by the small stream although some shells continued to come bouncing in between the trees to cause casualties amongst them.

Whilst the 2nd Battalion First Guards sheltered from enemy fire by the stream they were joined by the 3rd Battalion, under Colonel Stuart, whose cursing, angry men tripped and stumbled through the tangle of wooded undergrowth to form up on the right of the 2nd Battalion. With both battalions now on the edge of the wood Maitland led them in repeated attempts to attack the French guns that had been shelling them throughout the late afternoon. During these attacks both Askew and Stuart, commanding the 2nd and 3rd Battalions respectively, were wounded and had to be carried from the field, command devolving upon Colonels Edward Stables and Francis D'Oyly. Maitland's attacks were unsuccessful, however, and both battalions remained close to the edge of the wood.

By now the 2nd Brigade of Guards, under Byng, had come up and formed on the right of the 1st Brigade. The only troops of the 2nd Brigade of Guards to be engaged were those of the light company of the Coldstream, under Lieutenant Colonel Macdonell, supported by four companies of the regiment under Lieutenant

Colonel Mackinnon, and the light company of the Third Guards, led by Lieutenant Colonel Home. These troops quickly became embroiled in the fight at the southern end of the Bossu wood and in the struggle for a farmhouse called La Grande Pierrepont. Private Matthew Clay, of the light company of the Third Guards, was in the thick of the action:

We loaded our muskets and very hastily advanced up the rising ground in the open field; (the shots from the enemy now whizzing amongst us,) we quickly attained the summit, and bringing our left shoulders forward, the enemy retiring before us. We had now arrived near to a building against the walls of which the shots from the guns of the enemy (intended for us) were freely rebounding, being just within range of their guns, our skilful commander led us through an enclosed yard, (where several bodies of the enemy's cavalry lay, slain previous to our arrival). We immediately formed in the field into which we had entered and were at the same time joined by our light artillery guns.[21]

There ensued a confused fight between the Guards and the French infantry around the farmhouse, the fighting swaying first one way and then the next. The light companies of the 2nd Brigade of Guards eventually grasped the upper hand and forced the French back following a charge led by Lieutenant Colonel Dashwood, of the Third Guards, who turned to his men saying, "Now men, let us see what you are made of!" The French were thrust back at bayonet point but wet forced to halt themselves in the face of a large enemy cavalry presence, as Clay recalled later:

We continued pursuing the enemy over the slain, which were thickly spread around us. By this time our commander found it necessary to form us into squares to oppose the enemy's cavalry, who were constantly menacing us on our advance, our square being compactly formed and prepared to receive cavalry. Their cavalry now bearing off, the enemy's artillery would alternately annoy us with their shells which were skilfully directed..........Their cavalry now menaced us more daringly and prevented our taking fresh ground until their artillery had thrown their shells amongst us. By this means we had a more narrow escape than before, being compelled to remain longer in our position to resist cavalry. I being one of the outward rank of the square, can testify as to the correct aim of the enemy, whose shells having fallen to the ground and exploded within a few paces of the rank in which I was kneeling, a portion of their destructive fragments in their ascent [would] pass between my head and that of my comrade next in the rank; its force and tremulous sound causing an unconscious movement of the head, not to be forgotten in haste.[22]

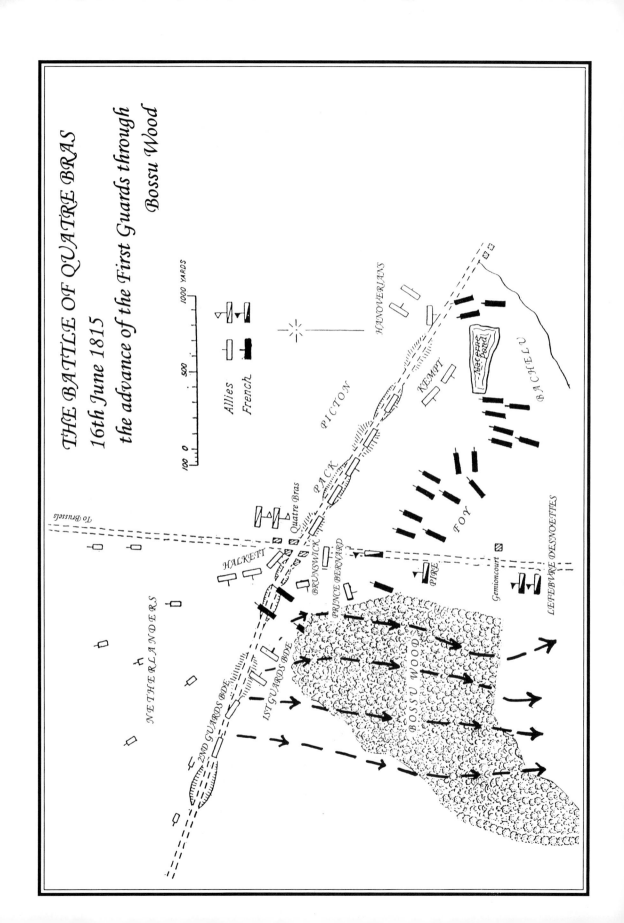

THE BATTLE OF QUATRE BRAS
16th June 1815
the advance of the First Guards through
Bossu Wood

Allies
French

1000 YARDS
500
100 0

To Brussels

Quatre Bras

HALKETT

NETHERLANDS

2ND GUARDS BDE

1ST GUARDS BDE

BRUNSWICK

PRINCE BERNARD

BOSSU WOOD

PACK

PICTON

KEMPT

FOY

PIRE

Gemioncourt

LEFEBURE DESSNOETTES

HANOVERIANS

BACHELU

Throughout the rest of the afternoon the 2nd and 3rd Battalions First Guards also kept up a constant firing on the French positions but were likewise prevented from advancing further by the constant hovering of the French cavalry. Indeed, the Guards were forced back into the wood on more than one occasion when, unable to form square, the men fell back to the shelter of the wood. Here, the First Guards took a heavy toll of the French cavalry and many riderless horses were taken by them for use by the officers of the regiment who had lost their own horses or whose mounts were blown.[23] One such mounted officer was not so lucky, however. Lord James Hay, acting as adjutant to Lord Saltoun, possessed a fine thoroughbred but it refused to jump a fence in the Bois de Bossu and reared up. As he struggled to control it Hay was shot dead by a French cavalry skirmisher. His body remained in the saddle and it was Saltoun, in fact, who discovered it when, riding up to the mounted motionless body, it fell across the neck of his own horse and rolled off onto the ground.

Another notable fatality was Lieutenant Colonel William Miller, of the 3rd Battalion First Guards.[24] Miller was shot during the closing stages of the battle and fell mortally wounded and was carried from the field by four Guardsmen. As he lay wounded he sent for his friend, Colonel Thomas, and said he would like to see the colours of the regiment once more before he `quit them for ever.' The colours were duly brought up and waved round his body, bringing a smile from Miller and as he was carried from the field he declared himself `satisfied.'[25] Miller was carried to Brussels where he died on June 19th. A brother officer of Miller, Captain Robert Adair, also of the 3rd Battalion First Guards, was struck by a cannonball towards the end of the day which shattered his thigh near the hip. Accordingly to Ensign Gronow, of the same battalion, Adair suffered terribly during the amputation as the shot had torn away the flesh and the bones were sticking out in splinters near the hip. The surgeon, a Mr Gilder, was forced to use a blunt knife owing to the number of amputations he had already performed during the action. Nevertheless, in spite of his sufferings, Adair was able to make light of his situation and joked, "Take your time, Mr Carver." Unfortunately, he died soon afterwards through loss of blood.[26]

As daylight faded so did the fighting. Wellington's strength at Quatre Bras had grown steadily throughout the afternoon and by evening Ney had been pushed back as far as Frasnes, Wellington establishing a line of picquets on the line from which the French had driven the Allies that very morning.

The cost had been high. Wellington's Anglo-Dutch army suffered 4,521 casualties of which 2,504 were British. The Guards Division sustained 548 casualties, most of which were amongst the First Guards who were suffered severely. The 2nd Battalion First Guards lost 3 officers and 23 men killed, and 4 officers and 256 men wounded. The officers killed were Captain T. Brown, Ensign Lord James Hay and Ensign the Hon. S.P. Barrington. The 3rd Battalion First Guards lost 3 officers and 20 men killed and 4 officers and 235 men wounded. The officers killed were Lieutenant Colonel William Miller, who died on June 19th, Captain E. Grose and Captain R. Adair.[27] As only the light companies of the 2nd Brigade of Guards were engaged casualties were light, seven men in fact, of the Third Guards.[28]

As usual, the battlefield at night was a wretched place with the groans of the dying and wounded being the only sounds to disturb the British troops, exhausted after the fatiguing march earlier in the day, as Matthew Clay recalled:

We were extended in line and lay down on our arms amongst the trampled corn. All being quiet, and diligently watching during the night, the only sounds we heard arose from the suffering wounded (in their different languages) who lay as they had fallen, some in the adjoining wood, others distant, and others nearer to us. In different parts of the plain or cornfield where we were posted, the deep and heavy groans of the more faint and expiring [mixed] with the loud calls for water from others less exhausted, whilst many hundreds of slain lay on every side, and a very formidable and watchful enemy before us.[29]

Ensign Short, of the Coldstream Guards, was on picquet duty that night and later recalled that:

The night passed off very well, though the groaning of the wounded was rather disagreeable or so, for the first time. I was very hungry the next morning having had nothing to eat since ten o'clock the day before, but a ship biscuit. I was called in about four o'clock. I then went to sleep and awoke about half past five, when I found Whitaker had sent me some bread and meat and a bottle of brandy, which I assure you was a great comfort, not being able to draw rations.[30]

Whilst Ney was in action against Wellington at Quatre Bras Napoleon, meanwhile, was attacking the Prussians under Blucher at Ligny. Here the fighting was bloody and losses on both sides heavy but at the end of the day Napoleon had given Blucher 'a damned good licking',[31] forcing him to retreat. This would seem to have been exactly what Napoleon had wanted, namely to separate Wellington from his Prussian allies. However, as Blucher retreated on the night on June 16th he fell back not on Liege to the east, as Gneisenau his Chief of Staff wished, but westward towards Wavre, the proud old Prussian having already promised Wellington that he would march to join him no matter what. The decision by Blucher to march west in order to form a junction with Wellington was the decisive moment of the whole campaign for upon the Prussian promise of assistance Wellington decided to stand and fight at the position south at Waterloo, at Mont St Jean. However, as the bruised and battered Blucher made his way slowly towards Wavre Wellington had yet to received news of the move and it was not until the morning of June 17th that he was told, as George Bowles, of the Coldstream, wrote:

On the morning of the 17th, my company being nearly in front of the farmhouse at Quatre Bras, soon after daybreak the Duke of Wellington came to me, and being personally known to him he remained in conversation for an hour or more, during which time he repeatedly said he was surprised to have heard nothing of Blucher. At length a staff officer arrived, his horse covered with foam, and whispered to the Duke, who without the least change of countenance gave him some orders and dismissed him. He then turned round to me and said, 'Old Blucher has had a damned good licking and gone back to Wavre, eighteen miles. As he has gone back we must go too. I suppose in England they will say we have been licked. I can't help it, as they are gone back we must go too.[32]

Within a few minutes Wellington had issued orders for a withdrawal northwards along the road to Brussels to the position at Mont St Jean, which he had already reconnoitred. As there seemed to be little activity in the French camp, and conscious of the fact that many of his men would have had little to eat or drink over the past twenty-four hours, he gave orders that the men should cook their breakfasts first. At 9am, when the cooking was finished, the Allies began to slip away from the position at Quatre Bras, leaving behind the cavalry under Lord Uxbridge and the horse artillery who were to cover the retreat.

June 17th dawned hot and sultry but as the retreating Allied army trudged up the road towards Mont St Jean the skies darkened and soon turned an inky black. The retreat had got underway without any interference from Ney who seemed to be paralysed and unable to comprehend the need for speedy pursuit. In fact, it was not until Napoleon himself arrived, seething at Ney's inertia, that the French stirred themselves into action. The Emperor led the pursuit in person, riding furiously at the head of his men, often close on the heels of the British rearguard.

A 'fox hunt' was how one of Wellington's men called it as Uxbridge's cavalry hurdled hedges and fences and rode headlong down narrow lanes to avoid capture by the pursuing French. It was all fast and furious stuff and the drama was added to when the heavens suddenly opened heralding the start of a torrential downpour that was to continue for the rest of the day and which did not let up until dawn the next morning. The moment was vividly described by Captain Cavalie Mercer, of the Royal Horse Artillery, who had halted to fire at the dark dense masses of French as they closed in. He later described the moment in his journal of the campaign:

The first gun that was fired seemed to burst the clouds overhead, for its report was instantly followed by an awful clap of thunder, and lightning that almost blinded us, whilst the rain came down as if a waterspout had broken over us. The sublimity of the scene was inconceivable. Flash succeeded flash, and the peals of thunder were long and tremendous; whilst, as if in mockery of the elements, the French guns still sent forth their feebler glare and now scarcely audible reports - their cavalry dashing on at a headlong pace, adding their shouts to the uproar.[33]

The Guards themselves had marched from Quatre Bras at about 11am on the 17th, the light companies remaining behind for a while as part of Uxbridge's rearguard. They retreated along the Nivelles road unhindered by the French and after a march of eight miles or so they arrived at the position on the heights of Mont St Jean which Wellington had chosen for the coming battle with Napoleon. Fortunately for the Guards they reached the position before the heavy rains began and so were able to gather wood for their fires and find shelter or erect their bivouacs on dry ground. The Guards were as shattered as everyone, having been on the march almost non-stop for the greater part of the last two days, during which they had fought a battle. There had been little time to eat, save at breakfast that morning, and so it was with some relief that each man cast off his heavy pack when the Guards arrived at the main position at Mont St Jean. No sooner had they done so, however, than the black clouds that had been threatening all afternoon, burst over them, soaking each man to the skin. Moreover, the night would get much worse, as lighting forked in the night sky and thunder crashed overhead, but as we have already seen, a storm on the eve of a battle had become something of a good omen for veterans of the Peninsula who had experienced such conditions on the eve of Salamanca and Vittoria.

A mile and a half a mile to the south of the village of Mont St Jean, and just to the east of the Nivelles road, was situated a large 17th century chateau, behind which Byng's 2nd Brigade of Guards was situated. The chateau was still empty at dusk on the evening of June 17th when Wellington suddenly ordered the four light companies of the two Brigades of Guards to occupy the chateau and its extensive surrounding grounds and gardens. Accordingly, the men of the light companies picked up their muskets and marched down the slope from the ridge where they had been positioned, some of them slipping on the ground that had by now begun to turn quite muddy as the rain intensified. They entered the old chateau by way of a pair of large wooden gates, the crunching of their boots and the rattling of their equipment echoing across the cobblestones in the courtyard and as they began to file out into the garden to make loopholes in the walls few of them could have realised how great a significance the place was to have on the outcome of the battle the following day.

The chateau was called Goumont but this was corrupted by the Guards to the name that would come down through history not only as one of the most famous episodes of the battle of Waterloo but also as one of the most glorious chapters in the long and illustrious history of the Foot Guards - Hougoumont.

NOTES

[1] Major H.L. Aubrey-Fletcher, *A History of the Foot Guards to 1856,* (London, 1927), 354.

[2] Ibid. 355.

[3] Wellington, *The Despatches of Field Marshal The Duke of Wellington,* (London, 1837-39), xii, 358.

[4] Lieutenant General Sir F.W. Hamilton, *Origin and History of the First or Grenadier Guards,* (London, 1874), iii. 8-9.

[5] Ibid. iii. 12-13.

[6] Ibid. iii. 14.

[7] David Chandler, *Waterloo; The Hundred Days,* (London, 1980), 72.

[8] Julian Paget, *Hougoumont - The Key to Victory,* (London, 1992), 15.

[9] The Earl of Malmesbury, *A Series of Letters of the First Earl of Malmesbury, His Family and Friends, from 1745 to 1820,* (London, 1880), ii. 445-446. The scene was recreated faithfully in the Dino de Laurentis' 1970 film, *Waterloo,* and was one of the film's more atmospheric scenes.

[10] Aubrey-Fletcher. *Foot Guards*, 362. In a letter to his mother Ensign C.W. Short, of the 2nd Battalion Coldstream Guards, wrote that, "the news came and they [the officers] all set off directly for their different posts and arrived at them about the time we were ordered to start, in their ball dresses." Short to his mother, NAM.

[11] Anthony Brett-James, [Batty] *The Hundred Days*, (London, 1964),

[12] Ibid. [Batty] 57.

[13] Ibid. [Macready] 62.

[14] Lt.Col. J.H. Stanhope, Add Mss. 34703, and C/Sgt Charles Wood, *Some Particulars of the Battle of Waterloo*, (Halifax, 1816), 4. Ensign Short claimed that the Belgians ran at the first shot."

[15] Aubrey-Fletcher, *Foot Guards*, 372.

[16] Hamilton, *Grenadier Guards*, iii. 17.

[17] Private William Blake, First Guards, to his sister, dated Paris, January 19th 1816. Private Collection, Ralph Weaver.

[18] Brett-James, [Batty] *The Hundred Days*, 57.

[19] Aubrey-Fletcher, *Foot Guards*, 372.

[20] The Prince of Orange later caused the virtual destruction of the 2nd Battalion 69th Regiment when, in spite of protests, he ordered it out of their square with a large number of French cavalry in close proximity. The 69th extended into line and were ridden over by the cavalry, losing its colours, the only occasion this ever happened in an army commanded by Wellington. Jac Weller, *Wellington at Waterloo*, (London, 19670, 65.

[21] Matthew Clay, *Narrative of the battles of Quatre Bras and Waterloo*. 2-3.

[22] Ibid., 3-4.

[23] Hamilton, *Grenadier Guards*, iii. 20.

[24] Miller was much liked by his men and was continually asking what could be done to make them more comfortable. "I do not care for the expense, money is no object to me," he said, and at the end of a march, his first care was to see that his men were well cared for. Colour Sergeant Wood, *Some Particulars*, 9.

[25] Hamilton, *Grenadier Guards*, iii. 23. According to Colour Sergeant Wood, in his *Some Particulars*, 9, the Colour was brought to him by Ensign Robert Batty, author of *The Campaign in the Western Pyrenees* and *The Campaign of 1815*, and whose sketches feature elsewhere in this book.

[26] Gronow, 145-146. According to Gronow, Adair was fatally wounded during the cavalry charges at Waterloo on June 18th but he was in fact wounded at Quatre Bras. Hamilton, iii. 22. says he later died in Brussels on June 23rd but in his appendix, iii.472. gives the date as June 16th.

[27] Hamilton, *Grenadier Guards*, iii. 22.

[28] Major General Sir Frederick Maurice, *The History of the Scots Guards, from 1642 to 1914*, (London, 1934), ii. 12.

[29] Clay, *A Narrative*, 5. Clay left a most graphic description of the battlefield of Quatre Bras at night, during which time he went off in search of water, all the time groping about in the dark amongst the dead and wounded. He eased the suffering of many of his comrades by placing them in more comfortable positions before finding water and returning to his comrades.

[30] Ensign C.W. Short to his mother, NAM. Short also went on to say that Wellington commanded at Quatre Bras wearing his ball dress, nor having had the opportunity to pull it off.

[31] Malmesbury, *A Series of Letters*, ii. 447.

[32] Ibid. ii. 447.

[33] Cavalie Mercer, *Journal of the Waterloo Campaign*, (London,1927) Mercer's account of the campaign is generally considered to be amongst the best written.

HOUGOUMONT

The night of June 17th 1815 was a miserable one. Inside the chateau of Hougoumont the rain splashed down on the cobble-stones as burly pioneers smashed up what wood was available to make firesteps or barricades. Whilst the rest of the Allied troops who had arrived from Quatre Bras took up their positions on the ridge of Mont St Jean, Hougoumont was turned into a hive of frantic activity as the place was converted into a defensible position. The Guards however, had only just managed to occupy the place, arriving there ahead of the French who were only too aware of the strategically important position of the chateau on Wellington's right flank. The French were sent packing by a few well directed volleys from the Guards but, undeterred, some French cavalry also tried their luck, only to be seen off likewise. To guard against any further French incursions Lieutenant Colonel James Macdonell of the Coldstream Guards, in overall command at Hougoumont, posted a picquet from the light company of the Third Guards, under Captain Evelyn and Ensign Standen, at the southern edge of the wood.

The chateau and farm buildings of Hougoumont formed a particularly strong defensive position.[1] They were enclosed by walls in the centre of which was the chateau itself with its attached chapel. Behind it was the farmyard which was protected on the other three sides by walls and farm buildings including the Great Barn on the western side of the yard. Entrance to the yard was by way of the great north gate. There was another yard in front of the chateau itself, with the south gate as its main entrance above which was the gardener's house. To the east of the buildings there was a garden surrounded by a wall and beyond that a much larger garden, also protected by walls. Beyond this complex of buildings and gardens there was a large orchard protected on the south side by a hedge and on the north side by a hedge and a deep ditch which became known as the Hollow Way. As well as the north and south gates there was an entrance into the buildings in the west wall through a door at the side of the Great Barn. To the south of the whole there was an extended wood through which the initial French attacks would come.

As the rain came down the Guards set about the walls of the orchard to make loop-holes, whilst elsewhere in the chateau other walls were dug out with bayonets to provide loop-holes and firing points for the Guards. There was to be little sleep for any of the men that night as they were set to work barricading entrances and bringing in ammunition, constructing firing steps and generally getting the place into a defensible state strong enough to withstand the legions of French infantry that would be thrown against it the following day. All the gates were barricaded except the north gate which was kept open to allow reinforcements and ammunition to pass through.

The troops detailed to occupy Hougoumont were the two light companies of the 2nd and 3rd Battalions First Guards, under Lieutenant Colonel Lord Saltoun, who were to hold the front edge of the orchard, the light company of the 2nd Battalion Coldstream Guards, under Lieutenant Colonel Henry Wyndham, whose task it would be to occupy the farm and chateau itself, and the light company of the 2nd Battalion Third Guards, under Lieutenant Colonel Charles Dashwood, who would defend the garden and the grounds surrounding the farm. Apart from Saltoun's men of the First Guards, all of the other companies of the Guards in and around Hougoumont were placed under the overall command of Macdonell.

The rain was unabating throughout the night and early morning and few of those who survived and later wrote of their experiences during the battle neglected to mention the miseries they endured. It could be said, in fact, that although the men were aware that with Napoleon leading the French army the forthcoming battle was liable to be something special, they were so preoccupied with the terrible weather that they hardly had any time to think about it. The Coldstream Guards, at least those companies not inside Hougoumont, spent the night in a bean field, with the crops sprouting through a few inches high. These young crops were soon trampled underfoot by the Coldstreamers and within a few hours the whole field was a quagmire.

The rain had barely stopped when a staff officer arrived at the orchard with a battalion of Nassau infantry along with a company of 300 Hanoverian Jagers and 100 Luneberg infantry. He brought orders to the effect that Lord Saltoun, along with his two light companies of the First Guards, was to rejoin the 1st Brigade of Guards situated on top of the ridge behind Hougoumont where the main Allied army was positioned. The defence of the orchard was then entrusted to the troops which the staff officer had brought with him. As Saltoun and his men trudged back towards the ridge they were met by Wellington and his Military Secretary, Lord Fitzroy Somerset, of the First Guards. "Hallo. Who are you? Where are you going?" asked

Wellington, at which Saltoun ordered his men to halt and lie down. He explained to Wellington the orders he had been given to which Wellington replied, somewhat surprisedly, "Well, I was not aware of such an order. However, don't join your brigade yet. Remain quiet where you are until further orders from me."[2] Apparently, Wellington turned to an aide an said, "That was one of my old Peninsular officers. See how he made his men lie down."[3]

Wellington then rode on to Hougoumont where he made a tour of the defences. As a result of his inspection the Nassauers, Hanoverians and Lunebergers were moved into the wood, relieving the picquet of the Third Guards, whilst a section of the light company of the Third Guards, occupying the garden, took up a new position at the haystack outside of the chateau's walls, just to the south-west of the farm. The reorganisation of the chateau's defences meant that the orchard was held by the light companies of the First Guards, under Saltoun, the garden and the chateau by the light company of the Coldstream Guards, and the lane to the west of the place by the light company of the Third Guards. This reorganisation was carried out with little interruption to the works being carried out on strengthening the place.

While the light companies of the Guards continued fortifying the chateau the rest of the four battalions of Guards, under Maitland and Byng, took up a position on the right flank of Wellington's line on the reverse slope of the ridge of Mont St Jean, a ridge that extended from Hougoumont on the right as far as the farms of Papelotte and La Haye on the left. The ridge was about three miles in length and was cut in half by the Brussels to Charleroi road. This marked the centre of the Allied position and in front of it lay the farm of La Haye Sainte which, along with Hougoumont, was one of the keys to Wellington's line and as such had been heavily fortified and occupied by men of the 2nd Light Battalion, King's German Legion, under Major Baring. There were nearly 70,000 Allied troops positioned along the ridge and with no shelter along its entire length all of them suffered during a miserable night of torrential rain which soaked everyone to the skin and lightning which startled horses and set many of them running amok over their riders as they lay on the ground.

There was, of course, a little shelter to be found by the Guards amongst the buildings of Hougoumont and even the Guards on the reverse slope of the ridge found a modicum of relief by virtue of a practice known to the Guards as 'pitching blankets'. Every man in Wellington's army carried a blanket of course, but those of the Guards had a button-hole and a tape in each corner.

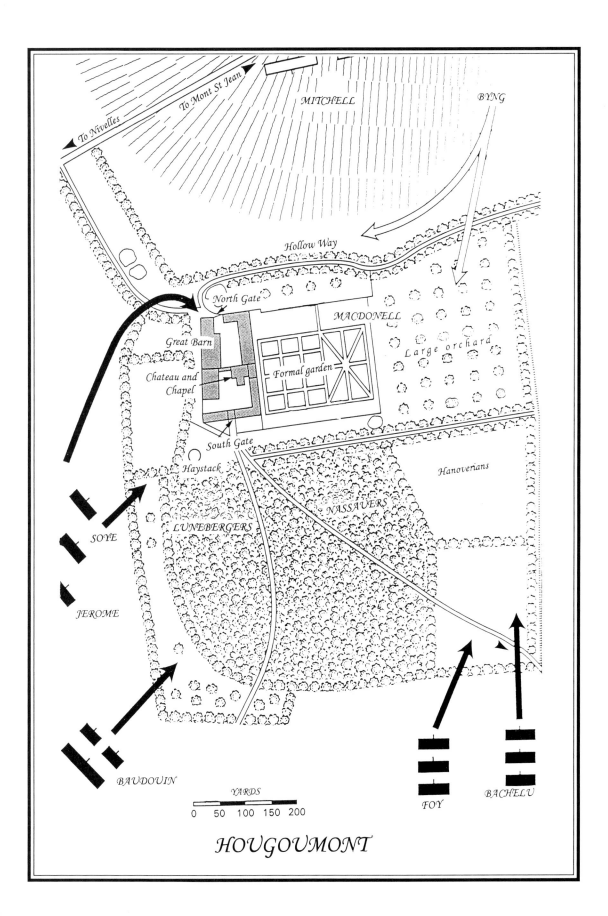

To Mont St Jean

To Nivelles

MITCHELL

BYNG

Hollow Way

North Gate

MACDONELL

Great Barn

Large orchard

Chateau and
Chapel

Formal garden

South Gate

Haystack

Hanoverians

SOYE

NASSAUERS

LUNEBERGERS

JEROME

BAUDOUIN

FOY

BACHELU

YARDS

0   50   100   150   200

HOUGOUMONT

When pitching blankets men were numbered in groups of four and each man drew lots to decide which two men should unpack their knapsacks and pitch their blankets. The two losers stood their muskets upright on the ground, pushed the knobs of their ramrods through the button-holes in the corner of the blankets and pegged out the other corners to make a form of ridge tent.[4] The four men then crawled into it and were kept reasonably dry for a while but when the time came to put the blanket back into the man's knapsack it was soaking wet, heavy and difficult to put back. However, it was beneath one such 'tent' that Ensign Gronow, of the First Guards, enjoyed a breakfast of cold ham and pie washed down with champagne, whilst many another Guardsman was afforded some welcome shelter from the terrible weather. Ensign Short, with the Coldstream Guards, recalled:

We were under arms the whole night expecting an attack and it rained to the degree that the field where we were was half way up our legs in the mud. Nobody of course could lie down and the ague got hold of some of the men. I with another officer had a blanket, and with a little more gin, we kept up very well.[5]

In all it was a miserable night but it was some comfort to Wellington's men to know that across the valley of Mont St Jean Napoleon's men were suffering likewise and, more significantly, that it would be his army that would have to attack up the muddy slopes once the battle started.

It was still raining when the first grey streaks of dawn began to filter through the early morning sky but by 9am it had stopped and soon afterwards the sun came out, its rays bringing a little welcoming warmth to the drenched soldiers of the two armies. Men stretched their chilled, aching bodies and soon the buzz of thousands of voices turned into a roar which was likened to the breaking of waves on rocks. Added to this sound was the crackling of musketry that rolled up and down the lines as thousands of infantrymen on both sides cleared their weapons of damp, dirt and mud. Matthew Clay, of the Third Guards, was no exception, and as he sat close to the Hollow Way behind Hougoumont, he fired his musket in order to clean it:

I discharged its contents at an object, which the ball imbedded in the bank where I had purposely placed it as a target. While so employed we kept a sharp lookout on the enemy (who were no doubt similarly employed) at the same time having well attended to those things usual for a soldier to do, (in the presence of the enemy) when not actively engaged, viz. examining the amount and state of ammunition remaining after previous engagements, also putting his musket in fighting trim, well oiled, flinted, etc. (bye the bye, the flint musket then in use was a sad bore on that occasion, from the effects of the wet, the springs at the locks became wood-bound and would not act correctly, and when in action, the clumsy flints became also useless. The shortest way of amending these failures, which were very disheartening, was to make an exchange from those that were lying about amongst the slain).[6]

Ensign Short got no sleep during a much disturbed night, and the next morning found himself tired and hungry and in a filthy state:

We had only one fire and you cannot conceive the state we were in. We formed a hollow square and prepared to receive cavalry twice but found it was a false alarm both times. Soon after daylight, the commissary sent up with the greatest difficulty some gin and we found an old cask full of wet rye loaves which we breakfasted upon. Everybody was in high spirits. We broke up the cask and got some dry wood and made some fine fires, go some straw and I went to sleep for a couple of hours.[7]

As the Guards and the rest of Wellington's army prepared for battle they were treated to the spectacle of a grand review as Napoleon rode up and down on his white horse as line after resplendent line of French soldiers cheered their emperor. This cut no ice with the impassive British soldiers, many of whom had seen such displays of French bravado go terribly and devastatingly awry in Spain and Portugal. Even those who had not seen action in the Peninsula were less than impressed by this show and were more concerned with the outcome of the day's fighting. However, if such shows were calculated to boost French morale the end result was to prove detrimental to their cause. Each delay was welcomed by Wellington who knew that as each hour passed his Prussian allies would be nearer to the field of battle. It has often been said that Napoleon was waiting for the ground to dry out before attacking, which may be true, but such delays caused by the waiting and by the review would cost him dear.

Whilst the French cheered themselves hoarse in front of their beloved emperor, Wellington rode down calmly to Hougoumont to make his final preparations. With him was General Müffling, his Prussian liaison officer. When the two men reached the chateau they were greeted by Macdonell who was told that an attack on his position was imminent. He was also told by Wellington that he must defend Hougoumont 'to the last extremity'.[8] As Wellington turned his horse around to return to the ridge Müffling asked him whether he seriously thought that the Guardsmen would be able to hold the place with just 1,500 men. "Ah," replied the Duke, "but you do not know Macdonell. I've thrown Macdonell into it."[9]

At about 11am[10] the first French attack got underway with an attack on Hougoumont by Reille's corps. This attack was intended to be a diversionary one with the object of goading Wellington into weakening his centre by moving troops to his right. However, as the struggle for the chateau escalated almost the whole of Reille's corps became involved, a total of about 13,000 men. Shortly after 11am one of Prince Jerome's brigades, that under the command of Bauduin, began to move into the wood south of Hougoumont covered by a strong line of skirmishers. As they advanced many a French soldier was killed by the round shot that came bouncing through the trees and by exploding shells fired by British artillery placed on the ridge above. The Nassauers and Hanoverians in the wood put up a strong fight but were steadily driven out of the wood and fell back upon the orchard. With the last Allied soldier driven from the wood the French thought they had the chateau within their grasp and as they struggled to get through the last clutch of trees their cheering reached a crescendo and drums beat a little faster. Officers urged their men forward and as they emerged from the trees they saw not a single Allied soldier between them and the south gate of Hougoumont. Cries of 'En avant!' and 'Victoire!' soared above the noise but at the moment of apparent victory it was snatched violently and devastatingly from their grasp.

As the French strained to get out of the wood the eyes of every waiting Guardsman were trained on them. Fingers twitched on the triggers of levelled muskets and sword-wielding officers waited with baited breath to give the order to fire. As Bauduin's men emerged from the trees the order was at last given and a storm of lead blew away the leading files of flailing Frenchmen. The French could hardly have expected to walk into the chateau but the greeting they received from the Guardsmen astonished them. From every broken window and gouged loop-hole, and from over every barricade, wall and firestep, the Guards poured out an accurate, heavy and sustained fire that swept the French away. But as French numbers grew as more of them debouched from the wood even the steady and controlled fire of the Guards could not keep them back and they were able to reach the walls of Hougoumont and its south gate. Many of the French set about the gate with the butts of their muskets whilst others climbed upon the walls of the garden. In both cases they were simply shot down as Macdonell's men fired and loaded as fast as they could amidst the fire and smoke of battle. Hands bled as bayonets were grabbed by men on both sides who tried to wrestle the muskets from their owners but no matter how bravely the French attacked they could find no way into the fortress. The only Frenchmen who succeeded in getting inside were promptly shot or bayonetted.

To the east of the south gate and garden, however, the Nassauers and Hanoverians, having already been driven from the wood, were forced from their positions in the orchard and fell back on the Hollow Way behind it. On the ridge above the orchard were the light companies of the First Guards under Saltoun who, as we remember, had been ordered to stay there by Wellington. However, a shout suddenly went up, "Light infantry to the front! The Nassauers are driven out of the orchard!"[11] Saltoun's men sprang into life, formed immediately and moved down the hill towards the orchard where they again met Wellington who greeted them with the words, "In with you, my lads," he said, "and let me see no more of you."[12] The light companies of the First Guards formed on the Hollow Way and charged the French with fixed bayonets, driving them back across the orchard and back into the wood. Following this they resumed the positions they had taken up the previous night in the orchard. It was noon and for the time being the tide of French troops had been stemmed, leaving about 1,500 of them dead or dying around the walls of Hougoumont.

Inside Hougoumont and its garden and orchard and outside the south-west corner of the chateau, the Guards checked their ammunition, counted and saw to their casualties and prepared for the next French attack which was not long in coming for in spite of Napoleon's orders that the attack on Hougoumont was merely a diversionary one Jerome was determined to take the place and now committed Soye's brigade to the attack.

Outside Hougoumont by a large haystack the 100 men of the light company of the Third Guards, under Lieutenant Colonel Charles Dashwood were suddenly attacked by Soye's brigade as it burst upon them from the woods on the Guards' right. Alongside Soye's brigade were the remains of Bauduin's brigade which had been battered during the first attack on Hougoumont in which Bauduin himself had been killed. A fierce fire-fight now ensued between the French and the Third Guards during which Lieutenant Standen waved his hat in the air with one hand and his sword with the other, and called out to his men to join him in charging the French. During the fighting Matthew Clay, and another man of the Third Guards, named Gann, took cover behind the haystack and began firing at the French. When the two men looked back towards the chateau they were horrified to see that they were alone, their comrades having retreated along the wood back to the north gate. Clay takes up the story:

We now halted. I unwisely ascended the higher part of a sloping ground on which the exterior wall of the farm was built, thinking of singling out the enemy's skirmishers more correctly, but very quickly found that I had become a target for them, my red coat being more distinctly visible than theirs. Remaining in this position I continued to exchange shots with the enemy across the kitchen garden, they having the advantage of the fence as a covering, their shots freely struck the wall in my rear. Our company from which we were separated had now opened fire from within. My musket now proving defective was very discouraging, but casting my eyes on the ground, I saw a musket which I immediately took possession of in exchange for my old one. The new musket was warm from recent use, and proved an excellent one, it having belonged to the light infantry of the 1st Foot Guards.[13]

Clay eventually rejoined his comrades by entering Hougoumont by way of a door in the west wall of the buildings. Whilst Clay and Gann had been engaged in firing at the French, Dashwood's men had fallen back fighting along the lane to the west of Hougoumont and, leaving the haystack behind them, they dashed to the north gate which they entered with a cheer, the French close behind them. As the Guards dashed through the north gate into the courtyard of Hougoumont many of them turned to engage the leading enemy regiment, the 1st Light Regiment. The Guardsmen, realising the perilous position they were in, sprang at their enemies and some ferocious hand-to-hand fighting ensued as fists were swung and swords and bayonets thrust home. Men were shot at point blank range and angry shouts mixed with the final, fading cries of dying men. In amongst the thick of the fighting was Sergeant Ralph Frazer, a veteran of Egypt who had fought with the Third Guards in eight major actions of the Peninsular War. In the midst of the chaos at the gates he saw the commanding officer of the French 1st Light Regiment, Colonel Cubières, riding his horse and waving his sword. Frazer immediately ran out from Hougoumont and leapt at Cubières, thrusting at him with his halberd. The Frenchman slashed wildly at Frazer who ducked beneath his thrusts and dragged him from his horse before mounting it himself and riding it back through the north gate in triumph.[14] Matthew Clay entered the courtyard shortly after this episode and noted the state of the place as he did so:

On entering the courtyard I saw the doors or rather gates were riddled with shot holes, and it was also very wet and dirty; in its entrance lay many dead bodies of the enemy. One I particularly noticed which appeared to have been a French officer, but they were scarcely distinguishable, being to all appearance as though they had been very much trodden upon, and covered with the mud.[15]

Initial French attempts to gain entry into Hougoumont had failed but the Guards there were still faced with the problem of a precariously short supply of ammunition. Fresh supplies had been ordered earlier in the day but now, with the French threatening the northern approaches from the main Allied position, any such supply would have to run the gauntlet of enemy fire if it were to be delivered safely. Fortunately, Ensign Berkeley Drummond, of the Third Guards, and Colonel Horace Seymour, of the Staff, managed to secure the services of a private of the Wagon Train, Joseph Brewster, who brought up a tumbril of ammunition. The man rode straight down to Hougoumont, all the time under fire, to deliver the ammunition, much to the relief of the beleaguered Guardsmen.[16]

The French had been thrown back and ammunition had arrived, but if the Guards thought the alarm was over they were very much mistaken for at this point came the closest the French came to actually taking Hougoumont. When Frazer and the last of the light company of the Third Guards were safely inside the gate was shut behind them but as the Guards were in the act of closing a huge French lieutenant named Legros, known as *L'Enforcer*, stepped forward wielding a pioneer's axe and with a mighty swing he shattered part of the gate and forced his way through followed by about 40 or so of his comrades who swarmed into the courtyard, cheering in triumph. As they advanced towards the chateau itself they were met by a withering fire from the surrounding barns and the windows of the other building that surrounded the yard. There was more savage hand-to-hand fighting as the Guards fought desperately to force them out. Eventually every single one of them was hunted down and killed except for one drummer boy who was taken prisoner. Legros himself paid for his bravery with his life and died fighting close to the chateau with his axe still in his hand.

While the fighting was raging inside Hougoumont other

French troops were trying desperately to get inside to help their comrades and dozens of them hurled themselves at the north gate in an attempt to break in. At this point came perhaps the most famous incident during the fighting at Hougoumont, namely, the closing of the gates, upon which, Wellington later openly acknowledged, 'rested the outcome of the day.'

Macdonell, sword in hand, stood close to the north gate and realised he had a potential catastrophe on his hands unless he could close the gates. He shouted above the din to three other Coldstream Guards officers, Lieutenant Colonel Henry Wyndham and Ensigns James Hervey and Henry Gooch, to help him at the gate. As they rushed towards it they were joined by two other Coldstreamers, Corporal James Graham and his brother Corporal Joseph Graham, and four men from the Third Guards, Sergeants Ralph Frazer, Bruce McGregor and Joseph Alston, and Private Joseph Lester.[17] The small group of Guardsmen fought and hacked their way to the gate and hurled themselves at it and straining every muscle they began to force it shut as the French clamoured for blood on the other side of it. Other Guardsmen came and added their weight to the struggle until finally they were able to drop the enormous wooden bar across it. The gate was shut and as a reinforcement all manner of wood and debris was stacked up against it as a barricade.

It had been a desperately close thing but the gate was shut although for Lieutenant Colonel Wyndham it was not the only close shave for as he strained to help close the gate a French grenadier scaled the wall and took aim at him with his musket. Fortunately, the Coldstreamer spotted him and, handing a musket to Corporal Graham, watched with relief as the Frenchman toppled back with a bullet in his head, courtesy of the marksmanship of Graham.[18]

Meanwhile, as the fight for Hougoumont raged below him, Major General Byng, commanding the 2nd Brigade of Guards, ordered down the remainder of the 2nd Battalion Coldstream Guards, less two companies that remained on the ridge with the Colours, from its position on behind Hougoumont in order to assist in its defence. This force consisted of three companies commanded by Lieutenant Colonel Alexander Woodford and these arrived at the north gate just after Macdonell had succeeded in closing it. There were still a large number of French troops outside but these were driven off down the lane to the west of Hougoumont by Woodford's men as they arrived. Daniel Mackinnon, commanded the grenadier company of the Coldstreamers:

The grenadiers and the other companies of the Coldstream under my command were ordered to charge the enemy who had surrounded the house. I was wounded in the act [and] also had a beautiful grey horse shot. However, I did the best that lay in my power and succeeded in repulsing them till relieved by the remainder of the battalion. The whole were then obliged to fortify ourselves in the farmyard which we were ordered to defend let what would oppose us......The ball struck me on the cap of the knee so you may suppose the pain is most excruciating, the inflammation is now very great therefore they cannot tell exactly what injury has been done but I trust in God and my good luck, a few days will make me quite easy about it.[19]

It may have been during this attack that the Coldstreamers sustained their only fatal officer casualty of the day when Captain John Lucie Blackman, of No.4 Company, was shot in the head and killed.[20]

Following this counter-attack Woodford's three companies entered the chateau by way of the west door at the side of the barn. Once inside, Woodford found himself the senior officer but as Macdonell had handled the situation well so far he decided not to assume to command and Macdonell was left in command for the rest of the battle. Ensign Short was with the 7th Company, one of the two companies of the 2nd Battalion Coldstream Guards that remained behind on the ridge with the Colours, but even here there was little respite from the enemy's fire:

We were ordered to lie down in the road; the musket shots flew on over us like peas. An officer next to me was hit on the cap but not hurt as it went through, and another next to me was also hit on the plate of the cap, but it went through without hurting him. Two sergeants that lay near me were hit in the knapsacks, and were not hurt, besides several other shots passing as near as possible. I never saw such luck as we had.[21]

At Hougoumont, the addition of the three companies of Coldstreamers allowed Macdonell to strengthen his defences, particularly along the east wall of the garden from where the Guards would be able to enfilade the orchard. In spite of the heavy fighting, however, it appears that instead of tending to their duties some of the Guardsmen still managed to find time to engage in some 'plundering', as Richard MacLaurence, of the light company of the Coldstream Guards, recalled many years later:

No sooner were the Guardsmen fairly within the chateau garden than the temptingly ripe cherries drew their attention and the soldiers were to be seen plucking them off the wall trees by handfuls, quite regardless of the shot and shells which were incessantly pouring in amongst them. "You scoundrels!" roared out Major [sic] James Macdonell. "If I survive this day, I will punish you all!"[22]

Shortly afterwards, however, the offending Guardsmen were busy once again as the French launched a third attack, this time to the south-west of Hougoumont around the eastern flank of the orchard. This posed a serious threat to Macdonell as a successful attack would isolate him from the main Allied position on the ridge.

The French attack began just before 1pm and was spearheaded by Gautier's brigade that moved stealthily towards the edge of the orchard to begin its outflanking movement. Unfortunately for Gautier's men, their manoeuvre was seen by the ever watchful Byng who immediately despatched two companies of the Third Guards, under Lieutenant Colonel Francis Home, to meet them. As the French came on their skirmishers were met by a galling fire from the Third Guards who not only drove them back but outflanked the French who were attacking the orchard and when the Coldstreamers lining the walls of the garden opened fire, enfilading Gautier's men, the French attack began to crumble and they were driven off which allowed Saltoun to advance once again in order to resume his position defending the orchard.

The third French attack on Hougoumont had thus been thwarted meaning that, 'less than 2,000 men in all had taken the sting out of the greater part of Reille's corps and had kept more than 10,000 Frenchmen occupied.'[23] And yet despite Jerome's despairing efforts to take Hougoumont he seemed to forget that Napoleon had meant the attack only as a diversion for it was only now, shortly after 1pm, that his main attack was to begin. We need not concern ourselves with the main battle, the more so since so much has been written about it. Also, we must concentrate on the part played by the Guards during the battle and as such we are fortunate that the two Brigades of Guards played a major part in the two most significant episodes of the day's fighting, at Hougoumont and late in the day during the attack of the Imperial Guard, a momentous climax in which the First Guards played the deciding role.

The outcome of the battle hung in the balance until late in the day but the struggle for Hougoumont can almost be said to have been a battle on its own. The combatants fought fiercely and desperately all day and seem have been consumed in their own 'private' battle, apparently unaware of what was going on elsewhere, as brigade after brigade was cast into the fiery realm of smoke and flame. The Guards hung on grimly inside whilst outside the French hurled themselves at the place until they began to despair and run out of steam. And yet some Frenchmen were actually convinced that they captured the place within a hour or so of the battle beginning.[24] The truth was, however, that it never did despite their efforts.

At about 2pm the French brought up a howitzer which soon began to cause much damage inside Hougoumont. As the firing continued Saltoun decided to lead an attack in order to silence or capture it but he ran into the greater part of three enemy brigades and was driven back across the orchard and on to the Hollow Way behind it. Following this abortive attack Saltoun was ordered to return to his brigade still situated on the ridge of Mont St Jean. It had been a hard day so far for him and his men but the day's fighting was not yet over for them as we shall see later.[25]

As Saltoun and the light companies of the First Guards made their way back to their battalions they were replaced in the Hollow Way by the remaining seven companies of the Third Guards under Colonel Francis Hepburn who decided that his first task would be to retake the orchard. This was duly accomplished and the Guards were able to line its southern edge once again. Soon afterwards, however, some changes were forced upon the Guards as a result of a severe wound to General George Cooke, commanding the 1st Division. Command of the division devolved upon Byng and in turn Hepburn assumed command of the 2nd Brigade of Guards, which proved somewhat convenient for him as the whole of the 2nd Brigade of Guards was fighting in and around Hougoumont. In fact, the force now defending Hougoumont had grown to around 4,000 men, for as well as the eight companies of Coldstreamers, the light company of the Third Guards and a battalion of Brunswickers - all inside the buildings - there were the remaining companies of the 2nd Battalion Third Guards and about fifty Hanoverians, all of whom were supported by two KGL battalions. With Hepburn now in command of the 2nd Brigade of Guards he now had nominal command of the Allied forces fighting in and around Hougoumont.[26]

Shortly after Hepburn assumed command the French launched another attack, this time by a division under General

Bachelu but this attack never really materialised, the French columns faltering before they reached the orchard. However, there was a much more serious development in the fight for Hougoumont at around 3pm when a battery of howitzers arrived in front of the place with the intention of shelling it with incendiaries. Within a few minutes the rooftops of Hougoumont were ablaze as was the chateau itself, the chapel and the great barn. This of course seriously affected the defenders inside who were forced to fight amidst the choking, suffocating smoke and searing heat of the fires whilst those Guardsmen firing from upstairs windows found the floors burning beneath them. Matthew Clay was one such Guardsman who had been placed in an upstairs room in the chateau:

We annoyed the enemy's skirmishers from the window, which the enemy observing, threw their shells amongst us, and set the building on fire we were defending. Our officer placing himself at the entrance of the apartment would not permit anyone to quit his post until our position became hopeless and too perilous to remain, fully expecting the floor to sink with us every moment, and in our escape several of us were more or less injured.[27]

Indeed, floors simply gave way and crashed to the ground and many a brave Guardsman died in the flames that now began to lick their firing positions. Shells exploded around them and as blazing timbers came crashing down into the yard burning ash and embers filled the air scorching the Guardsmen and starting fresh fires. A new horrific dimension was also added when the great barn, in which many of the wounded lay, caught fire. The screams of the wounded soldiers who lay burning helplessly inside shocked their comrades but such was the desperate nature of the struggle that not a single man could be spared to help them and they died where they lay. However, there was one man who was able to rescue one of the wounded men. This was Corporal James Graham, of the Coldstream Guards, one of the men that had helped Macdonell shut the gate earlier in the afternoon. Graham asked Macdonell's permission to fall out for a short time, at which his commander asked him why as it was a crucial moment in the defence of Hougoumont and no man could be spared. Graham replied that he would not have asked if it had not been his brother, Joseph, who had also helped Macdonell shut the gate. Graham was given permission to fall out and he was able to drag his brother from the burning wreckage of the barn to safety. Once this had been done Graham grabbed his musket again and returned to his post.

The flames soon spread to the chapel but instead of engulfing the wooden statue of Christ that hung on the wall they stopped at its feet, leaving them scorched but the rest of the statue untouched. Belgian peasants who visited the chapel after the battle considered this to be a miracle and it is indeed a mystery why the flames did stop suddenly. The flames also caused havoc in the stables where frightened horses ran back and forth into the flames to perish along with many wounded Guardsmen. Hougoumont had become something akin to a holocaust but in the midst of this inferno the Guards, their faces blackened not only by powder but by the thick smoke of the fires, stuck grimly to their posts, and still the French were unable to get in.

As the Guards struggled to contain both the enemy and the fires presently threatening to engulf Hougoumont the French were about to launch their massive cavalry attacks against the stoic squares of Allied infantry on the reverse slope of the ridge of Mont St Jean. It was about 4pm as Ney's cavalry galloped up the muddy slopes between Hougoumont and La Haye Sainte to begin the first of their prolonged assaults on Wellington's main position but the Guards were unaware of the spectacle going on to their left. In fact, only the Third Guards in the orchard saw anything of the charges and a few of them no doubt took the opportunity to loose off a few shots at them as they passed. But the Guardsmen inside Hougoumont were oblivious to it all. They seemed to live in their own small world, a microcosm of fire and flame, a cacophony of shouts and explosions where they seemed to lose all track of time.[28] Indeed, many of the defenders knew absolutely nothing of what was going on elsewhere on the battlefield. Indeed, when Ensign Wedgwood, of the 5th Company, Third Guards, wrote to Captain Siborne, the famous compiler of the *Waterloo Letters*, he said he was quite ignorant of the nature of the corps in its [Hougoumont's] vicinity, and went on to say that:

I remember that I was myself completely ignorant of what was going on or what the result of the action was likely to be until we saw parties of the French passing us in full retreat with the Brunswickers in pursuit on both sides of the house [Hougoumont].[29]

There was no lull in the fighting around Hougoumont even when the massed cavalry charges began. Indeed, even as Ney's horsemen disappeared over the ridge to engulf the Allied squares the battered remains of Bachelu's division were advancing through the wood to make yet another attack on the orchard. The French came on in a determined fashion, undeterred by their earlier failures and losses, and by sheer weight of numbers bulldozed their way passed the Third Guards, still under Hepburn, forcing them to retreat to the Hollow Way. However, as the French continued forward they were met by a destructive fire of musketry from the Coldstreamers lining the garden wall who blazed away furiously at their enemies, forcing them to abandon the orchard and as the French withdrew they were helped on their way at bayonet point by the Third Guards who, with a cheer, reoccupied their former positions in the orchard.

The defenders in the orchard had suffered heavily during this last attack but there was still to be one final effort by the French to take Hougoumont which came following the capture of La Haye Sainte by the French. This of course released a large number of French troops who now turned their attention to the Guardsmen still clinging to Hougoumont away to the west. The attack was made by Foy's division and once more it was to be the Third Guards in the orchard that bore the brunt of the attack. Perhaps it was just one attack too many by the French who must have realised by now that they were destined not to wrest the post from the Guards. The result of the attack was the same as the last one. The Third Guards were initially forced back upon the Hollow Way from where they in turn opened up a destructive fire on Foy's men, causing them to retreat once again following which Hepburn's men returned to the front edge of the orchard. They were not to be driven out again.

The fighting continued around Hougoumont following this last attack but by now the main attacks had ceased and the only danger to the garrison inside came from enemy firing which did little damage as the Guards were well protected by the walls and buildings of the place. The fire continued to burn fiercely, however, but apart from this the fight for Hougoumont had resulted in a triumph for the Guards. We shall return to Hougoumont later but first we must turn to the other momentous episode at Waterloo involving the two battalions of the First Guards who had been fighting on the ridge of Mont St Jean.

NOTES

[1] For convenience sake we will refer to various buildings comprising the position at Hougoumont as the chateau.
[2] Lieutenant Colonel Sir F.W. Hamilton, *The Orgin and History of the First or Grenadier Guards*, (London, 1874), iii. 31.

Above, Embarkation of the First Guards for Corunna at Ramsgate, September 8th 1808.

Below: The Battle of Talavera, July 28th 1809. The bareheaded officer in the foreground is Captain Robert Dalrymple, Third Guards, who was killed during the battle.

Plate 1: The Officers of the Guards (*See Appendix for notes on the uniform plates*)

Plate 2: The Guards - Sergeants.

Plate 3: The Guards - Privates.

Plate 4: The Guards at War.
Top: The retreat to Corunna, and (below), Quatre Bras.

Above: After the Closing of the Gates at Hougoumont, by Ernest Crofts.

Above: Sergeant Ralph Frazer, Third Guards, pulls the French Colonel Cubieres from his horse during the fighting outside Hougoumont, June 18th 1815. *Below*, The Coldstream Guards under attack from French cavalry at Waterloo.

Above: Daniel Mackinnon, wearing the uniform of the Coldstream Guards, in the late 1820s A hero of Waterloo he was one of the most celebrated characters in Wellington's Peninsular army. Painting by George Dawe.

Above: The Battle of Waterloo, June 18th 1815. The Defence of Hougoumont by the Coldstream Guards. Watercolour by Denis Dighton.

Below: The closing of the gates at Hougoumont, Waterloo June 18th 1815. Painting by Robert Gibb.

[3] Julian Paget, *Hougoumont - Key to Victory*, (London, 1992), 32.

[4] Matthew Clay, *A Narrative of the Battles of Quatre Bras and Waterloo: with the defence of Hougoumont*, (Bedford, 1853), 8-9. Clay was one of the unfortunate losers who had to pitch his blanket.

[5] Ensign C.W. Short, *Letter from Waterloo*, to his mother, June 19th 1815, NAM.

[6] Clay, *A Narrative*, 11.

[7] Ensign C.W. Short , *Letter*.

[8] Paget, *Hougoumont*, 35.

[9] Elizabeth Longford, *Wellington, The Years of the Sword*, (London, 1969), 450.

[10] From the many and varied accounts written afterwards, the Battle of Waterloo is estimated to have begun at anywhere between 10am and mid-day.

[11] Hamilton, *Grenadier Guards*, iii. 30.

[12] Paget, *Hougoumont*, 39.

[13] Clay, *A Narrative*, 13-14.

[14] Cubières survived the battle and seventeen years later met Colonel Woodford, of the Coldstream Guards, one of the defenders of Hougoumont. Cubières said that he owed his survival to the Guards who declined to fire on him as he lay on the ground. Major H.T. Siborne, *Waterloo Letters: A Selection from original and hitherto unpublished Letters bearing on the 16th, 17th and 18th June, by Officers who served in the Campaign*, (London, 1891), 262.

[15] Clay, *A Narrative*, 14.

[16] The timing of the arrival of this ammunition wagon is open to debate. Dan Mackinnon, *Origin and Services of the Coldstream Guards*, (London, 1833), ii. 216, later said that the tumbril arrived at about 1pm. Others, such as Julian Paget, *Hougoumont*, put it much later, after the chateau had been set ablaze by French howitzer fire. However, as the wagon is supposed to have passed through the gate and entered the courtyard this must be debatable as the gate had been heavily barricaded following Macdonell's 'closing of the gates'. At any time after this the ammunition would have to have been passed over the walls with the French in close proximity, an unlikely occurrence.

[17] Major General Sir Frederick Maurice, *The History of the Scots Guards, from 1642 to 1914*, (London, 1934), ii. 21.

[18] Apparently, Wyndham would never again close any door and would often sit for hours on end in draughty rooms, all because of his experiences at Hougoumont.

[19] Mackinnon to his brother, RHQ Coldstream Guards. Mackinnon only commanded the grenadier company. The other two companies sent down by Byng were No.1 Company, commanded by Lt-Col. Sowerby, and No.4 Company, commanded by Lt-Col. The Hon. E. Acheson.

[20] Captain E. Sumner, of the grenadier company, was also fatally wounded by lingered another eight days before he finally died on

June 26th. John Lucie Blackman's tomb can still be seen today inside the formal garden at Hougoumont although his remains were moved to the church at Evre in 1890. His letters are held by the National Army Museum, London.

[21] Short, *A Letter*, NAM

[22] MacLaurence went on to say that of the 134 men in his company, 'as smart a set of young soldiers as one could wish to see', only 13 marched out of Hougoumont at the end of the battle, led out by a Corporal Smith. Richard MacLaurence, in the *Newcastle Journal*, January 12th 1843.

[23] Maurice, *Scots Guards*, ii. 22.

[24] David Howarth, *A Near Run Thing*, (London, 1968), 112.

[25] Saltoun himself had four horses shot beneath him.

[26] Julian Paget mentions the fact that Wellington omitted to mention Hepburn in his despatch, whereas he mentioned Macdonell and Home as being the main defenders of Hougoumont. Apparently, Wellington later admitted that he regretted this but said that he never changed a despatch. Paget, *Hougoumont*, 52.

[27] Clay, *A Narrative*, 15.

[28] The defenders of Hougoumont seem to have endured remarkably similar experiences as the defenders of Rorke's Drift during the Zulu War of 1879, who were likewise caught up in a life or death struggle inside a small fortified place.

[29] Bm Add.Mss. 34705. Wedgwood to Siborne.

THE DEFEAT
OF THE IMPERIAL GUARD

While the fight for Hougoumont had raged below them the 2nd and 3rd Battalions First Guards - minus their light companies - stood impassively on the reverse slopes of the ridge of Mont St Jean. When the battle began at about 11am the 2nd Battalions of the Coldstream and Third Guards were with them but as the fighting around Hougoumont intensified these latter two battalions were fed into the battle there to help defend the place, leaving behind only those battalions with the Colours. We will recall that at about 3pm the two light companies of the First Guards, under Lord Saltoun, had rejoined their respective battalions[1] so that the two battalions were now reunited, save for those casualties sustained during the few hours' fighting in the orchard at Hougoumont.

The afternoon and evening of June 18th were to prove a trial of endurance for the First Guards as, along with the rest of Wellington's army, they had to stand and suffer for hour on end as round shot after round shot came flying in from Napoleon's batteries situated across the valley. Many battalions were ordered to lie down although many were never to rise again as a result of being hit by a shell or round shot. Colour Sergeant Charles Wood, of the 3rd Battalion First Guards, recalled picking up handfuls of new horse nails that had been bundled up together and fired. 'Unlawful carnage,' was how he described it.[2]

The First Guards formed with the 2nd Battalion slightly to the rear of the 3rd Battalion with both some way in advance of the main Allied line.[3] They occupied an exposed position and there was little cover from enemy artillery fire with round shot that was capable of knocking down whole files of men. The ground ploughed up around them but as the sods of earth flew through the air the Guards stood unmoved, breaking rank now and then only to pull their dead and wounded into the centre of their squares.

Shortly after 4pm the massed French cavalry attacks began but once more the stoic ranks of Guardsmen stood unbroken, opening fire to bring horses and riders crashing to the ground. The Allied squares refused to yield as Ney's horsemen swept around and between them and as the historian of the First Guards put it, 'as wave succeeds wave against an iron-bound coast, only to be broken and thrown back in spray, so did French squadron succeed squadron, only to be hurled back by the fire and bayonet of the British square.'[4] Lieutenant Colonel Stanhope later wrote of the Guards steadiness during this period of the battle:

When the French cavalry attacked us in squares, which they did with the most persevering gallantry, never retiring above 100 or 150 paces, and charging again, our men behaved as if they were at a field-day, firing by ranks and with the best possible aim, under a most destructive cannonade, an having several shells burst in the middle of us, not a man moved from his place.[5]

During the intervals between these cavalry charges French artillery would open fire and it was during one such period that both commanding officers of the two battalions of First Guards, Colonels D'Oyly and Stables, were wounded and had to be carried from the field. The latter of these two officers died the following morning. With both men carried from the field command of the 2nd Battalion devolved upon Lord Saltoun who, as we have seen, had returned to the his battalion following his early spell in the orchard at Hougoumont. The 3rd Battalion First Guards was placed under the command of Lieutenant Colonel Reeve.

It was during this artillery fire that a notable incident occurred involving Captain Colquitt, of the 2nd Battalion First Guards. Colquitt was lying down with his men under shell fire when suddenly a live shell landed amongst them. Without hesitating, he jumped to his feet, picked up the shell 'as if it had been a cricket ball,' and threw it over the heads of both officers and men. The shell exploded a few seconds later without doing any harm to a single Guardsman.[6] Nevertheless, casualties continued to mount amongst the First Guards and nerves needed to be steady. Colour Sergeant Wood recalled an incident which inspired his battalion following the death of Ensign Purdoe of the 3rd Battalion:

When the French 105th regiment advanced up the low ground, their cannon at the same time raked us with grape, canister, and horse-nails; and our line was so shattered that I feared they could not stand: in fact, I was for a moment really afraid they would give way; and if we had given way it would have gone hard with the whole line...Our Officers exerted themselves to the very uttermost, as also the Sergeants. Major General Maitland, Colonel Lord Saltoun, Colonel Reeve, and Brigade Major Gunthorpe, were in the front face of the square, in the hottest part of the contest; our loss at this time was most tremendous. It was at this juncture that I picked up Ensign Purdoe's coat, which was covered with his blood, lying on a dead horse. The Ensign belonged to out battalion; he was killed and stripped by the plunderers during some of our manoeuvres. I stepped about twenty-five paces before the line and waved the coat, cheering the men, and telling them that while our Officers bled we should not reckon our lives dear. I thought if anything would stimulate the men, this would be effective. They fought with all their might; and in half an hour, as I mentioned, we cut the 105th regiment to pieces.[7]

The French cavalry attacks continued throughout the afternoon and as Ensign Gronow of the First Guards recalled, the enemy lancers were particularly troublesome:

On one occasion I remember, the enemy's artillery having made a gap in the square, the lancers were evidently waiting to avail themselves of it, to rush among us, when Colonel Stables, at once observing their intention, with the utmost promptness filled up the gap, and thus again completed our impregnable steel wall: but in this act he fell mortally wounded......When we received cavalry, the order was to fire low; so that on the first discharge of musketry, the ground was strewed with the fallen horses and their riders, which impeded the advance of those behind them, and broke the shock of the charge.[8]

As the afternoon wore on Blucher's Prussians began to arrive on the extreme left of Wellington's position but for the latter's own army and the Guards the position had become desperate. It was equally so for Napoleon's troops however, but when his men captured the vital post of La Haye Sainte, a short distance in front of the centre of the Allied line, he seemed to have grasped the upper hand. Indeed, a short while afterwards he decided to play his final card; the Imperial Guard.

The men of the Imperial Guard were veterans of dozens of campaigns and had never been defeated in battle. However, they had yet to meet Wellington's Foot Guards and now the final act of Napoleon's final battle would be played out between these two elite bodies of warriors.

As evening came the Guards were joined at their position by Wellington who said to Saltoun, "Well, I think they are pretty well told out now," at which Saltoun turned to one of his officers and said, "I don't know; when I was outside the wood at Hougoumont, this morning, before the action began, I watched a column of men, as far as I can guess about 5000 or 6000, go into a hollow opposite; I have kept my eye on this spot all day, and have never seen them come out yet." No sooner had Wellington been told of this than the Duke, putting his telescope to his eye, said, "By God, he is right! they are coming out now!"[9] It was the Imperial Guard.

Wellington quickly realised that this was to be the great climax of the battle, the moment which might decided the fate of Europe. He scribbled off an order that brought Adams' Brigade - the 52nd, 71st and 95th Regiments - across to fill the space left by the 2nd Brigade of Guards, still inside Hougoumont. Adams and Maitland could see that they would bear the brunt of the Imperial Guards' attack and their fears were realised when Napoleon turned every available gun on their position and began to 'soften up' the two brigades as a prelude to the attack. The cannonade is estimated to have lasted for about forty-five minutes during which the Guards endured a furious storm of shot and shell, there being little cover on the ridge other than a sunken lane of which the Guards made as much use as possible, keeping their heads down as round shot bounced over them.

As the French approached Wellington ordered the Guards into a line, four-deep, which was achieved by the rear ranks of the squares simply wheeling around to form the line, a movement covered by a line of skirmishers.[10] The formation was such that in the event of any threat posed by French cavalry, the Guards would be able to redeploy into square. With the line thus being formed the men were ordered to lie down once more as the cannonade announcing the beginning of the attack by the Imperial Guard grew heavier.

However, at just after 7pm the French guns suddenly ceased and through the fading light of early evening, already made worse by the smoke of battle, those officers mounted on horses could see, in the distance, columns of French infantry, some 5,000 strong, approaching with Napoleon at their head. It was his Imperial Guard.

The regiments marching towards Wellington's Guards were the 2nd, 3rd and 4th Regiments of Grenadiers of the Imperial Guard, the 1st and 2nd Battalions of the 3rd Chasseurs and a single battalion of the 4th Chasseurs. The 2nd Grenadiers halted on a slight rising roughly halfway between Hougoumont and La Haye Sainte whilst the other five battalions carried on, approaching in five large squares, each with a frontage of two companies, as protection against Allied cavalry, the French having already seen the damage caused to D'Erlon's corps earlier in the day. They were also supported by Foy's division on the left and Bachelu's division on the right.[11] Napoleon had led them in person at the outset but as Allied guns were trained on the squares he halted and handed command over to Marshal Ney, now on foot having had several horses shot under him already during the course of the day.

The route taken by Ney took the Imperial Guard over the ground already churned up by his cavalry during their massed attacks earlier in the day but this did little to hamper the veterans of the Imperial Guard who came on 'apparently as regularly formed as for a field day'.[12] As the French came on the columns of squares separated, the Chasseurs inclining slightly to their left, the Grenadiers coming straight on towards the position occupied by Maitland's Guards.[13] The French were beginning to sustain heavy losses as they advanced towards the ridge as almost every available Allied gun was trained on their squares, blasting gaping holes in their ranks with grape shot. In spite of this, however, they continued to advance, 'preceded by a very strong line of sharpshooters who came on in a most gallant manner, shouting and keeping up a most destructive fire.'[14]

The French came on with shouts of "Vive l'Empereur!", the officers running backwards in front of the squares in order to keep their formation in check. Clouds of skirmishers screened the Imperial Guard as it advanced nearer and nearer to the crest of the ridge in the face of an ever increasing storm of shot and shell. The scenario was one that had been played out many times before in the Peninsula as the French neared the object of their advance, apparently unopposed by any enemy troops, only to receive a nasty shock at the moment of apparent victory. It was to be the same story at Waterloo and when Wellington said afterwards that the French simply came on in the old style, only to be driven off in the old style, he was not far from the truth.

Ney's veteran French troops arrived at the crest of the ridge which to them seemed deserted but at the last moment a British voice was heard above the sounds of battle and all at once a wall of red appeared to rise as if from the very ground, barring the French advance. The First Guards themselves had waited nervously as the French approached, oblivious to everything on the forward slopes of the ridge but hardly a single man amongst them could have failed to realise that the climax to the Battle of Waterloo was upon them. Wellington, as usual displaying his uncanny knack of being in the right place at the right time, took personal command of the Guards and when the tall bearskins of the Imperial Guard began to appear over the crest of the ridge he shouted to Maitland, "Now,

Maitland, now's your time," followed by "Stand up Guards!" at which the Guards scrambled hastily to their feet just a few yards from the heads of the startled French squares that checked back in amazement.[15]

Wellington's order was quickly followed by "Make ready, aim, fire!" and the words had barely left his lips when the long, four-deep line of British Foot Guards poured out a devastating, rolling fire that dropped hundreds of Frenchmen in an instant. The French squares staggered and appeared `convulsed',[16] and indeed, such was the effect of the Guards' musketry that the French squares were said to have been forced backwards.

Whether it was from the sudden and unexpected appearance of a Corps so near them, which must have seemed as starting out of the ground, or the tremendously heavy fire we threw into them, *La Garde*, who had never before failed in an attack *suddenly* stopped. Those who from a distance and more on the flank could see the affair, tell us that the effect of our fire seemed to force the head of the column bodily back. In less than a minute 300 were down. They now wavered, and several of the rear divisions began to draw out as if to deploy, whilst some of the men in their rear beginning to fire over the heads of those in front was so evident a proof of their confusion.[17]

It was the old story as the French columns, albeit squares on this occasion, which had previously led the Grande Armée to victory after victory came face to face with the British line. Mathematics alone decreed that a column, although much stronger numerically than a line, could only bring about its front ranks to bear on the enemy whereas the line, far more numerically inferior, could fire every single one of its muskets. The French squares, therefore, were completely enveloped by fire and as they struggled to deploy into line themselves Wellington's men pushed home their advantage. No sooner had the smoke cleared from the first few devastating volleys than Saltoun, seeing the confusion on the enemy ranks, shouted, "Now's the time, my boys!" and immediately his men leapt forward with fixed bayonets. But if the Guards relished the opportunity of setting about the Imperial Guard with cold steel they were to be disappointed, for although some Frenchmen did indeed perish on the point of a British bayonet, the French `gave us little opportunity of trying the steel,' as Powell, of the First Guards recalled, for they broke and fled in disorder. Colour Sergeant Wood later wrote that the French did not like the thought of the British bayonets and ran very fast in all directions.[18] Ensign Swinburne, of the 3rd Battalion, later wrote a graphic account of the defeat of the Imperial Guard:

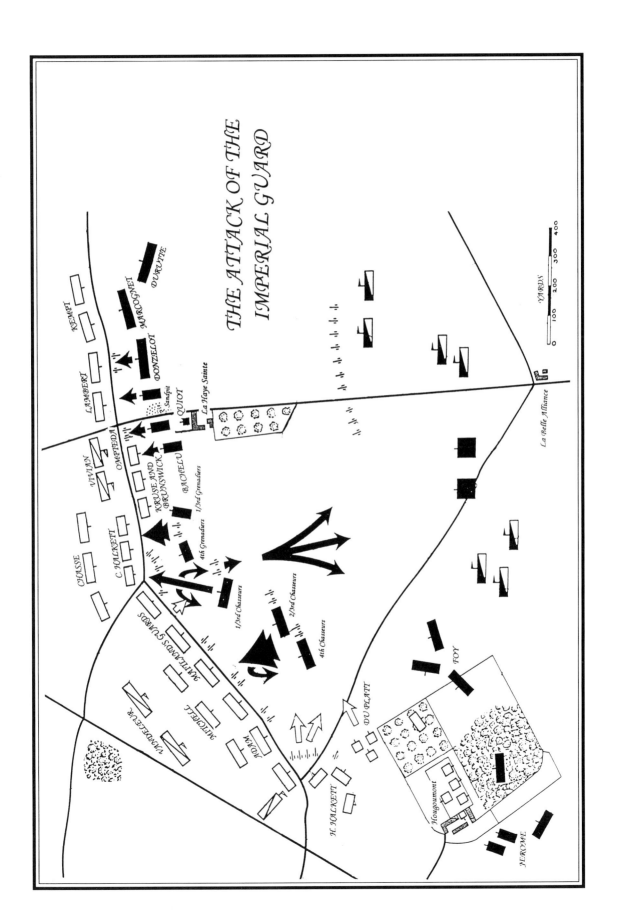

THE ATTACK OF THE
IMPERIAL GUARD

KEMPT
D'URUTTE
MARCOGNET
LAMBERT
DONZELOT
Sandpit
QUIOT
OMPTEDA
VIVIAN
KRUSE AND
BRUNSWICK
BACHELU
1/3rd Grenadiers
La Haye Sainte
CHASSE
C. HALKETT
4th Grenadiers
1/3rd Chasseurs
2/3rd Chasseurs
4th Chasseurs
MAITLAND'S GUARDS
VANDELEUR
MITCHELL
ADAM
DU PLATT
H. HALKETT
TOY
La Belle Alliance
Hougoumont
JEROME

YARDS
0   100   200   300   400

There was a call for skirmishers to check the French advance. I went forward with a few men pretty close to the French who continued advancing to the spot where our battalion was lying. I got back to the command of the company I had command of, shortly before were ordered to rise and fire a volley and charge. This the French received and I think they were not more than 15 yards from us. They were so close that most of our men fired from the charging position (I mean without bringing the musket to the shoulder). The fire was very destructive as there was a hedge of bodies lying over which we passed in the charge after them down the slope.[19]

Ensign Gronow also left a vivid account of the clash between the two elite units:

We were instantly on our legs, and after so many hours of inaction and irritation at maintaining a purely defensive attitude, - all the time suffering the loss of comrades and friends - the spirit which animated officers and men may easily be imagines. After firing a volley as soon as the enemy were within shot, we rushed on with fixed bayonets, and that hearty hurrah peculiar to British soldiers. It appeared that our men, deliberately and with calculation, singled out their victims; for as they came upon the Imperial Guard our line broke, and the fighting became irregular. The impetuosity of our men seemed almost to paralyse their enemies. I witnessed several of the Imperial Guard who were run through the body apparently without any resistance on their parts. I observed a huge Welshman of the name of Hughes, who was six feet seven inches in height, run through with his bayonet, and knock down with the butt-end of his firelock, I should think at least a dozen at least of his opponents. This terrible contest did not last more than ten minutes, for the Imperial Guard was soon in full retreat.[20]

As the Imperial Guard fled down the slopes of Mont St Jean many Frenchmen threw off their packs to facilitate their escape. Arms and ammunition were likewise discarded and as the First Guards pursued their enemy they had to climb over a great deal of discarded equipment, not to mention dead bodies.

However, as the Guards chased their defeated enemies it became apparent to Maitland that their right flank would be exposed to a second column of French infantry, that of the Chasseurs of the Imperial Guard, advancing in support of their comrades of the Grenadiers of the Guard. Maitland immediately ordered his men to halt and the right wing of the 2nd Battalion First Guards was thrown back in order to open fire on the French. Maitland's men returned to their original position to face this threat and as they opened fire on the face of this second attacking column Adams' brigade - the 52nd, 71st and 95th - away to their right, close to the blazing chateau of Hougoumont, threw forward its right flank and poured a withering fire into the left flank of the French column. The effect was shattering and soon Napoleon's men were fleeing for their lives in the direction of La Belle Alliance from where the attack had originally started.

The defeat of the Imperial Guard marked the effective end of the Battle of Waterloo. The undefeated had been defeated and when the cry went up, *La Garde recule!* the French army gave way and a general rout began, precipitated by the First Guards defeat of Napoleon's finest but hastened by the arrival in the west of Blücher's Prussians who pursued their old enemies with a bloody vengeance all the way back to France. The Imperial Guard made a gallant stand amidst the carnage and chaos of the Allied victory but even they were forced on by Prussian sabres and cannons. General Cambronne, who commanded Napoleon's Guard, was taken prisoner by the First Guards and was conducted to Brussels by a grenadier of the First Guards named Kent.[21]

As the general rout of Napoleon's army began the Coldstream Guards and Third Guards were still occupying Hougoumont, fighting on completely unaware of the carnage being meted out to the Imperial Guard atop the ridge of Mont St Jean by the First Guards under Maitland, admirably assisted by Adam's brigade and Halkett's brigade. However, as the evening wore on they suddenly heard a huge cheer from behind them as a figure on a horse raised himself in his saddle and waved his hat in the air. It was Wellington and by raising his hat in the air he was giving the signal for a general advance.[22] Apart from the cheers that went up from the Allied line the first hint of victory that the defenders of Hougoumont had came when scores of fleeing French troops passed by to the south of the chateau at which Hepburn's Third Guards scrambled from behind the defences to join in the pursuit. The men were exhausted by their efforts during the day, however, so Hepburn ordered his men to return to the smouldering wreckage of Hougoumont and the pursuit was left to Blücher's Prussians.

NOTES

[1] Lieutenant General Sir F.W. Hamilton, *The Origin and History of the First or Grenadier Guards*, (London, 1874), iii. 34.

[2] C/Sgt. Charles Wood, *Some Particulars of the Battle of waterloo, being an extract of a letter from C/Sgt C.W. Third Battalion First Regiment of Foot Guards*, (Halifax, 1816). 5.

[3] Hamilton, *Grenadier Guards*, iii. 35.

[4] Ibid. iii. 35.

[5] Ibid. iii. 517.

[6] John Raymond,(Ed), *The Reminiscences and Recollections of Captain Gronow, being Anecdotes of Court, Camp and Society, 1810-1860*, (London, 1964), 145.

[7] Wood, *Some Particulars*, 6.

[8] Raymond, *Gronow*, 71.

[9] Hamilton, *Grenadier Guards*, iii. 39.

[10] Major H.T. Siborne, [Powell], *The Wateroo Letters. A Selesction from original and hitherto unpublished Letters bearing on the 16th, 17th and 18th June, by Officers who served in the Campaign*, (London, 1891), 254.

[11] We are indebted to David C. Hamilton-Williams for this information which is based on contemporary French documents, confirming the fact that the Imperial Guard came on in squares, not in dense columns as is usually depicted. Vicomte D'Avout, *L'Infanterie de la Garde à Waterloo*, 'Carnet de la Sabretache,' Paris, 1905, 1-44. D'Avout based his findings on the collected letters and other primary source material of all surviving officers of the Imperial Guard who took part in the attack.

[12] Siborne, [Dirom], *Waterloo Letters*, 257.

[13] Ibid. [Maitland], 243.

[14] Colonel John Reeve, Add Mss. 34705.

[15] Wellington has often been quoted as saying "Up Guards, and at them," almost certainly a misquote but one, nevertheless, that we can almost imagine him shouting in a moment of almost boyish enthusiasm as he took command of the 1st Guards. In his letter to Siborne, Saltoun said he did not hear him say this words and added that he considered it 'a matter of no great importance' as to whether or not he did. Siborne, *Waterloo Letters*, 248.

[16] Ibid. [Dirom], 257.

[17] Ibid. [Powell], 255.

[18] Wood, *Some Particulars*, 5.

[19] Swinburne, Add Mss. 34708.

[20] Raymond, *Captain Gronow*, 72.

[21] Hamilton, *Grenadier Guards*, iii. 45. General Cambronne is traditionally supposed to have replied, "La Garde meurt, mais ne se rend pas!" (The Guard dies but never surrenders). A more earthy reply ("Merde!") is also reputed to have been shouted and is much more believable.

[22] When some of his staff queried the wisdom of the advance Wellington is reputed to have exclaimed, "Oh damn it! In or a penny in for a pound." Elizabeth Longford, *Wellington, The Years of the Sword*, (London, 1969), 479.

EPILOGUE

As night fell on the evening of June 18th, cries of "sauve qui peut!" were heard everywhere as the panic stricken legions of Napoleon's army melted away into the darkness. At La Belle Alliance, however, a happier scene was being played out as Wellington and Blücher, the victors of this tremendous but terrible day, met to congratulate each other. La Belle Alliance had been Napoleon's command post for much of the day but by now the defeated Emperor had been hurried away south towards France and his final exile.[1]

The three regiments of Foot Guards, meanwhile, spent the night in the positions occupied by them throughout the day. They, and the whole of the Allied army were exhausted to pursue the French and were only too pleased to leave that task to the Prussians.

At Hougoumont, the defenders who had defied the French throughout the day were at last able to take a look around them without fear of being threatened by the enemy. The fires continued to burn unchecked in many of the buildings, inside of which many of the wounded had been placed. Their charred bodies were dug out the following morning. Some of the Guards looked for water to drink or food to eat. Matthew Clay had put a portion of pork in his haversack that morning and now, at the close of the action, took it out and cooked it over a fire that still burned in a stable. However, Clay soon lost his appetite when he discovered that the fuel for this fire was provided by the corpse of one of his comrades who had been consumed by the fire earlier in the day. "My meat which was unsavoury in the morning, became much more so by its re-dressing," he later wrote. Fortunately, he found a piece of veal hanging in a cooking pot over a fire, smothered with dust and fragments of wood, but having cooked it he ate it nonetheless.[2] Others scoured the buildings for food, and the knapsacks of those who had fallen during the fighting were thoroughly searched. Later on, the survivors attended the evening Roll Call which was held to the sound of distant firing as the Prussians pursued the French, a sound that grew fainter by the minute as the chase sped south. Following the Roll Call Clay and his companions of the Third Guards, and no doubt the other battalions of Guardsmen also, lay down on the ground in their blankets and got a good night's sleep.

Wellington's army had suffered nearly 15,000 casualties of which 6,500 were British, whilst Blücher lost 7,000 men, which bears testimony to the part played by them at Plancenoit - where they were engaged for the greater part of the day on Napoleon's right flank - and in the pursuit afterwards. French casualties were put at about 40,000. As for the three regiments of Guards, casualties were not light. The 2nd Battalion First Guards lost 1 officer and 50 men killed, and 5 officers and 96 men wounded, whilst the 3rd Battalion First Guards lost 3 officers and 81 men killed, and 6 officers and 245 men wounded.[3] The 2nd Battalion Coldstream Guards lost one officer and 54 men killed, 7 officers and 242 men wounded, and 4 men missing.[4] The 2nd Battalion Third Guards lost 3 officers and 39 men killed, and 9 officers and 188 men wounded.[5] Altogether, the 1st and 2nd Brigades of Guards suffered a total of 1,034 casualties on June 18th. Their part in the battle was noted by Wellington with some approbation in his despatch to HRH the Prince Regent, written the day after the battle, in which he said:

It gives me the greatest satisfaction to assure your lordship that the army never upon any occasion conducted itself better. The Division of Guards, under Lieutenant General Cooke, who is severely wounded, Major General Maitland, and Major General Byng, set an example which was followed by all, and there is no officer nor description of troops that did not behave well.[6]

We have already mentioned some of the fatalities suffered by the Guards both at Quatre Bras and Waterloo, such as Hay, Miller and Stables, but there were others too, such as Captain Thomas Craufurd, of the Third Guards who was killed at Hougoumont. Craufurd was the nephew of the great Robert Craufurd who had commanded Wellington's Light Division during the Peninsular War. Captain John Lucie Blackman also died at Hougoumont and although his remains - along with Craufurd's - have since been moved, a tomb still lies within the orchard at Hougoumont today, marking the original sight of his grave.[7] Lieutenant Colonel The Honourable Sir Alexander Gordon, of the Third Guards, serving as ADC to Wellington was also killed at Waterloo. William Stothert, Adjutant of the Third Guards, and author of *A Narrative of the Campaigns of 1809, 1810, and 1811* was another officer who fell at Waterloo.

There was little to be done for the wounded the next day save for collecting them and bringing them to the various hospitals that had sprung up in the surrounding farms and villages and to Brussels of course for the army had to move on in pursuit of

Napoleon's defeated army. On June 19th the Guards marched to Nivelles and a week later had reached Peronne where the 1st Brigade of Guards was ordered to capture the town. The place was fortified with strong walls but when the light companies of the First Guards stormed the hornwork covering the main gate the town soon capitulated. On July 3rd Paris surrendered and twelve days later Napoleon himself gave himself up to the captain of HMS *Bellerophon*. Despite pleas to the Prince Regent for leniency he was subsequently taken to St Helena where he spent the final six years of his life before his eventual death on May 5th 1821.

The Allies themselves entered Paris on July 7th, the British troops setting up camp in the Bois de Boulogne. A Brigade of Guards, consisting of the 3rd Battalion First Guards and the 2nd Battalion Coldstream Guards formed part of the Allied army of occupation, the 2nd Battalion First Guards and the 3rd Battalion Third Guards having already sailed back to England. On Monday the Guards took part in a grand review of Wellington's army, some 65,000 men in all, and it was while the Guards were encamped at Paris that the Prince Regent, as recognition of the part played in the battle of Waterloo and in particular the defeat of the Grenadiers of the Imperial Guard, bestowed upon the First Guards the title of 'Grenadier', the full name of the regiment thus becoming 'The First or Grenadier Regiment of Foot Guards.'

On July 19th the Reverend John Norcross, of Framlingham, Suffolk, wrote to Wellington asking him to nominate, "any one of my brave countrymen who fought under your Grace's banners in the late tremendous but glorious conflict." Norcross intended to award him a pension for as long as he (the reverend) lived, the pension being paid annually on the anniversary of the battle. When Wellington replied on August 15th he had nominated both Sergeant Graham of the Coldstream Guards, and Private Joseph Lester of the Third Guards. Graham had helped Macdonell close the gates of Hougoumont and later rescued his brother from the burning flames of its barn. Lester was also one of those who helped close the gates and also saved Captain Hesketh, also of the Third Guards, by shooting the Frenchmen who had knocked Hesketh down and was about to bayonet him. Finally, Norcross chose to award the pension to Graham but it was short lived as he went bankrupt two years later. He did, however, leave a further £500 in his Will to be awarded to `the bravest man in England.' Once again Wellington was asked to make the nomination and as he himself later wrote; `The success of the Battle of Waterloo depended upon the closing of the gates at Hougoumont,' he said that as Macdonell had been mainly responsible for this, he could not help thinking that Macdonell should be awarded the £500.

The defeat of Napoleon at Waterloo and his subsequent banishment to St Helena brought an end to the Napoleonic Wars, a series of wars, campaigns and battles that had begun some twenty-two years earlier. For the three regiments of Foot Guards, however, Waterloo had been the culmination of seven years of fighting against Napoleon's armies, for although they had seen action at various times throughout the wars Waterloo marked the end of a continuous period of hard fighting stretching back to 1808 with Wellesley's landings in Portugal. Since then they had fought their way across the snows of Galicia with Sir John Moore, they had stood fast at bloody Talavera, Fuentes de Oñoro and Barrosa, had marched across Spain, fought their way over the Pyrenees and into France and now, finally, had thwarted Napoleon himself on the field of Waterloo. It is thus fitting that the final blow that brought an end to this tremendous period in history should have been dealt by the subject of our book, Wellington's Foot Guards, the 'Gentlemen's Sons'.

NOTES

[1] Napoleon had only just avoided capture at Genappe where he abandoned his coach at the very moment that the pursuing Prussian cavalry captured it. It was a scene very reminiscent of Joseph's near capture two years earlier following Wellington's victory at Vittoria.

[2] Matthew Clay, *A Narrative of the Battles of Quatre Bras and waterloo, with the Defence of Hougoumont*, (Bedford, 1853),16-17.

[3] Lieutenant general Sir F.W. Hamilton, *The Origin and Services of the First or Grenadier Guards*, (London, 1874), iii. 46. The names of those officers of the First Guards killed at Quatre Bras and Waterloo are inscribed on a plinth in the church at Waterloo.

[4] Colonel Daniel Mackinnon, *Origin and Services of the Coldstream Guards*, London, 1833), ii. 221.

[5] Major General Sir Frederick Maurice, *The History of the Scots Guards, from 1642 to 1914*, (London, 1934), ii. 37.

[6] Hamilton, *Grenadier Guards*, iii. 52.

[7] Blackman's letters are held in the collections of the National Army Museum, London. In his last letter, dated Enghien, June 15th 1815, he says he is in good spirits and has just drawn a further draft for £90 as it wouldn't do to go into a new campaign with no money.

APPENDIX

Notes on the uniform plates

PLATE 1. GUARDS OFFICERS IN THE PENINSULA

Left: Ensign, First Guards, in Service Dress.

This newly arrived ensign in Spain carries an umbrella which was quite common for officers of the Guards. During the retreat from Burgos in 1812 Captain Lord Saltoun carried a large, strong one which served as a walking stick and also saved him from many a good wetting as he had it waterproofed with oil varnish. The officers hat also has a waterproofed cover which kept the hats in good conditions. The officer wears blue pantaloons as the 1810 regimental orders permitted the officers of the regiment to wear them or overalls when on the march. His sword is worn on a fashionable black belt, and worn on his left breast is a miniature of his sweetheart.

Centre: Officer, Light Company, Third Guards.

Officers of the light companies were the only ones to wear the short jacket before the 1812 dress changes. The sword was carried in a frog although they later adopted slings and then black belts. He has the new light infantry waist sash with cords and tassels. The boots are made of the best soft leather. Footwear seems to have been a problem throughout the whole army during the Peninsular war. (See Chapter 3, *Military Dress*, for some of the problems and solutions.)

Right: Officer, Coldstream Guards, Campaign Dress.

This long serving dandy has stuck to the 'old red rag' but is wearing overalls which were in great vogue with infantry officers at the time. With sartorial freedom this Guards officer has chosen to wear a local Spanish straw hat and has it adorned with his full dress plume. He is a veteran of the Egyptian campaign an wears a captured Mameluk sword.

PLATE 2. SERGEANTS

Left: Sergeant, Coldstream Guards, Grenadier Company. Service Dress.

This sergeant, wearing improvised protection against the sun around his shako, is getting his men ready for another long, hot march. The heat of the Spanish sun in recalled in many a statement. Captain Bowles, of the Coldstream Guards, declared that he had marched upwards of 1,700 miles, losing six mules along the way through fatigue. "You will hardly believe that in the Coldstream there are only four officers who have stood the whole campaign," he wrote in December 1812. In 1811, when the Coldstream marched through valleys studded with shrubs and shrouded in dust. The men's haversacks became soaked with sweat that oozed through shirts and jackets. The heat grew so intense that the commanders decided to march at night. The 9ft pike was carried by sergeants of grenadier and battalion companies only.

Centre: Sergeant Major, First Guards, Battalion Company, Service Dress.

This sergeant major is just about to lead a burial service for his men. This took place many times in the Peninsula as there was a lack of chaplains in the army. Officers would also oversee the burial of the dead. Another reason was the fact that Methodism was very strong in the army and some sergeants even preached to their men. Wellington was worried about the possible effect upon discipline if officers and NCOs got together to hear exhortations of their juniors in rank. It seems that some good came out of all this religion, however. In the Guards, for example, a verse was pasted up in the sergeants' mess of the Third Guards by Sergeant Stevenson which read:

It chills the blood to hear the blast supreme
Rashly appealed to on each trifling theme,
Maintain your rank! Vulgarity despise,
To swear is neither brave, polite nor wise.

Right: Sergeant, Third Guards, Light Company, Campaign Dress.

This sergeant is shown during the Pyrenees campaign. He wears the old red rag, patched and darned, but with a new pair of trousers made from brown Spanish cloth. The footwear of the

Guards was to be improvised. In 1812 Spanish sandals were used. The soldiers placed their feet on the warm hides of freshly killed bullocks and then cut and fashioned the hide into a sandal. These were so popular with the men that later the following year the Guards - still lacking boots - were provided with a light hemp sandal made by the local people which was better suited for climbing the steep and slippery Pyrenees. A note on the waist sashes of the Guards: In 1802, sergeants of the First Guards wore crimson with a white stripe. The Coldstream wore plain crimson and the Third guards had crimson sashes with white and blue stripes. Some even survived up until Waterloo but by 1815 they were probably all crimson.

PLATE 3. PRIVATES.

Left:Private Matthew Clay, Third Guards, Light Company.

Possibly the most well-known private in the Guards at the time of Waterloo, as he would have looked on June 18th 1815. Clay was one of the last of the light company to enter Hougoumont before throwing off his pack to take part in the defence of the chateau. After falling into a water-filled ditch, neck-deep, Clay later described his appearance after battle. "We cleaned ourselves from our uncomfortable state, caused by excessive perspiration, marching through the clouds of dust, bespattered with dirt, laying on the wet ground by night, biting off the ends of cartridges, and being for many hours warmly engaged amongst spreading burning fragments of destruction in the chateau of Hougoumont." For a 20-year-old young man, it was a world away from full dress parades at Windsor or St James's.

Centre: Private, First Guards, Light Company, Service Dress, Marching Order.

This private of the light company is taken from a contemporary painting, a self portrait of William Payne, First Guards, 1814-15. Note the pattern on the wings of his jacket. The First Guards had a bastion lace pattern on their uniform so this could be the artist's interpretation of this or it could just show a lack of uniformity in the Guards. It is interesting to note that the same pattern is shown by the Victorian artist, W.B.Woollen, in a painting of the Guards at Hougoumont. The grey overall trousers were worn by the First Guards. The Coldstream and

Third Guards retained white overalls, as shown in paintings by Dighton and Atkinson.

Right: Corporal James Graham, Coldstream Guards, Light Company.

Corporal Graham was a particularly strong man, and took part in the famous 'closing of the gates' at Hougoumont. Dighton shows the Coldstream with waterproof shako covers with black tape strings tied under their chins. Men of the light companies would often kneel to fire the musket so a heavy toll would be taken around the knees of the men's trousers. This would all add up to a very ragged and patched appearance of the Coldstream Guards at Waterloo. As Coldstream Guards Quartermaster, Benjamin Selway, stated on May 8th 1815 of the man's jackets, "I think we shall be very fortunate if they will hang on the men's backs two months longer." The 2nd battalion Coldstream Guards were to begin their march to Quatre Bras still wearing the 'very much patched' clothing of the previous year. A far cry from the soldier on parade in Whitehall.

PLATE 4. THE GUARDS AT WAR.

Top: Officer, First Guards, Corunna.

On the retreat from Corunna this officer is wearing the old officers' watchcoat. Even officers of the Guards trudged along with their feet wrapped in torn blankets. One eye-witness remarked, "there goes three thousand a year."

Below: Officer, Coldstream Guards, Quatre Bras.

Many Guards officers fought at Quatre Bras still wearing their ball dresses. Sir William Fraser stated that, "My father saw many British officers lying dead at Quatre Bras in silk stockings and buckled shoes." Some may even have fought at Waterloo as it is recorded that Major Percy, who returned to England with the captured French eagles, was still wearing his full dress and silk stockings.

BIBLIOGRAPHY

UNPUBLISHED AND MANUSCRIPT SOURCES

ARMY MUSEUMS OGILBY TRUST.*Letter dated 14th April 1811 from William Perrott, 3rd Guards, to his Mother whilst serving with the Regiment in Spain.*

BLAKE, PRIVATE WILLIAM. *A Letter to his Sister, Paris, January 19th 1816.* In the possession of Ralph Weaver.

BRITISH MUSEUM. Add.Mss. 34703-34708. *Unpublished letters to William Siborne concerning the battle of Waterloo.*

MILLS, JOHN.*Letters and Diary of John Mills, of Bisterne, Ringwood, written to his Family from Spain, 1811 and 1812, while serving with the Coldstream Guards, and From Holland, 1813 and 1814.* In possession of his family.

NATIONAL ARMY MUSEUM, LONDON. *Letter dated July 12th 1815, from Private William Pritchard, 2nd Battalion 3rd Foot Guards, to his wife.*

NATIONAL ARMY MUSEUM, LONDON.*Typescript copy of letter from Lt. C.W. Short, 2nd Bn. Coldstream Guards, to his mother, dated Nivelle, 19th June 1815.*

NATIONAL ARMY MUSEUM, LONDON. *23 MSS letters of 29 Sept.1810 to 11 June 1814, written to his aunt Mrs Charles Drummond in London by Lt. & Capt. G.H. Percival, Coldstream Guards, from the Peninsula, 1810-11 and the Low Countries, 1813-14.*

NATIONAL ARMY MUSEUM, LONDON. *The Letters of John Lucie Blackman, Coldstream Guards, 1812-1815.*

NATIONAL ARMY MUSEUM, LONDON. *Microfilm copies of documents relating to Maj.Gen. the Honourable Sir Edward Stopford, 3rd Guards, 1809-1814.*

PUBLIC RECORDS OFFICE, LONDON. *WO.27. Inspection Returns.*

PUBLIC RECORDS OFFICE, LONDON. *WO.97. Soldiers' Documents.*

RHQ COLDSTREAM GUARDS. *Copy of a letter from Colonel Daniel Mackinnon, The Coldstream Guards, from the Field of Waterloo.*

RHQ COLDSTREAM GUARDS. *Brothel Account of Lord Alvanley, 2nd (Coldstream) Guards.*

RHQ COLDSTREAM GUARDS, *Standing Orders, 1808-1815.*

RHQ GRENADIER GUARDS. *A Diary of the March from Oporto, 1813, by Captain Colquitt, 1st Foot Guards.*

RHQ GRENADIER GUARDS. *Items relating to the Honourable Orlando Bridgeman, 1st Foot Guards, in the Peninsula.*

RHQ SCOTS GUARDS, *Standing Orders, 1808-1815.*

PUBLISHED SOURCES

ADAIR, MAJOR P.R. *The Coldstream Guards at Waterloo,* in the 'Household Brigade Magazine.' (London, 1965).

BATTY, CAPTAIN ROBERT. *Campaign of the Left Wing of the Allied Army, in the Western Pyrenees and South of Francve, in the Years 1813-14, under Field Marshal The Marquess of Wellington.* (London, 1823).

BLAKENEY, ROBERT, *A Boy in the Peninsular War,* (London, 1899).

BRETT-JAMES, ANTHONY. *Life in Wellington's Army.* (London, 1972).

BRETT-JAMES, ANTHONY. *The Hundred Days,* (London, 1964).

BRETT-JAMES, ANTHONY. *Wellington at War, 1794-1815, A Selection of his wartime letters,* (London, 1961).

CHANDLER, DAVID. *Waterloo: The Hundred Days.* (London, 1980).

CLAY, MATTHEW. *A Narrative of the Battles of Quatre Bras and Waterloo: with the Defence of Hougoumont, by Private Matthew Clay, 3rd Foot Guards.* (Bedford, 1853).

COWELL, JOHN STEPNEY. *Leaves from the Diary of an Officer of the Guards.* (London, 1854).

DALTON, CHARLES. *The Waterloo Roll Call,* (London, 1900).

DAVIES, GODFREY, *Wellington and his Army,* (Oxford, 1954).

DAWNAY, MAJOR NICHOLAS PAYAN. *The Standards, Guidons and Colours of the Household Division, 1660-1973.* (Tunbridge Wells, 1975).

DE LANCEY, LADY. *A Week at Waterloo in 1815. Lady de Lancey's Narrative,* (London, 1906).

FLETCHER, IAN. *Craufurd's Light Division. The Life of Robert Craufurd and his Command of the Light Division,* (Tunbridge Wells, 1991).

FLETCHER, IAN (Ed). *A Guards Officer in the Peninsula: The Peninsular War Letters of John Rous, Coldstream Guards.* (Tunbridge Wells, 1992).

FORTESCUE, J.W. *History of the British Army,* (London, 1910-30).

FOSTEN, BRYAN. *British Foot Guards at Waterloo, June 1815.* (New Malden).

FRASER, BRIGADIER D.W. *The First Guards - 2nd and 3rd Battalions, 16th/18th June 1815,* in the 'Household Brigade Magazine.' (London, 1965).

FRASER, SIR WILLIAM, *Words on Wellington,* (London, 1899).

FRAZER, SIR AUGUSTUS, *Letters of Sir Augustus Frazer,* (London, 1859).

GLOVER, MICHAEL, *Wellington's Peninsular Victories,* (London, 1963).

GLOVER, MICHAEL, *Wellington as Military Commander,* (London, 1968).

GLOVER, MICHAEL. *Wellington's Army. (Newton Abbott, 1977).*

GOW, LIEUTENANT COLONEL J.M. *The Third Guards at Waterloo,* in the 'Household Brigade Magazine.' (London, 1965).

GRATTAN, WILLIAM. *Adventures with the Connaught Rangers, 1809-1814*, (London, 1847)

GRONOW, CAPTAIN. *The Last Recollections of Captain Gronow, Formerly of the First Foot Guards.* (London, 1934).

HAMILTON, LIEUTENANT GENERAL, SIR F.W. *Origin and History of the First or Grenadier Guards*, (London, 1874).

HAYTHORNTHWAITE, PHILIP, *Uniforms of the Peninsular War*, (Poole, 1978).

HAYTHORNTHWAITE, PHILIP, *British Infantry of the Napoleonic Wars*, (London, 1987).

HIBBERT, CHRISTOPHER. *A Soldier of the 71st*, (London, 1975).

HOWARTH, DAVID, *A Near Run Thing*, (London, 1968).

JACKSON, LT.COL. BASIL. *Notes and Reminiscences of a Staff Officer*, (London, 1903).

JOHNSON, PAUL. *Marc Isambard Brunel.* (London, 1970).

KINCAID, CAPTAIN JOHN, *Adventures in the Rifle Brigade*, (London, 1830).

LARPENT, SIR GEORGE, (ED). *The Private Journal of Sir F. Seymour Larpent, Judge-Advocate General*, (London, 1853).

LONGFORD, ELIZABETH, *Wellington, The Years of the Sword*, (London, 1969).

MACKINNON, COLONEL DANIEL, *Origins and Services of the Coldstream Guards*, (London, 1833).

MACKINNON, MAJOR GENERAL HENRY. *A Journal of the Campaign in Portugal and Spain containing Remarks on the Inhabitants, Customs, Trade, and Cultivation of those countries, from the year 1809 to 1812.*

NAPIER, SIR W.F.P. *History of the War in the Peninsula and in the South of France, 1807-1814.* (London, 1886).

NAYLOR, JOHN, *Waterloo*, (London, 1960).

PAGET, JULIAN, *Hougoumont - Key to Victory*, (London, 1992)

PAGET, JULIAN, *Wellington's Peninsular War*, (London, 1990).

RAYMOND, JOHN, (ED). *The Reminiscences and Recollections of Captain Gronow, Being Anecdotes of Camp, Court and Society, 1810-1860*, (London, 1964).

STANHOPE, PHILIP HENRY, 5TH EARL, *Notes of Conversations with the Duke of Wellington, 1831-1851*, (London, 1888).

WELLER, JAC, *Wellington in the Peninsula*, (London, 1962).

WELLER, JAC, *Wellington at Waterloo*, (London, 1967).

WELLINGTON, ARTHUR DUKE OF, *The Despatches of Field Marshal the Duke of Wellington*, (London, 1837-39).

WELLINGTON, 2ND DUKE OF, *Supplementary Despatches, Correspondence, and Memoranda of Field Marshal Arthur Duke of Wellington, Edited by his son.* (London, 1858-64).

WARD, S.G.P. *Wellington's Headquarters, 1809-1814, Being a Study of the Administrative Problems in the Peninsula.* (Oxford, 1957)

WOOD, C/SGT. CHARLES. *Some Particulars of the Battle of Waterloo, being an extract of a letter from C/Sergeant C.W. Third Battalion First Regiment of Foot Guards.* (Halifax, 1816)

INDEX